NATIONS OF THE MODERN WORLD

AUSTRALIA   O. H. K. Spate
Director of Research School of Pacific Studies,
Australian National University

CEYLON   S. A. Pakeman
Formerly Professor of Modern History, Ceylon
University College; Appointed Member, House of
Representatives, Ceylon, 1947–52

MODERN EGYPT Tom Little
Managing Director and General Manager of
Regional News Services (Middle East), Ltd., London

ENGLAND   John Bowle
   A Portrait   *Professor of Political Theory, Collège d'Europe,*
Bruges

MODERN INDIA Sir Percival Griffiths
President of the India, Pakistan and Burma
Association

MODERN IRAN   Peter Avery
Lecturer in Persian and Fellow of King's College,
Cambridge

JAPAN   Sir Esler Dening
H.M. Ambassador to Japan, 1952–57

MALAYA   J. M. Gullick
Formerly of the Malayan Civil Service

MOROCCO   Mark I. Cohen
       and
Lorna Hahn

NIGERIA   Sir Rex Niven
Colonial Service, Nigeria, 1921–59; Member of
Northern House of Assembly, 1947–59

NEW ZEALAND James W. Rowe
*Director of New Zealand Institute of Economic
Research, Inc.*
Margaret A. Rowe
Tutor in English, Victoria University, Wellington

PAKISTAN Ian Stephens
Formerly Editor of The Statesman *Calcutta and
Delhi, 1942–51; Fellow of King's College,
Cambridge, 1952–58*

SOUTH AFRICA John Cope
Formerly Editor-in-Chief of The Forum; *South
African Correspondent of* The Guardian

SUDAN K. D. D. Henderson
REPUBLIC *Formerly of the Sudan Political Service; Governor of
Darfur Province, 1949–53*

TURKEY Geoffrey Lewis
Senior Lecturer in Islamic Studies, Oxford

THE UNITED H. C. Allen
STATES OF *Commonwealth Fund Professor of American History,*
AMERICA *University College, London*

YUGOSLAVIA Muriel Heppell
and
F. B. Singleton

AUSTRALIA

AUSTRALIA

O. H. K. SPATE

FREDERICK A. PRAEGER, *Publishers*
New York · Washington

BOOKS THAT MATTER

Published in the United States of America in 1968
by Frederick A. Praeger, Inc., Publishers
111 Fourth Avenue, New York, N.Y. 10003

Library of Congress Catalog Card Number: 68–19862

Printed in Great Britain

To
Mamie Sawer
and to
Virginia, Andrew, and Alastair
the wattle and the rose entwine

Preface

WHEN Sir Keith Hancock suggested to me that the time had come for a new *Australia* in this series, and that I might be interested in writing it, I was naturally extremely flattered – too flattered to decline. It was clearly not a matter of revising his book – for lesser men, if they have any sense, do not undertake to revise the classics – but of a new work, and perhaps, as Sir Keith suggested, a geographer's view might be appropriate in the context of rapid resource development in the 'sixties. I accepted the invitation with a fearful joy: joy, for I had long wished to attempt to clarify my own view of Australia, to 'get it out of my system'; fearful, for I was acutely conscious of a disparity of talent and of the small likelihood that I might match the high standard he had set.

In the event, although I trust that the pattern of development is not neglected in these pages (though changes are so rapid that any treatment runs serious risks of obsolescence), historical and political themes perhaps bulk more largely than I had anticipated. Despite their cynicism about their representatives, Australians are by and large a politically-minded people, and it seemed worth while, for example, to indicate divergences in the Australian political tradition from the British tradition which gave birth to it, or to emphasise for the British reader that Australia's war in the Pacific was not the same as nor (to Australian eyes) merely a part of Britain's war; and this was perhaps easier for an Englishman (if such he still is) called up in Burma and serving under South-East Asia Command to see.

It is, I hope, fair to claim that this book is written from the point of view of a man who is labour but not Labor, liberal but not Liberal, loving the country not less than the Country Party. While I have felt it only honest to indicate in a footnote my own opinion on that central and agonising dilemma of Australia today, the Vietnam war, I have tried in the text – doubtless with small success – to maintain a more detached view.

9

It is obvious that this book is not a work of original scholarship, and that the treatment of any specific topic must appear superficial to those who are expert in it. This is the inevitable penalty of the broad survey. There have been quite a number of such surveys in recent years, and the editors of *Australian Society* are justified in entering the caveat that 'The typical art form of the writer on Australian social affairs is the one-volume study which aspires to sum up a complex community in an array of subjective assessments of varying quality.' (One may, perhaps, justifiably file a counter-caveat at finding a sociological introduction to Australian life which says practically nothing at all about drink, sport, betting, and Trade Unions.) Having undertaken the assignment, all one can do is to be as honest and comprehensive as one can, accepting the hazards of impressionism.

Remarks which might be rude when uttered by a transitory guest may surely be allowed to a man who has taken out a long lease. It is easy enough to say what one dislikes about living in Australia – the politics, big business, the Unions, the pseudo-American rat-race of the capitals, the trite naivety of the small towns. . . . Many of these disagreeables would of course be met with in any country under the sun, but still some seem to have their peculiar local flavour. It is much more difficult to define what it is that has made so many people decide that Australia is *their* place for living. For one who came to Australia sixteen years ago, has remained, and in all human probability will remain till the end of his days, the writing of this book seemed to provide an opportunity of discovering the answer to this personal mystery. I am not at all sure that I am any the wiser now than when I set out on this journey of discovery, but at least the exploration has been enjoyable.

Mention should be made of a few points of usage. 'Common-wealth', unless specifically stated to be the British Commonwealth of Nations, refers to the Commonwealth of Australia. Similarly, except in one or two cases where the context should obviate ambiguity. 'State' when capitalised refers not to the abstract idea but to the States which make up the Commonwealth. The official spelling used by the Australian Labor Party and the Democratic Labor Party omits the 'u'; advantage is taken of this to distinguish between general and specifically political references: thus 'labour was in short supply', but 'Labor attitudes in this crisis', to give examples which might have occurred but do not. Historical references to sums of money are in Australian pounds (£1 sterling = £1.5.0 Australian); contemporary referencss in Australian dollars, adopted in February 1966 at the rate £A1 = $A2.00. Since the British devaluation of 1967, £1 stg = $A2.14, $A1 = £0.10.9 stg.

As some offset to the inevitable impressionism, anyone working in the Australian National University has an incomparable treasury of specialised knowledge to draw upon, and I have not hesitated to do so. My gratitude is owing, and proffered, to Professors L. F. Crisp, G. Sawer, and W. E. H. Stanner, Drs H. C. Brookfield, R. A. Gollan, and G. J. R. Linge, all of whom read some chapters in typescript; and to many others for 'heterogeneous Ideas and independent Hints'; I can only hope that, despite Dr Johnson's warning, I have succeeded in 'collecting in one point the several Rays of borrowed Light'. Needless to say, none of these gentlemen is responsible for any errors of fact or heresies of opinion. Alec Hope kindly allowed me to quote again his much-quoted poem *Australia*.

Thanks are also due to the editors of *The Australian Journal of Science* and *The Australian* for permission to use material which originally appeared in their pages; to Miss Joan Binns and Mrs Carol Taylor who produced the typescript; and to Mr Hans Gunther who drew the folding map.

Finally, the possession of an American wife, whose care for the moral and material welfare of the author is constant, carries with it the supplemental bonus of providing a point of reference not only to British but to American life.

Canberra
1967

O H. K. SPATE

Acknowledgements

Illustration No. 38 is by courtesy of Australia House, Strand, London. Numbers 10 and 11 are from the author's own collection. The rest are by courtesy of the News and Information Bureau, Department of the Interior, Canberra.

Contents

Maps

List of Illustrations

Part One

HISTORY

Chapter 1

The Land and its Limitations

Proem

In a magnificent image, the Australian poet Bernard O'Dowd called his country 'last sea-thing dredged by sailor Time from Space'. Sailor Time had his stout executive officers, and they came from the West: the tough masters of Dutch East Indiamen, and greatest of all that very practical geographer and very English Englishman Captain James Cook of His Majesty's Brig *Endeavour*. Whatever knowledge of the continent Malays and Chinese may have had – and that they had some is certain for the Malays and highly probable for the Chinese – the history of Australia is essentially a part of the European dispersion.

Both from Left and Right, from Ministers of the Crown and from crypto-Communists, there is much loose talk in Australia to the effect that it is 'a part of Asia'. Geographical proximity is of course of high importance, and relations with Asia are and will remain of most vital significance to the Australian people. But there are many geographical factors besides location; geologically and biogeographically the statement is simply untrue, and humanly speaking the most essential feature in Australian life is this: with New Zealand, she is the remotest outlier of Western, and specifically British, civilisation.

The outlier has of course its local note, its local genius: in this continent so ancient, so arid, so alien, no European culture could survive unchanged. The pattern of life is not strictly a British pattern, yet through it run strong and persistent British motifs: empiricism, an almost perverse tolerance of the unsystematic, a gift for improvisation and solidarity in crises. In another way the synthesis between the Great South Land and a northern people may be symbolised by those south-eastern hills and valleys where ti-tree and bramble, she-oak and willow, grow side by side: 'the wattle and the rose entwine'.

✼

The name Australia was first given currency by Matthew
Flinders, the first man to circumnavigate its shores at all closely, in
his book *A Voyage to Terra Australis*, published the day before his
death in July 1814; he derived the name from that of the Great
South Land which had haunted the imaginations of geographers
for centuries. Its story has the fascinations belonging to romantic
fable, to the history of ideas, and to a complicated tale of detection;
but its conclusions are inconclusive, and it has little relevance to the
Australia of to-day except as a source of poetic myth. There is small
reason (except academic curiosity, a good reason so far as it goes)
to speculate on possible Portuguese landfalls or on the frustrations
of de Lozier Bouvet, who carefully planned a voyage which would
have anticipated Cook by thirty years; or even to recount the more
solid sightings of the Hollanders, who by 1642 had fairly definite
knowledge of the coasts from the Gulf of Carpentaria in the north
to the east of the Great Australian Bight in the south: some two-
thirds of the entire coastline, but shores which were, and mostly
still are, uninviting in the extreme. It was left to Cook, with that
cool and thorough reasoning which set him above men his peers as
seamen and leaders, to deliberately seek out the temperate and
well-watered east coast. The history of Australia essentially begins with that exploration (April to August 1770) and with the
arrival at Botany Bay of the convict-laden First Fleet in January
1788.

Before then the continent had an anthropology, in great part lost
with the extinction of the Tasmanian and the tragical disruption of
the mainland aborigines; an archaeology, which we are only now
beginning to piece together; but no history: Terra Australis, nor
even New Holland, is not Australia. It was only the year before
Flinders established the name Australia – a quarter of a century
after the first white settlement, and only a century and a half before
the writing of these lines – that any recorded European had penetrated more than ten or twelve miles from hightide mark, except in
Tasmania and a tiny shut-in lowland extending for not much more
than thirty miles around Sydney.

Yet from this late and slow start, inauspicious in its felon origins
and most inconsequential in its actual foundation, has stemmed the
Commonwealth of Australia, a nation of twelve million people
occupying (it is true very unevenly) nearly three million square
miles. The themes of this book are the evolution of this nation, its

achievements and the problems which beset it, the promise (and the
perils) before it.

The lie of the land

The most obviously striking fact about Australia is its remoteness
from Europe, the begetter (the continent itself is the womb) of its
current civilisation. Of the four million or so people, mainly Europeans, who have immigrated into Australia since 1788, the great
majority have come across the Indian Ocean, and from Cape Town
it is 6,450 miles, from Colombo 3,600 (a week's steaming) to Fre-
mantle, which itself is 1,050 miles from Ceduna in South Australia,
the westernmost margin of the development in the south-east;
Sydney is 1,000 miles farther still. On the north, the nearest considerable Asian island, Timor, is only 500 miles from Darwin; but
the South Pole is nearer to Canberra than the nearest point on the
mainland of Asia, Singapore (or strictly speaking Johore). Beyond
New Guinea there lie some 7,000 miles of the Pacific before the
shores of any considerable Western power are reached, in California.
The nearest non-Asian neighbour, New Zealand, is 1,300 miles
away; and oddly enough this distance is in effect enhanced by the
apparently trivial fact that it is a little shorter from Sydney to
London by Suez than by Panama, and conversely for Auckland.
The difference, though small, is quite enough to make shipping lines
to Europe diverge, and again the economies are competitive, or at
least supplementary, rather than complementary. Hence Australia
and New Zealand are not, as they look from Britain, neighbours
merely semi-detached.

Mere mileage, however, has been no deterrent to European
sailors since Colombus, and more fundamental than simple distance
are the latitudinal position and the build of Australia. For modern
geographers it is a little old-fashioned to begin with latitude, and
yet the lateness of the discovery and settlement of Australia, and
many things in its development, depend in the last resort on the
facts that it is very compact, with its central bulk extending for
2,400 miles along the Tropic of Capricorn – that is, in the latitude
of what were called the South-East Trade Winds – but with its high
ground hugging the Pacific coast, so that the influence of the moist
air-masses from the sea is severely restricted.

When the Dutch came upon 'New Holland' early in the seven-
teenth century, as an incident of sailing to the East Indies, their

explorations were either in the too-tropical north or the drier
western two-thirds of the continent. From Magellan's voyage of
1519–21 onwards, the Pacific had been crossed from the South
American side ten times before 1770, but the tracks ran before the
South-East Trades and thus as it were slanted across the roof of
Australia, which on this eastern side was missed by Spaniards,
Dutch, British and French alike. The French did indeed display an
inconvenient interest after Cook's exploration of the east coast, but
by the time they were in a position to make that interest serious
(after the Napoleonic Wars) the British were engaged in pre-
empting the entire continent. Australia's position in relation to
prevalent and rain-bearing winds is thus responsible for the late
start of European settlement and its present concentration, which
except in the south-east is strongly coastal; and it is also largely
responsible for the unique fact that such settlement of an entire
continent took place under one flag.

The horizontal continent

The whole life of the continent has also been greatly influenced
by the distribution of high relief, or rather perhaps by the lack of it.
Humanly speaking, it may be 'the youngest continent'; in geological
terms it is the oldest. For aeons Australia, taken as a whole, has
been remarkably little affected by the vast mountain-building processes responsible for the Alps, the Himalaya, and the Andes; the roots
of ancient ranges lie below the ground, and contain much mineral
wealth, but the surface has been planed by the erosion of ages.

No other continent has anything like so small a fraction of its
surface lying over 2,000 feet above sea-level – 180,000 square miles,
a mere 6 per cent of the area. The loftiness of Mount Lofty behind
Adelaide reaches 2,334 feet; only in the south-east corner is there
any considerable area over 5,000 feet, and here Mount Kosciusko
attains 7,314 feet. But these misnamed Australian Alps have nothing Alpine about them; Kosciusko itself is only a rounded swell
sitting on the next highest plateau, and in good summer weather
one can drive to within a few feet of the summit in an ordinary car:
no other continent can claim as much, or as little. 'Snowy Mountains' is a better name for these bold rounded eminences; but when
Australians claim with probable truth that they have a snow area
larger than that of Switzerland, they often forget to add that only a
few square yards, if indeed any, are permanent snow.

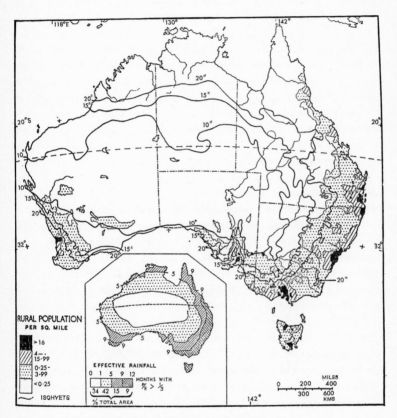

Australia: Rain and People

These mountains, on the border of New South Wales and Victoria, form part of the only really extensive area of high relief. This 'Great Dividing Range', lying along the Pacific coast, is much better termed the Eastern Highlands: there is no continuous range, and the divide itself is often quite unnoticeable. The Highlands are lower in Queensland than in the south, and set farther back from the coast, with rather more extensive coastal lowlands and valleys than in New South Wales. Generally, however, the really rugged areas are the fretted margins of plateaus; more rarely the cones and plugs of long-extinct volcanoes. The wetter seaward flanks of the Highlands are of course much more dissected than the 'Western Slopes' which fall away to the interior plains in long blunt-nosed ridges or mere undulations. The coast, especially in New South Wales, is often backed by massive scarps, cut by wild gorges which may head back into waterfalls which are imposing when there is much water; but beyond the crest the plateaus stretch away apparently without end. In the Blue Mountains behind Sydney 'the scenery lies *below*' in great canyons; or indeed in places not so much below as underground, in magnificent limestone caverns.

Two-thirds of the continent are occupied by the great Western Shield, mainly composed of ancient crystalline rocks forming vast plateaus broken here and there by ranges which nowhere reach 5,000 feet, although they may be very rugged, especially in the Kimberleys of Western Australia. Flanking the Shield are basins of younger sedimentary rocks, notably that behind Exmouth Gulf in the extreme north-west, which in 1954 was the scene of Australia's first oil strike; and in the south the Nullarbor Plain, a treeless cake of limestone so flat that the Trans-Continental Railway crosses it in the longest straight track in the world – 330 miles.

As a whole, however, Australia is very poor in accessible coastal lowlands. Except in the tropical north, where access from the sea is made difficult by mangrove swamps or by great tidal ranges, wherever littoral plains have any great width the coast is as a rule unindented, with few good harbours. South Australia, with the low-lying peninsulas flanking its two great gulfs, and Victoria, with extensive and on the whole well-watered plains in Gippsland, east of Melbourne, and in the basalt-covered Western District, are much better off than New South Wales. The most extensive lowlands lie in a huge belt between the Western Shield and the Eastern Highlands; this great downwarp is floored by relatively young sediments (corresponding in age to those of midland and southern England) which, where they can be watered, have a reasonably high soil potential. But water is the problem: the Great Artesian Basin in Queensland is of very little use except for watering stock, and apart from the tropical north (where rainfall is highly seasonal) only the southern portion of the vast lowlands, the Murray-Darling basin, is at all well-watered.

These rivers, which with their tributaries rise in the Eastern Highlands and flow inland, eventually debouching through shallow lagoons at the mouth of the Murray in South Australia, are indeed great rivers measured in miles: the Murray, the Darling, and the Murrumbidgee have a combined length of 4,100 miles. This is the only river-system of Australia at all comparable to those of other continents; there are four rivers in the USSR alone *each* with an average annual discharge greater than that of all Australian streams combined. Even the Murray system is unfortunately liable to extreme fluctuation: the Darling, which in high flood may cover a belt over forty miles wide, is frequently reduced to a chain of lagoons, and the Murray itself, in the less arid south of the lowland, has on occasion dried across. These vast interior lowlands are the analogue of the Mississippi valley in North America, but they have a far lower economic potential; nevertheless, they contain the great wheat-sheep belt which is the dominant concentration of Australian primary production.

Wind, rain, and sun

There is a striking index to the all-importance of rainfall in Australian life: weather reports give figures not in inches nor even in tenths of an inch, but in points – hundredths of an inch. By far the lowest of the continents, by that fact Australia is by far the driest.

Latitude and build are responsible for this. Could the Eastern Highlands be turned over, pivoting on their ends like a boomerang so that they were concave to the Pacific instead of parallel and close to it, there would be great perennial rivers in temperate and sub-tropical latitudes, with vast lowlands and alluvial deltas open to the rain-bearing air-masses from the sea; and Australia might by now carry three or four times its present population. Or again, if instead of the existing lay-out of relief there were central ranges high enough to carry glaciers and large snow-fields, not only would the south-east be more accessible to Pacific air-masses, but the north would reproduce the conditions of monsoon Asia; and there might be six or eight or ten times the present population. As the continent would then have been far more hospitable to Asian ways of life, candour compels us to admit that it would most likely not have been a White Australia.

The facts are distressingly different. The north has indeed its monsoons, and much of it has sixty inches of rain or even more; but this is concentrated in the five hottest months, and with no snow-fields to regulate the flow, many of the rivers are not perennial. The eastern coastal lowlands are well-watered, but narrow; the south-east and south-western corners have a typically Mediter-ranean-type climate, being reached by rain-bearing westerlies in winter. The southern part of the great interior lowland is affected both by these winter westerly depressions and by moist air-masses from the Pacific, but their influence falls off very rapidly away from the coasts, and high temperatures and great variability render the summer rainfall ineffective.

The results are summed up on the rainfall map which, when qualified by considerations of variability and effectiveness, is per-haps the most significant single document of the Australian environment. Variability of rainfall is of crucial importance: the usual formula holds, that the lower the rainfall, the less reliable it is; and to be paradoxical, one might say that in comparison with global conditions, in Australia variability is normally abnormally high. The middle of the Murray basin – in soil and terrain one of the most favoured parts of Australia – has a variability of over 30 per cent, which means that with mean annual rainfalls of 15 to 20 inches, roughly one year in five will have only 10 to 14 inches: in the first half of 1965 Canberra, in a generally reliable tract, had one-seventh of its normal fall; in the first half of 1967, one-third. The man on the land can never be sure that there will not be a run of drought years. On the other hand, great intensity of individual rain-storms also goes with low annual rainfall, and with the poor vegetation cover – much of it depleted by pastoral occupation – this means that in periods of high rainfall run-off is excessive, and floods can be as disastrous as droughts, though much more short-term in effect.

There is no moderation about the Australian environment: one aspect of it is summed up by a well-known cartoon of a man beating out a bushfire with a flood-warning notice.

High temperatures, and hence evaporation rates, greatly limit the effectiveness of rainfall for agriculture. On the standard Australian formula for effectiveness, only the extreme south-western corner, and a coastal strip from east of the mouth of the Murray to Cooktown in northern Queensland, have over nine months with effective rain, allowing for dairying and intensive agriculture. Within this is a girdle with over five months – a girdle broken by a long stretch of the almost desert west coast, by the Great Australian Bight and Spencer Gulf in the south, and by the Gulf of Carpentaria in the north. Although extensive pastoralism can be carried on in some areas with less than five months, this belt of five to nine months roughly corresponds with the areas in which extensive agriculture and pastoralism are reasonably possible, though still sometimes hazardous.

Irrigation is not much of an answer: it needs perennial water somewhere. Much of the continent has no co-ordinated drainage system at all, and some areas are without even dry stream-beds – the Nullarbor Plain, the Mallee of north-west Victoria. Most of the Western Shield is occupied by shallow enclosed basins, liberally dotted on the map with lakes which, on the ground, are sheets of salt. The greatest such basin is in the central lowland: that of Lake Eyre, thirty-nine feet below sea-level, into which drain long but usually dry rivers. C. T. Madigan has given a graphic description of an embayment of Lake Eyre where he found an old log, and around this only break in the flat waste of salt the local rabbits had crowded, to die of thirst. Yet in 1950 and again in 1953 most of the 3,100 miles of the lake floor were under water, and in 1963 floods prevented Donald Campbell's attempt on the world land-speed record. Once again local humour may point the moral: on an inland station, the new chum points to a cloud of cattle-dust along the creek-bed and asks the old hand 'What's that?' – 'Oh, that's the ruddy fish swimming up the ruddy river.'

One consequence of this alternation of drought and flood is liability to severe soil erosion, which has been fostered by reckless clearing and ring-barking of trees. This was done to allow pasture a freer field; it has often wasted the timber, produced no pasture, and given a free field to erosion –

> Flood, fire, and cyclone in successive motion
> Complete the work the pioneers began
> Of shifting all the soil into the ocean.

The south-east quadrant, which is the largest non-tropical area with reasonably good rainfall, is also most liable to extremes of temperature, although on the whole this is the least important limitation on Australian farming. In the eastern States, frosts are common south of 25°S in June, July, and August, and above 1,000 feet they can occur a good deal earlier and later. Drainage of cold air into enclosed valleys can produce damaging spring frosts; at Cooma seventy miles south of Canberra and 3,000 feet up, lambs have been killed by cold snaps in late spring. At Canberra itself (2,000 feet) one is occasionally glad of a fire at Christmas, though a few days earlier and later temperatures may be in the nineties.

In the south-east again, northerly winds in spring and summer can bring intense heat waves, with temperatures well over 100°F, or even, away from the coast, over 110°, and sometimes accompanied by dust-storms from the interior. In spring these can do great damage to flowering wheat by a few days of intense evaporation; these days of intense heat and strong winds are ideal bushfire weather.

All this adds up to a disconcerting picture: why did north European people ever go there? The first to go there were sent; but to redress the balance, it must be added that in those favoured margins where over ten of Australia's twelve millions live the climate, considered simply in relation to human comfort, is nearly everywhere most agreeable for most of the time. The discomforts are intense, but sporadic. For work and play, especially play, the lines are cast in pleasant places.

The face of the land: soils and vegetation

There are eighteen major soil groups in Australia, and 2,971,081 square miles. Five soil groups account for 1,677,185 square miles – the suspicious accuracy is official – or 56.5 per cent of the total area, and each of these five has the word 'desert' in its title.

'Desert' is a strong word: not all this 56.5 per cent is useless, at any rate for pastoralism, and some of these unleached soils would be fertile if water could be brought to them. Yet it is at least fair to say that over half the continent contains scarcely any land fit for agriculture (with foreseeable techniques) and very little fit for pastoralism of any intensity. Not more than 18 per cent of Australia has both water and fertile soils, and half of this percentage needs special treatment by the addition of trace elements; much of the better watered area is also quite rugged.

The better soils, the higher and more reliable rainfall, the denser vegetation, all conform to the pattern of concentric girdles – broken again on the west coast, the Bight and Spencer Gulf, and the Gulf of Carpentaria. The desert of the centre is discontinuous and includes a good deal of spinifex country; technically a grass, spinifex is as spiky as its name. This core is surrounded by vast areas of dry grasslands and mulga (acacia) scrub. A great belt of savannah country, grassland mixed with very open woodland, swings from south of the Gulf of Carpentaria into central Queensland, merging northwards into open monsoon woodland or the rainforest of coastal Queensland, southwards into the great parklands which dominate the rest of Australia apart from the forests of the south-east and south-west and the mallee, a peculiar scrub of low eucalypts found between the mulga belt and these better forests.

The parklands are most characteristically Australian. The trees, usually fairly wide-spaced except along streams, are mostly one or other of the 400 or 600-odd species of eucalypts; the best-known of course are the gums, losing their smooth thin bark each year and hence festooned with rags and tatters; but there are also stringy-barks and ironbarks and boxes, with a much finer-grained bark. In detail these parklands show great variety, since the distribution of individual species is very responsive to local changes in habitat; but in the large they are monotonous. Only an expert can distinguish more than a few of the commoner eucalypts, and to a layman the vegetation over vast stretches looks much the same.

Finally, there are the restricted areas of true forest. At its best, this is magnificent; the Victorian mountain ash, well-named *Eucalyptus regnans*, is the tallest, though not the bulkiest, tree in the world, reaching heights of over 350 feet; some have been claimed to exceed 400 feet. Even where it has been ring-barked, it is superb: great grey shafts towering nobly, even in death, above the regrowth. The karri of the extreme south-west is but little inferior, and on the east coast there are still stands of the smaller but very beautiful blue and spotted gums.

The glories of karri and mountain ash, the fine woodland along the frequented roads of the Eastern Highlands and littoral, mask the extreme poverty of Australia's timber resources, in the past (and to some extent still) barbarously mishandled. With under 200,000 square miles out of nearly three million under good tree cover, it is by far the least forested continent; and of the total, only two-thirds are potentially exploitable, and under 5 per cent are softwoods. Over most of the continent there is obviously little or no scope for afforestation, but in the wetter margins there is an active planting policy, especially of exotic softwoods.

The nature of the land
    The continent is not an easy one:

> A Nation of trees, drab green and desolate grey
> In the field uniform of modern wars,
> Darkens her hills, those endless, outstretched paws
> Of Sphinx demolished or stone lion worn away.
>
> They call her a young country, but they lie:
> She is the last of lands, the emptiest,
> A woman beyond her change of life, a breast
> Still tender but within the womb is dry.

In that terrible and unforgettable last image the poet, A. D. Hope of Canberra, captures the essential physical nature of the Australian land: an old land, worn and arid, carved out in horizontal planes, only on the margins better-favoured; a landscape often majestic and beautiful, more often impassive and even sombre, even in the bright clarity of the Australian sun; impressive by its very consistency in monotony, at once coarse in texture and very subtle in its modulations; but rarely smiling.

    One might well wonder how even twelve million people manage to scratch a living from so intractable a land. And yet – and of course – it is not all so grim; the breast is tender. There are in fact two Australias, summed up in Griffith Taylor's antithesis of Empty and Economic Australia; or one might say the desert and the metropolis, and between them the broad frontier zone of the bush.

    The Australia that most Australians know is the Australia where most Australians live: 15 to 20 per cent of the continent in the south-east and the extreme south-west. Naturally this is the Australia whose image is projected to the rest of the world; and it is undeniably an exceedingly pleasant land. Those grand forests, the rich dairying flats, the orchards, the leagues of wheat, the bright clean cities, the lovelies on the beaches – all these are real enough.

Real too are the stony gibber plains and the sandridges and the wastes of spinifex, the sheets of salt, drought and bushfire and flood. On a broad physical view of the continent the latter aspect, the limitations of the land, must prevail. On a human view, the note may legitimately be the very different one of ardours, endurances and achievement.

Chapter 2

Possessing a Continent

Before the Europeans

There can be little doubt that the aboriginal inhabitants of Australia came to the continent during the later phases of the last Ice Age, not less than 16,000 years ago or (in view of recent skeletal discoveries) even 32,000 years; owing to the locking-up of so much of the ocean waters in the great ice-sheets, large areas of the Indonesian seas were then dry land, with fewer and narrower water-barriers than now exist, and much of Australia was then better-watered. Various physical characters linking the aborigines with other groups under the question-begging term 'Australoids' seem of doubtful significance, save perhaps as regarding the Veddahs of Ceylon.

The first arrivals brought with them no domestic animals except the dingo, whose feral descendants were the only non-marsupial mammals when the Europeans came; and, more significantly, they had no agriculture. Their economy was solely one of hunting, fishing, and gathering; but within this narrow range they developed considerable skills, living in tribes or 'hordes' with a developed sense of territory and sometimes of family rights. In the more arid areas the territory of even a small group would extend over hundreds of square miles, and 'tests of manhood . . . include the recital in unbroken succession of the names of all the water supplies'. Simple as the material side of their life seems, it was yet highly ingenious when set against the sheer difficulty of survival in most of this inhospitable continent; and their social life, expressed in kinship systems, ceremonials, creation myths, and art, was often very complex indeed. In this context it is no exaggeration to speak of a high level of creativity.

The aborigines may have numbered some 300,000 when European settlement began; today there are about 46,000 full-bloods, while the distinct Tasmanian race ceased absolutely to exist in 1876. The pattern of non-coexistence, tempered by well-meaning but ineffective official gestures, was set in the first years of European settlement, and until recently it can hardly be said to have bothered white Australians very much. There is now at least an incipient change of heart; and, if we here wave the aborigines so cursorily off the stage, they will reappear later.

To set the stage for the European settlement, we must try our hands at the difficult art of controlled forgetting; must think, if we can, of an Australia without corrugated iron roofs or wire fences, without one single sheep or rabbit; a continent with no straight lines, but only the irregular and often blurred frontiers of vegetation belts; a land in which the only signs of human activity would be notchings and fellings of trees, ephemeral shelters of bark and boughs, scratches and patches of colour on rock-faces, rings and patterns of stones, more or less defined footpaths; such, apart from portable artefacts, was the material legacy of the aborigines. From the air, scarcely any of this could be seen. Perhaps the rough scrabblings of camps between dune and marsh could be picked up here and there; more widely, faint plumes and pencillings of smoke rising from the bush; the most striking evidences of man's handiwork would be an occasional wall of smoke and flame on the front of a bushfire lit to drive the game, and in the more open scrub and grassland the scars of older burns. The vast land-mass was barely flecked with the faintest traces of human occupation. The Tank Stream dawdled into the placid waters of Sydney Cove across what is now Martin Place, hub of a conurbation of two and a half million souls.

This metropolis, and indeed all of Economic Australia, grew from a start as unpromising as that first Thanksgiving at Plymouth Rock, or even the fever-ridden hamlet at Jamestown. Compared with these American beginnings, that of Australia had only one factor in its favour, and even that must often have seemed dubious. It had a government, however ineptly interested, behind it.

The gaol
The motivation for settlement in 1788 may well have been more than the reason usually given, that it was essential to find somewhere (more healthy than West Africa, which was considered) for disposing of the criminals who had formerly been transported to the now independent American colonies, and were now overcrowding British gaols. Some indeed hold that transportation was the mode

rather than the motive of settlement. The great voyages of Cook, Bougainville, and others were not solely disinterested scientific endeavour; behind them lay also commercial considerations, mercantilist sparring for position in vast realms of unknown potential. By the 1780s, some of this potential was being glimpsed, and not only by the British: whaling, sealing, and that preoccupation of the century, 'marine stores' such as flax, hemp and timber. For a preeminently maritime power like Great Britain, a base in the east of New Holland was a logical development.[1]

Be this as it may, the First Fleet was thrown round the world with no more forward planning than was derived from the fact that, eighteen years previously, Captain Cook and Sir Joseph Banks had spent a week at Botany Bay and liked the look of the place. Captain Arthur Phillip, 'Governor of our territory called New South Wales' (which had been named and taken possession of by Cook rather casually, like so much in Australian history), looked again and took only a day or two to decide that Botany Bay was hopeless: not enough water. He moved a few miles to Port Jackson, named but not entered by Cook, and there, on 26 January 1788, Australia began with some 750 convicts and 450 marines and officials. Establishing the precise human numbers is a pointless academic puzzle, but we have Phillip's official return for the beasts: seven horses, two bulls, five cows, forty-eight sheep and goats, seventy-four swine, 291 assorted poultry, and five rabbits.

The cattle, unlike the convicts, could live off the country: they went bush, and when the naturally increased herd was found a few years later it was promptly protected as an essential food reserve. The sheep and rabbits were given short shrift by convicts, aborigines, and dingoes, probably in that order. There were just two people who had really practised agriculture – British agriculture – and not one plough or harrow; most of the seed-wheat, damaged by the long voyage, failed to germinate. More than once in the first two years the settlers nearly starved; the first relief ship was wrecked on the way out and when, after thirty months (and weeks on half-rations), a ship was sighted, she carried 'an unnecessary and unprofitable cargo' of 222 female convicts, mostly 'loaded with the infirmities of old age'. Luckily the other transports of the Second Fleet were not far behind.

[1] This view, pioneered by K. M. Dallas, is best presented in G. Blainey, *The Tyranny of Distance* (Sun Books, Melbourne, 1966), pp. 21–33.

Somehow they survived. Young Captain Tench could even write 'To proceed on a narrow, confined scale, in a country of the extensive limits we possess, would be unpardonable: extent of empire demands grandeur of design.' As the extensive empire was the huts of Sydney, plus about thirty acres of soil so poor and so poorly cultivated that it barely produced next year's seed, this may be irony; and certainly most would have agreed with Tench's commander: 'in the whole world there is not a worse country . . .'

For twenty-five years the colony struggled on. After Phillip, the first Governors were also naval officers, lacking his quiet yet resolute optimism, but honest irascible men, fully competent on the quarter-deck, less competent to guide economic development and to handle the specially raised New South Wales Corps which provided the most permanent and the toughest official cadres in this enclave of exiles. Some progress was made; the ex-convict James Ruse showed that it was possible to be a self-supporting arable farmer, and by introducing the merino sheep James Macarthur set a pattern of export production which still largely prevails. An unamiable man, perhaps something of a paranoiac, Macarthur yet had something near genius in his single-minded pursuit of economic advance – his own first, beyond any doubt, but to him that was the general good, and in the circumstances this was valid enough. He saw clearly that a non-perishable export commodity was essential; for the England of the Napoleonic Wars, with supplies from Saxony and Spain wholly or largely cut off, that commodity was wool, which alone could stand the long voyage and the high transport costs to England – as well as, later, the eight or ten weeks' journey by bullock-dray from interior to coast.

Macarthur and his fellow-officers of the New South Wales Corps bought up government stores the moment they arrived, made rum almost the currency, and bullied successive Governors into granting them most of the land and the assigned convict labour to run it. With the home government distracted by the struggle against revolutionary and Napoleonic France, there was little effective check on their activity; and there was no other group with the economic power and grasp to act as entrepreneurs. Only they could stand out against the extortion of the masters of trading vessels, and if this meant, as it did, a Rum Corps monopoly, at least money was kept in the colony and invested there; without them it is difficult to see how even the very modest expansion of the first fifteen years could have taken place.

The Rum Corps has received sweeping denigration from radical Australians, and certainly some of its officers seem to have been gentlemen in a merely technical sense. One may not uncharitably suspect that during the Napoleonic Wars good material would scarcely have come or been sent to such a corps. The group compares unfavourably with the Peninsular generation which followed, men like Brisbane, an ineffective Governor but an amateur astronomer who took a real interest in cultural development; Surveyor-General Mitchell, the most scientific of the earlier inland explorers; William Light, son of Francis Light of Penang by a Portuguese-Malay girl (traditionally a Princess of Kedah!), a gallant officer, a man of culture and many parts, who as founder and surveyor of Adelaide gave Australia her first effective lesson in town-planning.

For twenty years the Rum Corps ruled the roost. As Governor, Bligh of the *Bounty* tried to curb its power and favoured the few free settlers who were beginning to farm the Hawkesbury flats thirty or forty miles from Sydney; Macarthur and the Corps deposed Bligh. His successor, Lachlan Macquarie, was sent out in 1810 – with his own regiment – to wind up this little *coup*. High-minded and highly angular, he promoted public works with perhaps more vision than judgement, and took the view, common sense now but heresy then, that once a convict had purged his crime by serving his term of transportation, any career or office for which his talents fitted him should be open. Admirable as Macquarie's ends were in the long run, this was treachery to his class, the official and landed class; and he pursued his aims with so little tact that he could plausibly be charged with looking on the colony as a preserve for ex-criminals: no gentleman need apply. What with this and what with his expenditure on public works, he fell foul of the home government and was recalled in something like disgrace. Yet he had left some solid material foundations, and given a social lead, a hope never forgotten by the emancipist ex-convicts who sang

> Macquarie was the Prince of Men,
> Australia's pride and joy;
> We ne'er shall see his like again,
> Here's to the *old* Viceroy!

But perhaps his name and fame were saved not by the bibulous odes of Michael Massey Robinson but by an event that would have happened in any case: the penetration of the Blue Mountains which surrounded the County of Cumberland, 'the gaol', like a wall for convict and free alike.

The gaol-break

The County of Cumberland was as full as it well could be on current techniques of husbandry, and swept by plagues of drought and caterpillars, when in 1813 the barrier was at last forced. The expansion which followed was almost an explosion. It was not on a broad front inland from the coast; rather it forced its way by a few defiles through the rugged and forested coastal scarps, fanning out over the more open plateaus beyond; apart from Sydney and New-castle, most of the few coastal settlements long remained (and some still are) mere pockets between sea and bush.

Beyond the Blue Mountains lay scores of thousands of square miles of rolling parkland, empty for the taking: the aborigines counted for nothing. Bathurst, the oldest inland city, was founded with modest pomp by Macquarie in 1815 – a year after Cleveland, Ohio, five years before Indianapolis – and already by 1823 land was being taken up around Canberra, 200 miles to the south. Attempts to control the movement by the proclamation, in 1829, of the Nineteen Counties as the 'limits of location' were futile; the Counties were a block of 34,505 square miles, extending about 150 miles inland from Sydney; but already in 1830 half the flocks were beyond their limits. As Governor Gipps wrote in 1840:

> As well might it be attempted to confine the Arabs of the Desert within a circle, traced upon their sands, as to confine the Graziers or Woolgrowers of New South Wales within any bounds that can possibly be assigned to them; and as certainly as the Arabs would be starved, so also would the flocks and herds . . . and the pros-perity of the Colony would be at an end.

The land-takers had to be legitimised by the issue of tickets of occupancy giving simply the right to graze stock over a roughly defined area; the holders of these tickets were 'squatters' – a word which in Australia, unlike the rest of the world, connoted not poverty but wealth, though not invariably undue respectability.

By the 'forties this very open pastoralism had spread right through New England (the north-east of New South Wales), while to the south it had entered the Riverina, the country between Murrumbidgee and Murray, and on the latter river it was meeting a new advance from Melbourne.

The continent claimed

By this time New South Wales and Sydney had rivals. In what became Victoria, the Henty family, from Sussex via Western Australia, set up a whaling and farming base at Portland, in the extreme west, in 1834; next year Melbourne itself began as offshoot from Tasmania, then still officially Van Diemens Land. Both these ventures were completely unauthorised and were recognised only reluctantly, as the Port Phillip District, by Sydney and Whitehall. Within a decade the squatters of Port Phillip were so impatient of neglect by Sydney that they elected Lord Grey, the Secretary of State for the Colonies, to represent them in the New South Wales legislature. Grey could hardly take up his duties, but neither could a Port Phillip squatter, separated from the capital by 500 almost roadless miles; the point was well taken, and in 1850 Grey acceded to the demand for a separate colony of Victoria.

Victoria's parent Van Diemens Land itself began in 1803–4 as the backwash of an unsuccessful settlement at Port Phillip, and became a separate colony in 1825. By 1840, Hobart was a town of taverns and shipyards, tough, lively, rowdy as befitted a major whaling base in a convict colony. In the lowlands, gentlemen farmers and their convicts were busy growing the wheat which did not do so well around Sydney (the Tasmanian climate, both for plants and men, was so much more akin to Britain's) and incidentally endowing the island with a neglected heritage in the form of much good Georgian building. Tasmania was used for the tougher convicts and recidivists, like the settlement at Moreton Bay (1821) which became Queensland in 1859.

The other two colonies were not penal in origin. South Australia was founded in 1836, designed with loving care to reproduce all the features of English society minus its religious discriminations and its poverty; its over-weening aristocracy was ruled out by nature. The machinery to achieve this half-Radical half-Whig end had been devised by Edward Gibbon Wakefield who, having bungled his elopement with the desirably wealthy Miss Ellen Turner, occupied his enforced leisure by writing, in Newgate Gaol, *A Letter from Sydney*. The key to Wakefield's thinking, expressed with elegance and force, was that great land-grants were useless without the labour to run them; convicts were useless and anyhow too few. Sell the land, therefore, at a uniform and reasonably high price, and use the proceeds to bring out the free labour needed by the capitalist or yeoman farmers who were to be the core of the new society. The ideal was not ungenerous: the society was to be free of convictism, self-governing and self-financing, and the industrious poor, morally and materially more independent than in England, could by diligence and thrift (but not too quickly) win their way to a modest competence in this new land.

The Wakefield group had all the right contacts and were adepts in manipulating them, but Wakefieldism had a longer and more significant career in New Zealand than in Australia: in South Australia it broke down largely because the gentlemen farmers, many of whom to begin with couldn't farm, preferred to squabble and speculate in town lots at Adelaide, and paradoxically the success of land sales in the first years flooded the colony with more immigrants than could well be handled. Nevertheless the colony did attract sufficient people of solid capacity to take a lead in agriculture. Already by 1842 John Ridley had invented the stripper, which largely overcame the shortage of labour for the wheat harvest, and German immigrants were extending viticulture: Buring, Lindemann, Seppelt are still important names in the Australian wine industry. So when the gold rushes came, South Australians found that feeding the diggers more than compensated the lack of gold of their own, and this without the social troubles which would have disturbed their somewhat complacently tidy little society. And Adelaide has remained acutely conscious that, unlike Sydney and Melbourne, it was founded by gentlemen for gentlemen.

There was some French exploration round the coasts early in the century, just enough to worry about: Western Australia began as a military outpost at Albany, soon overshadowed by the initially unhappy Swanland settlement at Perth in 1829. But progress in the west was desperately slow: having come most of the way round the world, voluntary emigrants naturally preferred going the little farther to the established eastern colonies, and in 1849–50, when Victoria and New South Wales were turning away the convict transports, Western Australians had to swallow their pride and ask for them. But really striking advance had to wait till the gold rushes of the 1890s.

Finally, in the far north there had been abortive military settlements at Melville Island and Port Essington in 1824–29 and again in 1838, motivated partly by nervousness about the French and partly by pipe-dreams of tapping the trade of the East Indies. The only settlers to remain were the imported draught buffaloes, whose feral descendants are still hunted, along with the native crocodiles, for their hides.

Thus by 1840 there was at least some settlement in every colony: the British claim to an entire continent had been initiated when Europe was engrossed in the Revolutionary and Napoleonic wars, and was completed almost unnoticed in 1829 by the annexation of all that part of New Holland not included in New South Wales – a trifle of 1,495,054 square miles, most of which is now in Western Australia and the Northern Territory. It occurred to nobody that the aborigines had prior rights; only John Batman at Melbourne went through the motions of a treaty, 'purchasing' 600,000 acres for the traditional red flannel and trinkets. His claim was disowned by the Crown, but that did not mean that the local natives came into their own: to Europe the whole continent was *res nullius*, an empty thing, there for the first taker. The British claim was being made good by actual occupation, and with the separation of Victoria and Queensland and the transfer of the Northern Territory to South Australia (1863) the political map was complete. 'Actual occupation', however, was thin: in 1850 there were only 405,636 whites in all Australia.

Convicts, emancipists, and exclusionists

The society which developed in the first three decades was and had to be rigidly authoritarian, tempered at the top by the internal bickerings of a tiny oligarchy. After the first few years convicts actually doing time were never a majority, except briefly in Van Diemens Land; but in 1821 over 82 per cent of the adult population of 22,719 had been transported. Between 1825 and 1850, however, free immigrants numbered 223,000, transportees less than half as many. Altogether a total of some 160,000 convicts were sent to Australia, all but 10,000 of them to the eastern colonies (excluding unsmirched South Australia) and before 1850. The convict-descended component in the modern population is therefore very slight, the more so as most were males and many were not in a position to found families.

As to what manner of men they were, that has been much disputed. Undoubtedly some were the brighter lads of the village, those with pluck to raid the squire's coverts or burn the rector's haystacks; there was a very small leaven of politicals – Irish rebels, Scots Reformers, Tolpuddle Martyrs, Chartists; and some were men of family gone wrong: to the 'gentleman's crime', forgery, Australia owed a number of professional men, among them the best of her early architects, Francis Greenway, a protégé of Macquarie's whose portrait appropriately adorns Australian currency notes, and the versatile James Blackburn in Tasmania.

To exaggerate these elements is comforting doctrine. By and large most of the convicts came from the submerged urban proletariat, and there seems little point in extenuating their records: some got seven years for offences which would not now receive as many months or weeks, but many were undoubtedly tough professionals. An educated man with introductions might get a ticket-of-leave almost at once, and become a minor public servant; at the other end of the scale were the real hells, mainly for recidivists: the chain-gangs on the roads, Moreton Bay, Port Arthur (now Australia's most impressive ruin) in Van Diemens Land, and most dreadful of all Norfolk Island, where in the worst periods conditions were so frightful that the Chief Justice of Australia declared to an official enquiry his belief that convicts committed murder without malice, simply to escape in the only way possible – by getting hanged. Between these extremes, convicts assigned to squatters might find themselves in the hands of a sadist, or might have a rudely comfortable life with the chance of a small competence on discharge.

Small as the numerical contribution of the convicts was in the long run, the fact remains that the first formative era of Australia was the era of the lash. Authority made the laws, its victims banded together in a tacit but complete confederacy. A hostility to the arm of the law, a distrust of 'authority', a code of 'mateship' – still strands in Australian *mores* – were fostered by other factors, notably the rough comradeship on the diggings and among the itinerant bush workers, but in their essence go back to convict days. So *Bold Jack Donahue* fathered *The Wild Colonial Boy*, most popular of the earlier bush ballads, and their spirit survived their time. The transmutation of the later bushranger Ned Kelly into a serious myth for poets and painters of the stature of Douglas Stewart and Sidney Nolan is but another example.

In a way, the convicts were more trouble once they had served their terms than while they were still under penal authority. With a steadily if slowly expanding economy, there was no great difficulty with the rank and file; it was the educated emancipist who had to have a career opened to his talents, and this inevitably led to conflict with the oligarchy – even in trade, since in New South Wales, as the Rum Corps had shown, there was no false prejudice against a gentleman following the main chance. The exclusionist oligarchs, however, had their own grievances against arbitrary power: they wanted trial by jury (at least amongst their peers), some voice in policy, some freedom of the Press in order to attack the Governor. They were very far indeed from being democrats or even reforming Whigs; and yet, while they resisted violently Macquarie's policy of advancing emancipists even to the bar or the local bench, they still needed allies. Hence a curious three-cornered struggle, often bitter and squalid, of shifting alliances – exclusionists and emancipists against each other and against the bureaucracy, a struggle complicated by the changing personalities of Governors and by the apparently unpredictable interventions of the home government, whose information and instructions were naturally nearly always out of date.

Separation of executive and judiciary, and nominated executive and legislative councils, came in the 1820s; by 1843 New South Wales had a Legislative Council with a majority elected on a very narrow suffrage, so that the more outrageous petty interferences of Whitehall (such as the decision on where to put lighthouses) were now curbed. But by this time a new political element was rising into significance, the free immigrants, mainly business-men, professionals, and artisans in Sydney and Melbourne. The political struggle had to some extent shifted to economic matters such as the future of transportation and land tenure, in which the squatters were concerned with securing more liberal terms and more assured tenure from the Crown; it was to return to constitutional issues in the 'fifties, when W. C. Wentworth, once the darling of the reformers, was to advocate a hereditary 'bunyip aristocracy'. New lines were being drawn: the old emancipist quarrel was becoming a matter of history, but the big squatters wanted the revival of transportation (which had ended in 1840) or even the importing of Asian labour. Against this, of course, the wage-earners and the respectable and radical middle class were adamant, and when as a result of mass meetings the transport *Hashemy* sailed on from Sydney to Moreton Bay (1849) the retreat of the squattocracy had begun. If the legacy of convictism was the agin-the-government mateship of the lower orders, that of the emancipist struggle and the oligarchic cliques was a certain raffishness in public life, contrasting markedly with the staidness of politics in Victorian England.

Gold and votes

Although it is virtually certain that earlier gold discoveries had been officially hushed up (it would never have done to let the convicts know they had been sent to El Dorado), the first openly avowed finds were made in the 1850s in New South Wales and Victoria; and between 1850 and 1860 the population nearly trebled, to 1,146,000. The lion's share in this expansion was Victoria's: she leapt from 76,000 to 538,000 souls, an increase of 600 per cent, neglecting of course aboriginal souls, as the Commonwealth Census still did until 1961.

This great injection of both capital and labour naturally resulted in an inflationary expansion, even though its first effect was an immense drain of every sort of labour to the diggings. Its social and political effects were profound. Until the gold decade, Australian society in some ways seems a survival of the eighteenth century: around Sydney a settled society of large land-owners and officials, who between them wielded political power; in the bush a frontier but still hierarchical society with the squatter for the squire. Only in Sydney, Melbourne, and Adelaide was there a pale replica of the middle-class radical England of the 1830s. The gold rushes changed all this.

The influence on this change of really left democratic ideas and movements, such as Chartism, has quite probably been exaggerated by the radical school of Australian historiography. This orthodoxy, which has been as dominant as the Whig view of English history was in the last century, is now under serious revision, on the one hand through more econometric analyses of economic history such as those of Noel Butlin, on the other through increasing attention to less clear-cut ideological values, as in Manning Clark's *History of Australia* which, despite a highly personal and at times over-intense presentation, is yet the first serious attempt on the grand scale to place Australia in relation to great movements of thought. Nevertheless the radical view, like the Whig, should not be too lightly discounted in its broad outlines, though specific interpretations are open to challange.

Thus the affair of Eureka Stockade in December 1854 hardly bears the weight sometimes placed on it. A protest by the Ballarat diggers against the arrogance and injustice of the gold field officials culminated in the hoisting of a rebel flag bearing the Southern Cross and an attack by troops in which twenty-two miners and six soldiers were killed. It was dramatic in a country whose history lacks spectacular event of this sort, but hardly a turning-point in Australian history: rather an incident, turned to violence by official bungling, and the drama made it a myth. No doubt it played its part in a general ferment, to which the struggle against transportation had also contributed; but the agitation was much less in New South Wales (after all, the diggings were much farther from Sydney than Ballarat from Melbourne), and less still in South Australia where there were no diggers and transportation had never existed. Yet in 1855 all three colonies received constitutions with lower houses elected on wide franchises, and quiet South Australia had even a slight lead in the introduction of manhood suffrage and the 'Australian ballot' (1856); these came to Victoria in 1857 and New South Wales in 1858. But the general ferment cannot be denied, and that this liberalism was not just an automatic reflex of unsolicited generosity from the home government is shown by the fact that Tasmania lagged.

In 1865 an imperial Act finally confirmed the validity of any colonial law which did not violate an expressly applicable imperial statute, and such statutes were very few. Colonial Governors had wide powers of refusing bills, or reserving them for assent in London, and in some cases (for example constitutional amendments) reservation was required. But these requirements themselves came within the scope of colonial amendment powers, and in any event the Governors gradually came to depend more and more on the advice of their local ministers, less and less on that of Downing Street; in particular, they left purely legal objections to the validity of legislation to the decision of the local Courts, with ultimate appeal to the Privy Council. Hence by 1890, when Western Australia attained fully responsible government, the six colonies were to all intents six independent states so far as local matters were concerned, and had begun to negotiate independent commercial arrangements with each other and with other countries. But they

accepted without question the sole authority of the imperial government in the higher realms of foreign policy, in particular war and
peace.

'Unlocking the land': the agrarian dream

If Eureka was but an incident, the total effect of the gold decade
was a revolution whose immediate beneficiaries were not so much
the diggers and the bush democracy (many of whom were too
mobile to secure a vote) as the middle class and artisans of the
capital cities. The next move, however, was agrarian. As the alluvial
gold failed, there were increasing numbers anxious for access to the
land locked away in great squatting properties, which had acquired
some security of tenure in 1847. The squatters and their clients
were of course numerically very weak, and in the 1860s the colonial
legislatures passed ambitious Acts for closer agricultural settlement.
Although there was variation in local detail, and with later amendments, the general effect of the Robertson and Duffy Acts in New
South Wales and Victoria was that almost anybody could select an
agricultural holding, usually of 320 acres, on very easy terms and in
New South Wales even before survey. Common sense yielded to a
beautiful dream of Australian plains filled with a sturdy and independent yeomanry.

Much of this selection was not *bona fide*. The acres might be
carefully chosen to include the water-points on a grazing property;
this picking out of the eyes was known as peacocking, and the
object was often not agriculture but blackmail by forcing the squatter to buy back. To meet this sharp practice, many squatters did
their own peacocking, using dummy selectors – in some cases their
unborn children. The potential for corruption was large and
obvious, and the squatters had more money for graft, or could
borrow it from the banks and pastoral companies which increasingly
held real control of the land: paradoxically, after two decades of
closer settlement, over half the alienated land of New South Wales
was held by 552 men with over 18 million acres. The squatters'
defence was that they were compelled into dishonesty, but it is
probably a rationalisation to date a general decline in public
morals from the selection era: the earlier history of Australia would
provide a fine anthology of skulduggery, from the Rum Corps
on.

Closer settlement in all mainland colonies over-reached itself.

Coupled with the folk heresy that 'rain follows the plough', it led in South Australia to a disastrous extension of wheat-growing far beyond the line which the perspicacious (and naturally unpopular) Surveyor-General Goyder had suggested as the safe limit for arable; hence in the 'middle north' every hill-top has its stone ruin, and the landscape recalls the Scots border after an English raid, or the Shenandoah after Sheridan had gone through. It was not simply a matter of defeat by corruption and political manoeuvre, though naturally this explanation was and is popular; more fundamentally, very much of the country thrown open to selection was just not suitable to small-scale arable farming with then existing techniques.

The American Middle West was too constantly before Australian eyes; as Griffith Taylor has pointed out, 450 miles west from New York in the Ohio valley, one is just approaching the finest agricultural areas of the United States; at that distance from Sydney, one is back o'Bourke, in an environment more akin to the Arizona semi-desert. Unlike the Middle West, the Australian frontier was, and largely still is, a 'big man's frontier'. The costs implied by distance to markets, the high overheads of bringing in bulk supplies, the constant risks of droughts, bushfires, and floods, all conspire to make Australia by and large inhospitable to the small farmer. For many a *bona fide* selector, bush farming was a long-drawn-out agony of disillusion: the pathos comes out even through the knockabout fun of Steele Rudd's *On Our Selection*.

Nevertheless, taken as a whole the selection Acts have had an unduly bad press; the nineteenth-century official enquiries, on which so much condemnation is based, were sometimes partial in more than one sense. Closer examination of the record suggests that in some areas the Acts did indeed foster a good deal of solidly based farming settlement; there were competent and successful selectors, in greater numbers than the blanket view of total failure allows, and without them the countryside would not have been ready to carry out the real advance which came with improved techniques towards the close of the century. By and large, the Acts did not achieve their avowed aim of creating an independent self-reliant yeomanry; even to-day, with the most modern techniques, arable seems almost lost in the vastness of the continent: 30 million acres, half of it wheat, only about 1.6 per cent of the total area. But the selectors and their sponsors did put down the first seedlings, tender and even perhaps sickly; for survival and growth, they needed – and they received – continued applications of State aid and, later, of new and greatly improved techniques.

An Australian dilemma

Here we touch on a fundamental duality in Australian life, one deep-rooted in its historical geography. On the one hand, the conditions of bush life enforced a self-reliant individualism ready to turn its hand to anything, and the habit of mind summed up in the national motto 'she'll do'. The man on the land, were he squatter, selector, or bush worker, had perforce to do many things with what tools and rough materials lay to his hand. He might have to build his house or sink a well, cure a sick horse or set a broken leg, perhaps even tend his wife in childbirth and teach his children. There was no room here for professional graces; anything would do so long as it worked. This individualism, the often narrow economic sectionalism bred in a long tradition of struggles from emancipists versus exclusionist gentry to shearers versus squatters, the empirical amateurishness and casualness – all these persist now that Australian society is not only urbanised but largely metropolitanised. They are offset by other bush qualities: astonishing individual generosity, a genius for individual and collective improvisation in crises such as a bushfire or a war.

On the other hand, as the selectors found that their land was not so easy to run as to get – again for obvious geographical reasons – it became clear that individualism and improvisation were not enough. It was by State action that they had got their land; let State action make it possible for them to run it profitably. This meant railways, water-supplies, irrigation, bounties, tariffs, agricultural research. Railway policy is an example: the first lines were begun by private enterprise, including that of politicians who preferred it that way; but high construction costs, labour shortages, and the great distances between pay-load centres soon brought them near or right into bankruptcy, and governments had to come to the rescue if lines were to be built at all; but the first take-over Acts were in temporary terms envisaging an eventual return to private enterprise. Hence a French observer as early as the 1890s could speak of 'Socialism without doctrines' as the note of Australian society; and so to a large extent it still is. Men will vote against the Australian Labor Party for its doctrinaire retention of socialism in its platform, while

supporting or even demanding essentially *étatiste* policies from a
Liberal government.

But these essentials, railways and the rest, meant organisation
and bureaucracy, and in this land of vast distances and few people
the countryside had neither the men nor the money to run the
machinery needed. These had to come from the existing administrative and commercial centres, the great port-capitals, which in
turn had to accept the task since their commerce depended on
primary exports and hence on continued expansion of rural industry. But the effect of the centralisation of services – rendered so
much easier by the telegraph – was to reinforce the trend to metropolitan concentration which had been strong from the very beginning.

By the end of the first century, then, the main pattern of settlement had been blocked out; most parts of Australia which are now
peopled had at least some population. Many bad mistakes had been
made in the selection and closer settlement policy, and the struggle
between squatters and selectors was inconclusive: shorn of political
power (except by way of obstruction in upper houses elected on
narrow franchises), the squatters, or financial agencies at home or
abroad to whom many were in mortgage, were economically protected by the hard facts of geography: a big man's frontier. Wool
was still dominant, but no longer the monopoly it had been;
although the land industries were, as they still are, predominantly
extensive rather than intensive, advances in scientific agriculture
and pastoralism were already afoot, and were to constitute perhaps
Australia's largest single contribution to human welfare. Large
towns were few, practically only Sydney, Melbourne, Adelaide,
perhaps Brisbane might be counted; but in them consumption
industries were being built up. The society and the economy were
far more diversified and articulated than they had been before the
1850s.

But the attempt, conscious on the part of the Wakefieldians and
implicit with some others, to transplant in Australia the balanced
hierarchy of England had failed. A few oases reproduced faintly
something of the English scene and the pre-industrial English ethos:
the Tasmanian lowlands, the rolling hills north of Adelaide, isolated
patches in New South Wales and Victoria where climate and terrain produced an environment not too wildly dissimilar from

'home'. Elsewhere – nearly everywhere – the dream had dissolved before the intractable geography and the historical accident which had substituted for steady growth the inflationary influx of the gold decade; and by the same token had doomed such conservatism as Wentworth's project of a local peerage to serve as an aristocratic balance to the weight of democratic numbers.

From the start there had been a tension between the values of the 'currency lads' born in the colonies and the 'sterling' sent from Britain; now the stage was set for the confluence of various myths – *The Wild Colonial Boy*, Eureka, Ned Kelly, mateship, and more visionary imaginings of an Austral land unstained by Europe's hates and wars – into the image of a brash young nation.

Chapter 3

Founding a Nation

THE 'NINETIES' in Australia were anything but *fin de siècle*. The period must not be defined too closely. In the preceding decade we have such premonitions as the founding in 1880 of *The Bulletin*, the first overseas forays in Queensland's imperially disavowed annexation of Papua (1883) and the sending of a New South Wales contingent to the Sudan (1885), the founding of the Association for the Advancement of Science (ANZAAS), the introduction of impressionist painting by Tom Roberts and others in the '9 × 5' exhibition of 1889. And as Vance Palmer points out in *The Legend of the Nineties*, the two books which most incarnate the shaping spirit of the decade did not appear until the next century: Joseph Furphy's incomparable novel *Such is Life*, half-picaresque and half-philosophical, in 1903, and in 1912 Bernard O'Dowd's very uneven but powerful poem *The Bush*:

> Our youngest hearts prolong the far pulsation
> And churn the brine of the primordial sea:
> The foetus writes the précis of creation:
> Australia is the whole world's legatee.

The 'nineties proper opened with a great depression, most acute in Victoria, and closed in the century's worst series of drought years; yet arable farming became more firmly based than ever before. They saw the most critically significant strikes in Australian history, the founding of the Australian Labor Party, and in 1899 a Labor government in Queensland, a world 'first' even if it did last less than a week. Alongside the sharpening of an isolationist and radical national identity in the Labor movement and the *Bulletin* writers there was the more cautious and conservative movement, still with 'imperial' undertones, towards Federation. The decade was far from one of steady progress, yet in it modern Australia took shape.

The economy: progress and slump

In 1891 the non-aboriginal population of Australia was 3,241,000; of this total, 1,158,000 were in New South Wales. Melbourne was much the largest city in Australia, with 491,000 inhabitants to Sydney's 383,000, respectively 43 and 33 per cent of the colony total. From being simply ports and administrative centres, these cities had become financial metropolises, but second-hand ones depending on the continued influx of British capital.

Much of this capital was devoted to the needs of the land. In the pastoral industries, fencing, water-supply, and dummying against selectors all called for money, which could be had at a price from the city banks and from great wool merchants such as Dalgety's; once mortgaged, however, the individual squatter was often kept mortgaged by drought or low prices, and wool prices fell fairly consistently from 1870 till the end of the century. There were added risks and costs such as those presented by erosion and the rabbit plague which, beginning in Victoria about 1860, had swept up to Queensland by 1886; these were only partially offset by technical improvement in breeding and machine shearing, which became widespread in the 'nineties. The result was that the squatter very generally became a manager for some financial or 'stock and station' agency. Balladry may gloss the cold statistics –

> When first I was a squatter, some twenty years ago,
>   Then Fortune followed gaily in my train,
> But I speculated heavy, and I'd have you all to know
>   That I've lost that little freehold on the plain;
> Oh the stockyard's tumbled down and the woolshed's
>   fallen in,
>   I've written to the mortgagees in vain . . .

This, and the generally increasing tightness of the squatter's financial position, had some bearing on his relations with his labour, and it fostered the tendency to centralisation in the capitals. The pastoral industry has never been a large direct employer relative to its output, but it needs an infrastructure of marketing, finance, and supply; the telegraph facilitated central organisation and control, and this is one factor in the paradoxical paucity of medium-sized towns in a highly urbanised country. There are few Australian equivalents of the larger European subregional centre, or even the Middle West service centre of the 20–30,000 population class.

The waning of the older goldfields led to a great deal of slap-dash prospecting all over the continent, and a great diversification of the mining industry: gold mainly in eastern Queensland and from 1885 in Western Australia; copper first in South Australia and later in Tasmania; tin in Queensland, New England (NSW), and Tasmania; silver-lead-zinc in Tasmania again but most importantly at Broken Hill, opened up in 1883 and still to-day an urban outlier in the semi-desert, as are the gold towns of Kalgoorlie and Coolgardie in Western Australia. All these were for export; meanwhile the coalfields of the Hunter valley, discovered in 1796 and exploited in a small way around 1800, and those west and south of Sydney, with smaller fields in the other colonies, met local demand and bunkering as well as some exports to Pacific countries. Although mining investment was quantitatively much less than that in construction, manufacturing, or pastoralism, its highly speculative nature played its part in the great depression: a sober regard for facts was no part of the outfit.

The main field of public investment was in railways; mileage grew from 994 in 1870 to 9,757 in 1890 and, despite financial stringency, to 12,955 in 1900. Unfortunately, by a fortuitous muddle, Victoria and South Australia adopted broad gauge (5′ 3″) with 3′ 6″ lines in the remoter parts of the latter colony and in Queensland, while New South Wales adhered to the standard 4′ 8½″.[1] With some exception for obvious geographical reasons in Queensland, the system in each colony focused on the capital, once more reinforcing metropolitan concentration; there was of course much log-rolling, but the railways helped very greatly in the establishment of a really settled market agriculture by substantial farmers instead of semi-subsistence selectors.

Noel Butlin's studies of investment from 1861 to 1900 show conclusively that 'the building of cities absorbed the greater part of Australian resources devoted to developmental purposes', and nowhere was this more true than in the greatest of them all, Mel-

---

[1] The reason is that in 1848 New South Wales, having agreed with South Australia on standard gauge, imported an Irish engineer who put across the broad gauge of that country. South Australia and Victoria (now separated) conformed, but after they had ordered their rolling stock New South Wales accepted a Scots engineer's plea for the cheaper standard gauge, without bothering to inform her neighbours. See G. Blainey, *The Tyranny of Distance* (Sun Books, Melbourne, 1966), pp. 244–47, and E. Harding, *Uniform Railway Gauge* (Lothian, Sydney, 1958), pp. 23–32.

bourne. It was true that Victoria had adopted early – in the 'seventies – a high protectionist policy and had built up the largest manufacturing industry in the continent, even though this was almost confined to light consumption and engineering lines and was little more advanced in organisation than that of free trade New South Wales; but this was a relatively small component of economic activity. Over-capitalisation on the land (often in the form of over-stocking to keep up output in the face of falling prices), politically rather than economically motivated railways, wildcat mining speculation (also in face of falling silver prices), were important factors in the depression, but its depth and catastrophic nature were due to the wild inflation of city land-values, more particularly in Melbourne. Dealings were financed by inexperienced and often irresponsible land-banks and building societies, relying on a continuation of British lending. As the crisis, brought on by over-extension, deepened, this naturally began to dry up, although the effect of British withdrawals was probably a contingent rather than a primary cause of the crash.

There had been a number of Australian failures, mainly of land and finance companies, in 1891–92; but the major crash began when the Commercial Bank of Australia, one of the largest Melbourne firms, suspended in April 1893. By May the Victorian government was compelled to proclaim five bank holidays in a row, although three of the stronger banks in part ignored them. More astute government action in New South Wales cushioned the shock to some extent, but Australian credit as a whole was very severely shaken. In Victoria the results were almost catastrophic: while the population of Australia increased by 18.75 per cent in 1891–1901, Victoria's growth was only 5.35 per cent, less than a quarter of the natural increase; for Sydney and Melbourne the increases were 26 and a mere 1 per cent. The ornate new offices of central Melbourne, and thousands of suburban villas and cottages, long stood tenantless. Recovery was slow, achieved mainly by grim cheeseparing.

The droughts of 1895–1902 were devastating in New South Wales and Queensland: sheep numbers in the former fell from over 60 million to under 27 million, and Queensland's 22 million in 1895 fell in like proportion. Over-stocking and rabbits as well as drought ruined the vegetation cover and led to severe wind-erosion and great dust-storms, and it seems that the dry Western Division – the country between Lachlan and Darling and beyond the latter – never fully recovered from these years. But improved breeding increased the weight of fleeces, so that the New South Wales wool clip fell in weight by the remarkably low figure of only 6 per cent. Since 1885 refrigeration had permitted the export of frozen mutton, as well as the expansion of the beef industry, especially in northern Queensland.

Even more notable was strictly agricultural progress. A more rational approach to closer settlement, by survey and classification of land before subdivision, put farming in New South Wales on a firmer footing. In South Australia, where the rapid areal expansion of the 'seventies was followed by permanent retreat from the northern portion of the settled Counties, new areas were opened in Eyre Peninsula and in the south-east, where the mallee scrub was cleared by heavy rollers and fire, and tilled by the 'stump-jump' plough invented in 1876; McKay's combined harvester-thresher came into use in 1891. South Australia led the way in the application of superphosphate, supplemented by nitrogen-fixing subterranean clover in the 'super and sub revolution'. Also significant to the progress of the wheat industry was the pioneer breeding work of William Farrer, devoted to producing rust- and drought-resistant strains of high yield; the culmination of sixteen years' work was 'Federation' wheat in 1902.

Under the guidance of Alfred Deakin, Victoria had commenced irrigation in the mid-'eighties, bringing the Chaffey brothers from California to start citrus and vine growing at Mildura on the Murray: technically successful, the project ran into marketing and (with the depression) financial difficulties, and the full development of this 'Sunraysia' oasis, as well as intensive irrigation in the Goulburn valley, had to wait till the twentieth century. Extensive irrigation – the use of water for stock as well as domestic supplies – was an essential factor in the opening up of the Wimmera, the mallee country of north-western Victoria.

Apart from wheat, the most striking agricultural advance was the expansion of sugar-cane along the tropical Queensland coast; although small producers supplying central mills were replacing larger holdings with individual small mills, the industry was based on indentured 'kanaka' labour from the Pacific islands, brought in by 'blackbirders' whose methods were sometimes not easily distinguishable from slaving. The eventual suppression of 'kanaka' labour owes less to humanitarianism than to the 'White Australia' ethos which the Australian radical movement made peculiarly, though not exclusively, its own.

The rise of Australian Labor

The prehistory of the Australian Labor movement was not greatly dissimilar from that of Britain, allowing for differences of scale and the scarcity and mobility of workers. By 1870 craft unions were fairly strong in the capitals, and if anything were even more respectable than British unionism of the day. The later history, though showing some parallelism of phase – for example, syndicalist influence from 1911 on and a peak of militancy around 1921 – was very different, and few things are more disconcerting to the immigrant social democratic intellectual from Britain than the general anti-intellectualism of Australian Labor. As in many aspects of Australian life, the original British pragmatism is writ more large, to the extent that it has itself become, paradoxically, an impediment to re-thinking.

The solid construction and routine efficiency of the Australian Labor Party machines, State and Federal, play a big part in this. As we shall see, large steps towards the Welfare State were quickly obtained by an empirical approach, and it was natural to succumb to the temptation; nor is it at all clear that better results would have been attained by more devotion to theoretic principle and less to politicking. However, once the gains had been institutionalised, and partly owing to the historic accident of the great depression of the 1930s, this has led to an essentially defensive stance (and the defences are powerful) in the mid-twentieth century. It is now hard indeed to recognise the Australian Labor Party as Keith Hancock's 'party of change'. This general pragmatism is not confined to Labor: it is shared by its rivals, the Liberal and Country Parties, though not by the break-away Democratic Labor Party; and it is naturally even stronger in State than in Federal politics.

This was by no means so apparent in the 'nineties, when Labor had a very lively interest in ideas and ideological attitudes were very fluid. As in Britain, the immediate forerunners of a Labor Party were election or representation leagues of a somewhat 'lib-lab' cast, with a variety of more ideological ginger groups prompting from the wings. These groups were inspired largely by Bellamy's *Looking Backward*, which had the place in Australian socialist affections of William Morris's *News from Nowhere* in British, and by Henry George, though in this isolationist decade there was a strong home-spun contribution represented by such lively and idiosyncratic journals as *The Hummer* of Wagga Wagga and *The Boomerang*, William Lane's paper, at Brisbane.

The older craft unions had concentrated much of their energy on the Eight Hour Day effort, which began as early as the 'fifties and by 1875 had had a good deal of piecemeal success in most colonies. As in Britain, Trades Councils were a natural development, but these were usually of local, mainly metropolitan, significance, and sometimes astonishingly parochial: in 1893 the Melbourne Council even refused the unemployed the use of the Trades Hall. A great change was ushered in by the New Unionism of the 'eighties, which like its British analogue appealed to the unskilled and semi-skilled and was much more militant than craft unionism. Its most important figure was W. G. Spence, a very able leader and organiser, who began by forming the Victorian and then Australian Miners' Association and moved on to enlist the semi-nomadic bush-workers, most notably in the Amalgamated Shearers' Union:[1] by 1889 the ASU and allied Queensland unions had organised the great majority of shearers, seasonal workers who had the tactical advantage of being concentrated as at a factory, and yet free to pull up their roots and move on to another shed at will. Waterside and other urban transport workers were also organising.

The great strikes of 1890–91 took place against a background of falling wool prices and gathering depression. They began in August 1890, when in Melbourne the Marine Officers' Association, meeting with little response to respectful remonstrance, announced its intention of affiliating to the Trades Hall; from Adelaide to Newcastle unions and employers' organisations were soon locked in a bitter struggle on the fundamental issue of 'freedom of contract' versus the right to organise on more than a local shop or craft basis. In September the Sydney Labor Defence Committee called out the shearers, but these were vulnerable to penalties for breach of contract under antiquated Masters and Servants Acts, and had themselves been the financial mainstay of the striking or locked-out workers in the capitals. The colonial governments showed themselves determined to protect 'free labour' not only with police and

[1] By a pleasing irony, one of his lieutenants was a grandfather of Sir Robert Menzies.

specials but with the local armed forces, and by November the unions admitted defeat.

In Queensland the main clash came later, and in early 1891 the bush seemed almost on the verge of civil war, with shearers' camps under a rough quasi-military discipline and the government proclaiming a state of insurrection and sending strongly armed militia units to outback towns. There was plenty of free labour from the south, where unemployment was growing; under a hitherto forgotten Act of George IV – who had died three decades before Queensland was born – many strikers were heavily fined and jailed. Here defeat was long drawn out but complete; in the south, largely owing to Spence's union of caution and diplomacy with determination, something was saved: though the claim to full unionism had to be abandoned, the improved working conditions gained before the conflict were largely maintained.

Outwardly a failure, the strikes were more materially significant in the formation of Australian radicalism than Eureka; they contributed also to the hold of 'mateship' and the bush ethos in an increasingly urban society. The immediate result was a shift to political action; this would have been a natural reaction, and paradoxically enough the possible alternative of a quasi-syndicalist 'big unionism' was inhibited by an uncharacteristic ideological impulse – the departure of many seasoned union leaders with William Lane to found a New Australia overseas. To Lane, the new continent had shown itself sadly unfree from the immemorial vices of old Europe, and perhaps the ideal commonwealth might be born in the isolation of the Paraguayan bush. They sailed, ironically, in the *Royal Tar*, on a pathetic adventure which awaits a worthy historian.

Meanwhile, Labor Electoral Leagues were formed in New South Wales under the auspices of the Sydney Trades Council, and in June 1891 secured a striking success with the election of thirty-one of their candidates. To the unions, Labor members were more their own delegates than representatives at large, and it was expected that they would form an opportunist but solid bloc throwing its weight behind any government willing to meet specific demands such as extension of union recognition, factory legislation, payment of members, and abolition of plural voting. This was made virtually impossible by the facts that the major issues of parliamentary politics were the fiscal problem – free trade or protection – and the federation movement; in the latter Labor had little interest, on the former it was itself deeply divided, and the confusion was compounded by the strong influence of the single-taxers, still riding the wave stirred up by Henry George's triumphal visit in 1889.

Adroit old parliamentary hands trapped the inexperienced Labor members into open discussion of their differences on the floor of the House, and the party did not become really effective until the famous pledge of obedience to caucus decisions was enforced – a measure regarded by leaders of other parties with open scorn but probably secret envy. The pledge naturally led to splits, but the nineteen members of 1894 were much more to the point than the thirty-one of 1891. All the same, this tension, so early arising, between the unionists who paid for and organised Labor's intervention and the parliamentarians who were its spokesmen in a wider and less self-regarding circle still persists, and not only in Australia; as it is admirably put by R. A. Gollan, 'Labour policy is the resultant of many forces. Of these the two most important are those of which politicians are conscious and those that unionists experience.'[1]

New South Wales provided the model for the Australian Labor Party, which despite its recent disarray has been the central factor in the party politics of the Commonwealth. In Victoria, craft unionism remained stronger than in New South Wales, and there was a stronger progressive tradition in a more coherent Liberal Party: working-class politics thus remained for the time more 'lib-lab' than truly Labor. Queensland was different: initially, under Lane's almost charismatic influence, the platform was more avowedly socialist; but the unusually gross local inequities of plural voting led to some emphasis on electoral reform, and Queensland's 'peculiar institution' of 'kanaka' labour to an even stronger one on the exclusion of any sort of coloured or indentured labour, and here again Lane's racist influence was marked. Other colonies tailed after these three.

'Socialism without doctrines' thus needs qualification. In Victoria at least, perhaps in South Australia, the phrase could equally well apply to older liberal parties, and there is much point in Gollan's remark that 'Penal colony beginnings determined that the state should be both centralised and positive.' As regards the Labor movement, there were in the 'nineties rather too many doctrines floating about for any one of them to dominate: a self-styled Marxist could

[1] *Radical and Working Class Politics ... 1850–1910* (Melbourne University Press, 1960), p. 213.

point to Sidney Webb, Laurence Gronlund, Bernard Shaw, Annie Besant, and even W. H. Dawson (*Bismarck and State Socialism*) as his real masters. Labor thus presented the paradox of a party increasingly solidarised by the pledge but still essentially opportunist; it was not until 1921 that it formally wrote socialism into the platform instead of innocuous phrases about collective ownership of monopolies. But long before that, and in a wider sense than Sir William Harcourt meant in 1894, 'we are all socialists now'.

Australia rampant

The Hummer, The Boomerang, The Clipper, nothing could be more off-beat and 'offensively Australian' than these names; by contrast, after a slow start, the liveliest journal that Australia has produced belied by its contents the staidness of its name. The editors of *The Bulletin* might have preferred to have it said that they produced Australia, or at least Australianism.

Iconoclastic to the point of asserting republicanism, isolationist with 'Australia for the Australians' on its masthead, shrewd and hitting hard at cant wherever it came from, capable of more than an occasional shot at its own clients and contributors, yet with a humane streak or rather more, and always conducted with the utmost verve and pungency, *The Bulletin* (now if anything Establishment) after a slow start became an unprecedented and unrivalled forum for all who rebelled against the colonial or imperial Establishment. It could be stridently xenophobe, more especially against Chinese and other lesser breeds who might turn out to be inconveniently greater, and in this context was capable of sublime self-contradiction: 'There is only one circumstance demanding from Australia any effort in the way of defence, and that is the circumstance of our being a British dependency.'

Apart from Chinese and the British connections, *The Bulletin* disliked Japanese, Governors, colonial knights, most of the clergy, the larrikins (the Mods and Rockers of the day); it liked bushmen, unionists, and any available Bohemians, most of whom were on its strength anyhow. As Vance Palmer puts it, 'Upon the paper had descended the mantle of a good many prophets and its task was to sew them into a wearable garment.'[1] It was naturally a coat of all colours except yellow and True Blue; *The Bulletin* of to-day is less polychrome, since the red has been deleted.

[1] *The Legend of the Nineties* (Melbourne University Press, 1954), p. 90.

Behind the tumult of self-conscious showmanship there was the serious purpose of building up an Australian culture. It was a reading age, and *The Bulletin* met this need, not least by its editorial policy of keeping contributions short and above all readable. Most accounts agree that in the bush, where books were few (though often solid enough), it was the intellectual and cultural staple, though 'constant readers' may have been few; but conversely *The Bulletin*, the most sophisticated journalism that Australia had yet seen, proclaimed itself the great sounding-board of the bush ethos, contributing to 'the curious down-grading of the cities' and of the middle-class image noted by Hartley Grattan. No doubt there is exaggeration in the legend, but the journal certainly succeeded in projecting its own immodest estimate of itself.

The writers of *The Bulletin* were a remarkable group, who owed little to England except the words of the language and the unsophisticated ballad metres which dominated their verse; but for the first time there was a specifically indigenous literature of some enduring literary value. Much was naive and sentimental 'mateship', well exemplified in Henry Lawson, whose best stories, however, attain a high and sharp realism: the dry irony of *The Union Buries Its Dead* is not easily forgotten. 'Tom Collins' (Joseph Furphy) and Bernard O'Dowd were frequent contributors and between them, in very different ways, sum up the spirit of the age: a down-to-earth and salty democratic idealism in *Such is Life*, a quasi-mystical idealism in O'Dowd's strange crabbed quatrains, strewn with capital-letter personifications; he sees in Australia a 'vast and unpolluted stage' for new civilisations of unprecedented splendour, and yet asks the most awkward questions –

> Are you a drift Sargasso where the West
> In halcyon calm rebuilds her fatal nest?
> A new demesne for Mammon to infest?
> Or lurks millennial Eden 'neath your face?

Much of O'Dowd's verse is loaded with a quaint mythologising drawn from many (and not always digested) sources; Furphy, a man of the bush and the small country town, shows (if self-consciously) an astonishing range of reading; clearly, the indigenous isolation and the lack of 'culture' must not be over-stressed. These are clearer in the simple rhythms and direct diction of the balladists, of whom the best was A. B. ('Banjo') Paterson; their verse on occasion has the satisfying quality which comes from a completely realised internal consistency, however homely its outward form: a small world perhaps but a real one.

The intensely nationalist approach is of its age, not for all time, except perhaps for *Such is Life* (was ever a more universal title?); it has been overlain by cosmopolitan influences and probably could have flourished only before the protection of distance was broken by radio and air travel. Already there were premonitions of cosmopolitanism: beside the robust balladry was the still small voice of Christopher Brennan, most Symbolist of all poets in English; there was French influence also in the painting of Tom Roberts and Charles Conder; the universities, still overwhelmingly expatriate-staffed (at any rate at the top), and the law were enclaves of the more traditional British values; the American contribution came in powerfully with Bellamy and George; and the constitution of the Commonwealth of Australia was framed by men with a wealth of American and Canadian federal precedent at their finger-tips.

The coming of the Commonwealth

After the drama of the shearers' strikes and the brashness of *The Bulletin*, the first thing that strikes one about the federal movement is its genteel tone. Those bearded frock-coated parliamentarians, frozen into attitudes of eternal statesmanlike peroration, seem to belong to a different world; and indeed the movement, vital as it was to those actively engaged, seems largely to have passed over the heads of the populace at large. Here and there, and especially in border towns whose trade was fenced in by colonial tariffs, there was a genuine popular enthusiasm; but in the final referendum only 43 per cent of qualified voters opted for Federation, and 17 per cent against it. The movement had its moments of drama, but the attention of the audience was largely elsewhere.

The great federations, nominal or real, of the nineteenth century were typically European-settled countries of great area in relation to population: the United States of America, Mexico, Brazil, the Argentine, the Dominion of Canada. Australia certainly fits this pattern, and so obvious is federation as a solution to the problems posed by small numbers and vast distances, and so striking was the mobility between the colonies, whether by sea or by overlanders driving stock or prospecting for gold or jobs, that to hindsight it seems surprising that tentative proposals in the 1840s were left so long in abeyance. After all Canada had to cope with much greater difficulties – the enclave of French Catholicism in Quebec, the lack of direct sea communication between Vancouver and Montreal – and yet achieved Federation by 1867; but then Canada had an external threat on its marches with the United States, a threat at its height in the 'sixties when Confederates could raid Vermont from Ontario and Fenians could return the compliment.

In Australia there was some desultory discussion between 1850 and 1880, and in 1885 a Federal Council was set up with legislative authority – entirely permissive – for such things as relations with the Pacific islands, enforcement of legal judgements, divorce and commercial law, patents and copyright, and so on. It was ineffective since New South Wales, the mother colony, took sulky advantage of a tactless speech by the Victorian Premier and stayed out; and had it been effective, it would probably have impeded the building of any more substantial federal structure, especially as it completely dodged the key question of tariff policy.

The issue was re-opened in 1889 by Sir Henry Parkes, who had proposed the Federal Council in 1880 and then reneged, ostensibly because of its ineffectiveness. Parkes, a Birmingham ivory-turner with vague Chartist connections, had come out in 1839 and taken a lead in the *Hashemy* agitation of 1849, proceeding through a succession of happy marriages, bad verses, near bankruptcies, and dropped aspirates to become, not least in his own view, the Grand Old Man of New South Wales politics. The ostensible motivation of his speech at the little town of Tenterfield (October 1889) was the recent report of a British general on the colonial defence forces, which obviously could only gain by some central control. This was a strong argument in the context of French and German expansion in the New Hebrides and New Guinea, though the less charitable hinted that Sir Henry was in need of a new cry, a suspicion not allayed by his visit to Melbourne for his health – in January, a month less than salubrious in that city. At all events, he soon found his cry: 'the crimson thread of kinship runs through us all', and he had laid his ground well.

The soil of Victoria was fertile to the concept: at this date Melbourne was still making the economic running, largely owing to its tariff-protected industries which stood to gain from a larger market, though by the same token Sydney was reluctant. Tasmania and Queensland followed the lead, or lack of it, given by New South

Wales (where Parkes was now out of office), and the constitution so carefully drafted by the National Australasian Convention at Sydney in 1891 lapsed, though it remained as it were on the agenda of the decade.

So far the movement had been in the hands of professional politicians of some standing, of whom the most convinced and effective were Alfred Deakin in Victoria and Edmund Barton in New South Wales. The next move was taken on the initiative of the Australian Natives' Association, a body strongly influential in Victoria, and to some extent under the spur of the depression. The border areas along the Murray were amongst those most affected by the intercolonial barriers to free commerce, and the conference which met in mid-1893 at Corowa, on the New South Wales side of the river, had for the first time some popular drive behind it. (It is revealing, incidentally, that only three non-metropolitan towns have given a local habitation and a name to a significant event in Australian history: Ballarat (Eureka), Corowa, and Tenterfield.)

The Corowa delegates proposed a new approach: since the colonial parliaments and their leaders were elected on quite other issues, a directly elected convention should draft a constitution which, if approved by referenda in three or more colonies, should be submitted to the imperial Parliament for implementation. This procedure was accepted by a premiers' conference in 1895, and in June 1898 referenda were held in four colonies (Queensland and Western Australia abstaining for local reasons) and passed in all of them – but in New South Wales by a majority well short of the agreed minimum. Some tricky bargaining ensued to meet New South Wales' objections to the draft, and in 1899 referenda were held in five colonies. Affirmative majorities were overwhelming in Victoria, Tasmania, and South Australia, adequate in New South Wales and Queensland; Western Australia did not vote until July 1900 and was only just in time to be an original member of the Commonwealth.

The constitution eventually adopted was a fairly cautious and conservative document, though less so than the 1891 draft. Debate had centred mainly on the fiscal question and on the role of the Senate. Apart from a traditional aversion to agreeing with Victoria, New South Wales' objections were based largely on her own adherence to free trade, or at most a low revenue tariff, and in view of the feelings of the other colonies, such attitudes could not stand out indefinitely against the general recognition of the need for union to cope with defence and external affairs. In Western Australia, the presence of many 't' othersiders' from the east on the new gold-fields forced the reluctant hand of Perth, in part by a separatist threat; she secured a concession allowing her to phase out her own tariffs over five years. With the special interests of an isolated primary producer, Western Australia had less to gain from a high all-Australian tariff than the east, and has at times been restive: in 1933 a State referendum gave a two-thirds majority for secession, but with engaging inconsequence the same voters threw out the government which had recommended it, and as recently as 1966 separatist murmurs were heard when the Commonwealth inter-vened on iron-ore contracts to Japan at prices it considered too low.

It was obvious that the Commonwealth could not but have a common tariff, and that meant the eventual end of free trade. It was expected that running expenses would be low – even Deakin is said to have accepted an annual figure of £0.2.6 per head! – and even with no revenue but customs (though it was empowered to levy what taxes it thought fit) this meant a big surplus: the contem-plated disposal of this accounted for more than a few field-days. The smaller colonies were naturally particularly interested, and the final compromise – that two-thirds of it should be returned to the States – came from the Tasmanian premier. This 'Braddon Blot' was particularly obnoxious to New South Wales, and one of the compromises reached between the two referenda was its limitation to ten years.

That there should be a Senate with equal representation of the States was as obvious as that there should be a common tariff; but what was to be its role? Bernhard Wise, a strong federalist, put the difficulty well: 'the ghosts of past controversies still walked the political fields; the "Liberals" and "Conservatives" alike discussed the function of a Federal Senate as though it were a local Upper House' entrenched in a property qualification. The 1891 draft was excessively conservative: the Senate was to be elected not directly but by the colonial parliaments (in some of which the Upper House was distinctly oligarchical), and whether the Executive was to be truly responsible to the popularly elected House of Representatives was left open. There were not wanting hints, from far Left and far Right, that such a Federation would be a useful, perhaps the only, means of securing the rights of property against assaults which might be successful in the more 'progressive' colonies. Such considerations were responsible for the sceptical detachment of *The Bulletin* and the distinct coolness of the Left in general; only one Labor leader took part in the conventions. These elements were advancing in the stronger colonies; they were all for an Australian *nation*, and in a more unitary structure might expect to drag up the more backward components; but the checks and balances thought appropriate by the politically (if not always literally) Elder Statesmen of 1891 seemed to them a brake on the progressive movement.

George Reid, the paunchy and tricksy Premier of New South Wales, does not appear in a dignified light in the formal histories; but the speech in which he displayed the disadvantages of Federation to his colony, and ended by saying that anyhow he'd vote for it, not only earned him the sobriquet of 'Yes-No Reid' but may have builded better than he knew. The too-thin New South Wales majority of 1898 put him in a strong bargaining position. Direct election of the Senate and executive responsibility to the House were essential to meet more principled radical objections, and the limitation of the power of the Senate over finance bills and resolution of House/Senate deadlocks (by double dissolution and if need be by absolute majority of a subsequent joint sitting) are due to the stalwart South Australian radical C. C. Kingston. But Reid's insistence on the limitation of the 'Braddon Blot' to ten years opened the way to the widening of Commonwealth powers, without which the full Australian effort in two world wars would have been difficult to obtain except by the complicated procedure of constitutional amendment; and referenda on such matters have been nearly always resolved in the negative.

A few remaining points may be noted. One of them, 'Section 92', is more than a detail: the precise interpretation of the apparently direct words 'trade, commerce and intercourse among the States shall be absolutely free' has been of much practical economic significance, as well as a munificent resource for constitutional lawyers. The title 'Commonwealth of Australia', with its Cromwellian associations, was looked at askance by conservatives (and is decidedly inconvenient now that the British Empire has become the Commonwealth of Nations), but from a public relations angle may be fairly counted as one of Sir Henry's happier inspirations. The siting of the capital, obviously a very sore point in the conditions of competitive colonialism, was settled by a classic federal compromise: Sydney and Melbourne cancelled out, so it must be in New South Wales, on territory ceded to the Commonwealth, but not within a hundred miles of Sydney. (The resultant jockeying which led to Canberra is another story, entertaining but irrelevant here.) Finally, it is a fair comment on the empiric 'it will settle itself' attitude of Australians that while such an obvious, and from a States' Rights point of view uncontroversial, matter as a uniform divorce law, adumbrated under the Federal Council, was specifically included in Commonwealth powers, it was not until 1959 that the Commonwealth got around to passing a measure of such import to the happiness of many thousands of Australians.

After the 1899 referenda, it was all over bar the shouting, of which there was plenty, and a rather unpleasant compromise with Joseph Chamberlain over the right of appeal to the Privy Council from the Australian High Court, appointed guardian of the constitution. With many processions and much booming of guns, the Commonwealth of Australia was formally proclaimed on the first of January 1901.

Many admirable men had given much devotion, many opportunists some, to its creation; and many men have given their lives, in the most literal sense, to the idea of Australia as the way of life of a continent. It is not likely that many have died for the Commonwealth of Australia simply as a political entity: that sort of patriotism is not the Australian way. Yet to some it was more than a dream, it was a vision; to Deakin, to O'Dowd, to Brunton Stephens in 1877:

> She is not yet; but he whose ear
> Thrills to that finer atmosphere
>   Where footfalls of appointed things,
>   Reverberant of days to be,
>   Are heard in forecast echoings
>   Like wavebeats from a viewless sea –
> Hears in the voiceful tremors of the sky
> Auroral heralds whispering, 'She is nigh'.

With the new century the Commonwealth was launched onto an existence far more agitated than could have been foreseen by its progenitors. O'Dowd's vision was not to be; although until World War II, and even since, many have thought Australians too prone to halcyon calm, millennial Eden is not yet.

Chapter 4

The Commonwealth: The First
Three Decades

T HE NEW-BORN COMMONWEALTH was a healthy but perhaps
hardly a lusty child. It had sprung from lawful spousals, and
in practical affairs there was lacking that quasi-revolutionary
energy so often associated with new and illegitimate states, and this
lack has persisted; in matters of political organisation, Australians
often give the impression of being tired rather than adventurous.
There was, however, plenty of quiet efficiency; the transfer of
powers and services from colonies to Commonwealth went smoothly,
and even more smooth and striking was the transfer of politicians
from local to Federal Parliament. Although it was to become clear,
by the time of the anti-Labor Fusion of 1909, that the major issue
was to be if not the existence of governmental intervention in
economic life (long conceded or even sought by entrepreneurs),
then at least its extent and ultimate objectives, this was at first
masked by cross-currents between the parties on the fiscal question,
and their practical agreement on 'White Australia'.

It would be pointless to trace the political history in any detail.
To begin with, there were 'three elevens on the field': free traders,
uneasily aware that the pass had really been sold by the very formation of the Commonwealth; protectionists of varying conviction;
and Labor, still formally uncommitted on the issue. On the whole
the running in the first few years was made by the protectionist
Deakinite Liberals, a group with a strong tradition of moderate but
not irresolute social reform, and so able to bid for Labor support,
generally with success but not without upsets such as that which
led to the first, brief, Labor ministry in 1904. But, if Labor was
divided on tariffs, both free traders and protectionists had their
conservative and progressive elements: Reid, for example, only
reluctantly acquiescent in a tariff which he would have liked confined to revenue, and much given to displaying the 'Socialist tiger',
was yet responsible for the Conciliation and Arbitration Act (1904),

originally a Labor plank and the foundation for a vast and complex structure which is still a main economic factor. On the other hand, Sir John Forrest, who had the natural instincts of a Tory, yet managed to be a member of Liberal Cabinets until 1907.

In this flux of opportunism, it is a little surprising that so much was achieved that has endured, even though subject to strain and at least academic questioning. Basically the protectionist, arbitration and wage-fixing, and migration policies are still with us. Much of the credit must go to Deakin's political tact and adherence to principle and, later, to the quiet power of Andrew Fisher backed up by the more fiery energy of William Morris Hughes. At least the foundations of the modern Australian Welfare State (a structure perhaps less impressive than many Australians assume) were laid by these three men, who made some conscience of what they did, by Reid's less conscientious but still fruitful intervention, and by the insistence of Mr Justice Higgins, President of the Commonwealth Arbitration Court, on his 'New Province for Law and Order'.

'Australia for the Australians'

It is simplest to take first what was after all the first badge of Australian nationalism: 'White Australia'. Conceding that any nation has a right to determine its own composition, and if it has not got a large-scale colour problem is well advised not to buy into one, it is difficult to-day to appreciate the fervency with which all but a tiny minority rallied to the cause. Fundamentally, it was the defence of a culture, and if this be a sin, what modern nation, in Asia or in Africa, can justly throw the first stone? It is fashionable, and to some extent true, to go beyond this, to pass it off as basically merely socio-economic and to deplore the unfortunate (and unofficial) misnomer of 'White Australia'; yet it cannot be denied that there were ugly racist tones in its enunciation.

The Labor attitude (and it was well to the fore) was understandable enough: Labor had no love for cheap labour of any kind, white or coloured, and 'coolie labour' was the easiest to keep out. It was not so long since Chinese, 2 per cent of the Victorian population in 1891, had formed 20 per cent of the work-force in some trades, at 40 per cent less wages than those of Australians in the same trades. Yet the racist side was most strident on the Left, with William Lane and the *Bulletin* radicals; in New Australia, Lane even disapproved of contact with the Paraguayan 'natives' who had after all given him asylum. While Deakin was defending restriction on the ground that the Chinese were dangerous not from their bad but their good qualities (by which he seems to have meant that they worked harder) and hence more of a menace, a Senator, the Commonwealth hardly born, was proclaiming them 'a nation of yesterday'. What real contention existed was between the extremists who wanted things done overtly (and offensively) and the realists willing to act on Joseph Chamberlain's hint that a dictation test would do the trick; this prevailed until it died of ridicule when applied to inconveniently leftish and literate Europeans who ran through the gamut of languages available to the local officials. It was not formally abolished, however, until 1958.

It must at least be said, and this is a credit on the non-racist side, that no attempt was made to interfere with Asians already resident: descendants of the 'Ghan' camel-drivers brought to help on the Overland Telegraph are as accepted Aussie bushmen as anyone else in the Centre, and in towns the local café keeper, if not Italian or Greek, is as like as not a Chinese who may also be a pillar of church, chapel, or football club.[1] Here assimilation has been successful; but the 'kanaka' indentured labourers on whom Queensland sugar was dependent posed a different problem. There was much more debate on the special 'kanaka' case than on the general principle, and the protests of the sugar interests against repatriation to the islands were met by the provision of a bounty on sugar grown by white labour. Italians provided a useful reinforcement for the heavy manual work in tropical conditions, and the practice thus begun of passing sectional costs to the consumer has since been extended with less ideological justification.

Arbitration: the house that Higgins built

The tariff legislation of the first Parliament was little more than a compromise between the hard need for revenue, not only to meet Commonwealth expenses but to reimburse the States, and the remaining free trade feeling of old-guard politicians; but protection is an appetite which grows with that it feeds on. Partly no doubt for tactical reasons – to hold Labor support for a policy well this side of socialism – but also in fulfilment of his own broad view of socio-economic progress, Deakin in his second ministry (1905–08)

[1] Incidentally, restriction was never applied to Maoris, as being New Zealand citizens.

introduced the concept of the 'New Protection', by which tariffs to an industry were to be offset by an excise on manufactures, which would be rebated subject to satisfactory wage-levels in accordance with the awards of the Arbitration Court. It is true that this ingenious device was soon declared unconstitutional by the High Court's decision in the 'Harvester Case' (1908), but Labor was definitely won over and the fact of protection has never since been a serious political issue (except to the early Country Party), though there has been dispute in plenty as to its modalities. In face of the High Court decision, the Arbitration Court remained the palladium of the Australian working man – who from time to time supplemented its often lengthy procedures by more direct action.

The concept of a compulsory arbitration system for industrial disputes, derived from Bismarck's Germany via New Zealand, became popular in several colonies in the 'nineties and had some support in all Federal parties. But the Conciliation and Arbitration Act as finally passed in 1904 was in the main a Deakinite-Labor creation, though disputes over its details had brought down both Deakin and Labor governments in that same year; it was an accident of political in-fighting that it reached the statute book under the short-lived Reid-McLean (free trade) ministry. Its compromises on Trade Union preference in employment and on union contributions to political funds appeared very dilute to Labor stalwarts, but union practice rather than positive legal sanction eventually established both principles, not without distaste and minor harassments from non-Labor interests but without the reversals which have marked British legislation on these issues. The conciliation side of this legislation has had relatively little effect – certainly the strike weapon has never grown rusty, though Australia's strike record is by no means so outrageous as it looks from outside, and no strike actually against a Court award took place until 1916. But under the very active leadership of Henry Bournes Higgins, President from 1907 till 1921, the Court very soon became the great pace-maker in industrial affairs.

In a long series of judgements beginning with the Harvester Case, Higgins enunciated the principle of the basic wage 'below which employers ought to be forbidden by the State to employ its citizens'; the employee must be considered 'a human being in a civilised community', and on this basis his normal needs included a wife and three children. It is easy enough to ridicule this reasoning by calculating that by 1920 this meant providing for half a million non-existent wives and an equivalent number of unconceivable children (whence the case for family endowment as an alternative), and by pointing out that in some cases the choice might be between receiving the basic wage and receiving nothing when the mine shut down. Nevertheless the principle was thoroughly in accord with the whole Australian ethos and has become a built-in part of Australian society.

Even more complicating was the obvious rider of 'margins for skills', to which were added all sorts of claims for special allowances, dirt-money, danger-money, clothing and gear; even Mr Justice Higgins at times showed signs of restiveness at such demands. The result is that the arbitration system has become if not a jungle at least a maze where the sensible uninitiate fear to tread, a sort of quasi-autonomous metabolism within the body politic, and almost everything comes directly or indirectly within its ambit, from the question as to whether sailors' mattress-covers should have tapes or press studs up or down to the salaries of professors. The quarterly (now annual) determination of the basic wage, tied to the cost of living index (in itself a field wide open to dispute), and the ensuing rounds of margin awards, form a factor in economic life fully comparable to the wool cheque and the interest rate.[1] There are stresses and maybe even cracks in this imposing edifice, but the claim of Henry Bournes Higgins to be a main architect of modern Australia cannot be gainsaid.

Labor arrives

By 1908 the Deakin-Labor marriage of convenience was breaking up; a brief Labor government in 1908–09 was the signal for the 'Fusion' of the old Reid party (now led by ex-Labor Joseph Cook), the Forrest dissidents, and the Deakinites. Despite Deakin's desperate and sincere attempts to make the new bloc a decently progressive force, it was in reality a not too principled alliance in which his genuine Liberals were sold out to a 'party of resistance'; as he himself wryly observed, he had behind him 'all my old opponents since Federation'. His own third ministry was merely a stop-gap, and in 1910 Andrew Fisher formed the first Labor government not dependent on the sufferance of Deakin or Reid.

[1] The principle of basic plus separate margin awards was not dropped, in favour of a 'total wage', until June 1967. It remains to be seen whether it will result in more flexibility, as well as more realism.

The new administration was strong in personality and sense of purpose; it attained a very creditable record of legislation, in part the fulfilment of business unfinished by Deakin. This included confirmation of the arrangement, replacing the 'Braddon Blot', for allotting surplus revenue to the States on a *per capita* basis (with special grants to poorer Tasmania and Western Australia); the establishment of the Royal Australian Navy and the Royal Military College, to provide the officer cadres for a compulsory service citizen army (for home defence only); the taking over of the Northern Territory from South Australia; the definitive locating of the Federal capital at Canberra. Of its own motion, Labor set up the Commonwealth Bank, took over the note issue, and introduced a land tax designed to assist in the break-up of large holdings for closer settlement. But the major items of its programme – the general extension of Commonwealth as against State economic powers, and the nationalisation of monopolies – were twice defeated in constitutional referenda; an attack at once on States' Rights and free enterprise was too much for a generally benevolent electorate.

In the 1913 election Deakin, whose powers were failing, yielded leadership of the Fusionists (now formally the Liberal Party) to Joseph Cook, who secured a majority of one in the House, while Labor had 29 of the 36 Senators. Unable to govern effectively, Cook forced on a double dissolution which misfired; Labor came back with 42 to 32 in the House, 31 to 5 in the Senate. But the election was actually in progress when, an hour before noon on 4 August 1914 (and hence only an hour after London's ultimatum on the other side of the world) the first British shot of the war was fired – at a German merchantman leaving Melbourne.

Gallipoli to Versailles

Even before he became Prime Minister, Fisher pledged 'the last man and the last shilling' to the support of Britain, and this expressed the spirit of a *union sacrée*. There had been no consultation by Britain, but that did not enter the reckoning. It is a little difficult to understand the universality of the response; the Boer War, despite pride in the still 'colonial' contingents, had not been universally popular – perhaps the Boer Republics were after all uncomfortably close to the bush ideal of government. But in 1914 it was not simply 'that vast human sigh of relief . . . marking the onset of every great conflict' and the ending of intolerable tension of which Liddell-Hart speaks; Australians were simply too much out of touch with the long European crisis since Algeciras and Agadir for that to affect more than a few. It is true that Germany in New Guinea had tended to replace France in the New Hebrides as the local menace; but such real foreboding as existed attached rather to Britain's ally Japan. Perhaps in the last resort it was simply the old original sin which equates manhood with the fighting man (there is surely a little of this in all of us); Rupert Brooke's 'Now God be praised Who has matched us with His hour' – with the rider that Europe had already experienced many such hours, Australia none.

At all events, it may be said that it was Gallipoli which finally assured Australia that she was a nation in her own right; it is impossible to overstress the psychological impact of this dramatic, if tragic, entry onto the world stage. Even in the mid-'fifties, a juke box in a country town could retail

> My loved one lies so far away,
> And now he sleeps by Suvla Bay

to a girl who by no possibility could have known a loved one there. Australians fought with distinction on the Western Front and in the Palestine Campaign, and produced at least one great commander in Sir John Monash; but no other actions of theirs had material significance comparable to the almost bloodless walkover in German New Guinea, moral significance comparable to the futile slaughter at Gallipoli. But, though this deep feeling of having been blooded into maturity at Anzac Cove has persisted till the Anzac Day on which these words were written, the immediate glamour did not. After the war the Melbourne poet Furnley Maurice answered by implication O'Dowd's questions:

> While I protected your body
> No one remembered your soul . . .
> Australia, speak!
> Is this the country I went forth to save?

In most respects Australia, an essentially unindustrialised country, had to improvise almost everything for modern war. The details of the multiplicity of boards and committees devoted to war organisation are of local and temporary interest only; their resultant was to strengthen the Commonwealth *vis-à-vis* the States and in relation to economic activity generally, but in a piecemeal and *ad hoc* manner which was far from compensating Labor for the loss of the pre-war referenda foreshadowing overall control. Government intervention went pretty far, not only in such matters as censorship; the High Court even took the view that the defence power extended to fixing the price of bread. Finance was mainly by borrowing, including internal loans on a scale exceeding any expectations; the Commonwealth considerably extended its taxing range, and overseas developmental borrowing for the States was centralised in Commonwealth hands. If, as some say, true federalism is dead in Australia, it died under the pressures of the first war; but there is probably inconvenient vitality left in the corpse. And in one matter, of most direct military import, the government over-reached itself: conscription. The bitterness over conscription, for which William Morris Hughes was in a large part responsible, still has its effect in politics fifty years later: 'the evil that men do lives after them'.

There is a most remarkable parallel between Hughes and that other diminutive Welsh wizard Lloyd George. Both extremely able men of intense dynamism, capable of the most complete dedication to a cause with which their urges to power and command were identified, but not too scrupulous as to means when self-assured of the rightness of the end, they both began the war as the offsiders[1] to highly respected but less dynamic leaders whom they supplanted; both ended it at the head of governments composed of a rump of their original followers and a main body of their old foes; and both, trying to maintain some of their old radical drive, lasted just until their new allies could get rid of them, to finish as legends, admired for their adroitness (and for undeniable services) but not greatly trusted. Hughes certainly showed much greater resilience, being often in office and in 1943 nominal leader of the United Australian Party; his private life doubtless left more energy for public affairs than did Lloyd George's. Labor properly enough never forgave Hughes: repentance should precede absolution, and if Billy Hughes ever repented of anything, the evidence has not yet come to light.

The conscription crisis arose from the insatiable demands of the Western Front. Hughes, Prime Minister since October 1915, had scored a personal triumph in England as the blunt colonial keen on

---

[1] This Australianism has nothing to do with being offside in soccer; it derives from the offside bullocks in a team, and applies to a working partner or mate: in this context, it is not only more lively but more formally accurate than 'second in command'.

the war and nothing else, and seems to have been completely captured by the 'Westerners' there – this was before Lloyd George's disillusion with the Passchendaele generals. It was later officially ascertained without doubt that the figures for necessary replacements were greatly inflated, but on their basis it could well be held that voluntary enlistment would not be enough. Yet, to Labor in particular, the idea of compulsory *overseas* service was alien, and to many anathema. The ministry itself was deeply divided; yet with war idealism not yet overcome by war weariness, the referendum held in October 1916 seemed to have a good chance of success. Despite a somewhat uninformative formulation of the question, it failed.

The causes were complex. The division was by no means on straight party lines: 32 Labor and 12 anti-Labor electorates of 1914 voted 'No', 10 Labor and 21 anti-Labor 'Yes'; country areas, suffering from a loss of workers from shearing and harvesting in a good season, tended to vote 'No'.[1] Irish resentment at the execution of the Easter Week leaders was intense, and in the Irish-born Archbishop Mannix of Melbourne Hughes met a man with a nerve as steely as his own. Mannix's influence had doubtless been exaggerated as regards its immediate actual effect, but it became a symbol whose potency is not yet dead.

Hughes anticipated a no-confidence caucus vote by walking out, taking with him about a third of the parliamentary Labor Party (and more than a third of its tried leaders) and carried on, as 'National Labor', with Liberal support; in January 1917 he recognised the logic of the position by joining with his old enemies to form the Nationalist Party. This swept the 1917 elections, but its victory was really conditional on promises that overseas conscription would not be introduced without a second referendum. Once more – and once more on questionable figures – this was thought necessary. Devices of censorship, intimidation, muzzling of opponents (even the Labor Premier of Queensland) were resorted to, and an even more disingenuous form of question – simply 'Are you in favour of' a policy not remotely described in the paper. They failed, and even more decisively. In accordance with a campaign pledge, Hughes resigned, but the Governor-General had no alternative to recommissioning him. Meanwhile, embittered Labor raised demands for a negotiated peace, and in 1917 there were very serious

[1] I. Turner, *Industrial Labour and Politics . . . 1900–21* (Aust. National Univ. Press, Canberra, 1965), pp. 113–16.

strikes which owed something, perhaps much, to the agitation of the Industrial Workers of the World and similar syndicalist groups, and indicated a growing disillusionment with the arbitration system. It may have been well for Hughes, it was certainly well for Australian society, that the war ended as soon as it did; indeed it can be strongly argued that the crisis of the West, moral as well as political, would not have been nearly as catastrophic as it has been had there been a negotiated peace in 1917.

This may be irrelevant; but the crisis of 1916 is not irrelevant to the Australia of 1966. Far more than any other political conflict, even those of the great depression, the conscription crisis left lesions in the body politic not yet healed. Hughes's tactics in themselves lowered the standards of political life and ensured continued bitterness; certainly he had provocation, and extreme provocation, from the extreme Left, but less egocentric labour leaders have learnt to live with their lunatic fringes, and his reaction was undiscriminating in the extreme, not sparing reasoned and moderate opposition – with the natural result that it too became extreme. First Cook, then Hughes (and his followers Pearce and Holman), later Lyons (and Ramsay Macdonald) – the sequence greatly strengthened the always latent and often patent distrust of the unionist rank and file of Labor (and its NCO's and field officers) for the unduly brilliant parliamentary leader; a factor which to-day inhibits those who would refashion the movement into a form capable of facing the realities of a time suburbanised as well as urbanised. The Labor Party had been central to national life; the split threw it off centre; it regained, painfully, a central position under Curtin; and again, and in no small part due to the legacy of Hughes and his like, became off centre with Evatt and Calwell. This was not just a misfortune for the Labor Party: it was a misfortune for Australia, long deprived of a really effective opposition and hence subject to the ills which come of too-long continuance of governments which can (politically but not nationally) afford to be complacent.

Australian political memories are long: the Democratic Labor Party, Victorian and Catholic based and at least as much dedicated to stopping the spread of Communism in Asia as the post-1950 Liberal governments, showed in a 1966 opinion poll a majority of 61 per cent (the national majority was 57 per cent) against sending conscripts to Vietnam, by far the most divisive question of that day. The heirs of Mannix and the ghost of Hughes survived to bedevil Holt.

It is difficult, even at this distance of time, to come to reasonable terms with Hughes: a man of great gifts, given over, at Versailles, to the narrowest chauvinist cause, which he served with all the selfish truculence and with rather worse manners than those of any Balkan politician, and yet convinced in all sincerity that he was securing the future of his country. It is sad to reflect that at this time he probably came nearer than any other Australian politician to being a national hero. His vulgar (on his part) verbal exchanges with Woodrow Wilson are best left in a decent obscurity; their practical effect was unsatisfactory. While desiring and working for renewal of the Anglo-Japanese alliance, he secured the rejection of the Japanese proposal to insert a declaration on racial equality into the League Covenant; the compromise he could have secured would have hurt nobody, the outright rejection played straight into the hands of Japanese imperialists, and 'White Australia' was double-branded as racist, which might have seemed not to matter then but does now. On New Guinea, his demands for direct annexation of the old German portion had to be compromised into a Class C Mandate. Whatever his motives, it is clear that the current Australian problem in New Guinea would certainly be much simpler were it not for the distinction between indubitably Australian Papua and the Trust Territory of New Guinea, and it is unduly cynical to assume that the relatively enlightened present attitude of Australians to their colonial problem is mainly due to the necessity of reporting annually to the United Nations. A negotiator less brash, more prepared to give the soft answer and to make concessions in form, might have got more on what was after all the most minimal of issues to the statesmen of Europe, however much a matter of principle to Wilson. As for reparations, Hughes – a faithful epigone of Lloyd George's propaganda of squeezing Germany till the pips squeaked – claimed £464,000,000; he accepted under duress £100,000,000; and Australia received £5,571,720. Hughes was at once a great man by his intensity of will; a little one in his causes and his intellectual vision.

From war to depression

Australia came out of the war with a marked shift in her economic structure. In 1911, primary production still claimed 30 per cent of the work-force; by 1921 actual numbers had fallen from 609,000 to 600,000 and the percentage to 26; conversely manufacturing industry had risen from 569,000 to 726,000, from 28.7 to 31.2 per cent. It is true that much of this expansion was petty stuff, and war development had been desperately hampered by lack of machine tools and the facilities to produce them, despite the establishment of the Broken Hill Proprietary steel works at Newcastle in 1911 and the immediate automatic protection afforded by the war.[1] The immediate post-war years showed much the same sequence of coupon election, short-term boom, unemployment and labour unrest as in Britain. Around the world (though it could not be seen at the time) 1921 was really the end of post-war and the beginning of inter-war; and in that year the industrial wing secured the adoption of a definitely (and prominently) socialist plank in the Australian Labor Party platform.

There was a shift in the political spectrum. Labor ceased to inherit the 'national' mantle of the Fisher years; but the Nationalists themselves had new competition from the quite sudden rise of the Country Party. Dissatisfaction at war-time bulk buying schemes (especially for wheat), fear of the 'Red' Labor machines entrenched in the capitals, distrust of the high capitalist policy of protected industrial development at the cost of rural producing interests, brought into the 1919 Parliament 10 Country members; with 35 Nationalists facing 26 Labor representatives, Hughes could form a government only with the sufferance of this bloc. Sufferance was guaranteed by the ideological impossibility of a Labor-Country alliance, but in view of his own party's conservative reluctance to support him in his effort to carry on his erstwhile Labor approach, Hughes was fatally hampered. A referendum, much on the lines of those of Fisher and calculated to steal Labor's clothes by proposing the nationalising of monopolies, was defeated. In 1922 Labor and Country Party each gained four seats in the House; government of any shade was possible only on Country Party terms, and these included first and foremost the deposition of Hughes. Stanley Bruce took over as Nationalist leader and Prime Minister; the Country Party leader, Earle Page, was Treasurer, and his party had four of the remaining ten Cabinet posts. With two brief intervals (the first Lyons and the first Menzies Cabinets) the lop-sided pattern of anti-Labor ministries thus set has persisted till to-day.

The next decade was an anomalous period. Nationalist as the

[1] In India, production from the Tata works at Jamshedpur also began in 1911, and the war sequence was strikingly similar.

government was by title, in some ways Australian nationalism was at slack tide; Bruce, like Menzies later, was a 'King's man', content to follow the British lead in external affairs, and this was much easier in a period relatively free from major international complications. Culturally the decade lacked distinction: the sense of Australian particularism, which in the 'nineties and the first years of the Commonwealth had been a stimulus, now became a restrictive yardstick, critical judgement being too often exercised more with the quality, or even quantity, of dinkum Aussie local colour than with intrinsic values. Perhaps this was compensation for the loss of the old radical excitements, and this was also the period of the most uncritical boosting. The coincidence that Australia and the United States are almost the same in area led to potentialities being assessed by a simple rule-of-three sum, with all the essential variables left out. Griffith Taylor, Australia's leading geographer, found that his honest (and very forthright) efforts to instil a little common sense about the real nature of the arid two-thirds of the continent made him so unpopular that he left his foundation Chair at Sydney for the freer, if not wider, horizons of North America. Perhaps the most solid and permanently valuable achievement of the Bruce-Page government was the establishment of what grew into that household word of Australia to-day, 'CSIRO', the Commonwealth Scientific and Industrial Research Organisation.

Nevertheless, there was a good deal of development, even if mainly of a 'filling-in' kind and with some bad mistakes in the old field of closer settlement, especially 'soldier settlement'. The decade saw the beginnings of civil aviation, which obviously had a key role in a country of such vast distance and scattered population, and in 1928 the opening of another steelworks at Port Kembla. The Bruce-Page ministry was a 'business-man's government' in a relatively favourable sense; it devoted a good deal of attention to co-ordinating development, formally establishing the Loan Council to handle all external borrowing, State as well as Commonwealth; untypically, this centralising move was for once supported by a referendum. It reorganised the Commonwealth Bank, handing over to it the note issue which from 1911 till the establishment of the Note Board in 1920 had been a direct Treasury function. But it left the Bank somewhat aloof from any close relation to government policy; whence troubles when depression and a Labor government coincided. The Bank became a convenient agency for handling external financial affairs, but internally became not so much the central bank it might have been but just another trading bank which happened to be State-backed and (under Country Party pressure, Page being Treasurer) particularly prominent as a source of rural credit.

The Tariff Board, set up by Hughes, was meant to provide a permanent clearing-house technically equipped to pass informed judgement on the ever-proliferating claims to protection from industries infant or senile (no industry ever seems to be in its healthy prime). By this time the Country Party's general suspicion of tariffs was being replaced by a more sophisticated appreciation of the advantages of getting in on the receiving end. The small size of the internal market presented a fundamental problem: desirable industries could grow by protection to meet the local demand, but then it was unthinkable to 'undevelop', and to *grow* meant foreign markets, often very difficult to attain on Australian costs. Hence elaborate bounty schemes on export production, accompanied of course by high internal prices; sugar, dried fruits, butter are classic examples. But again rising consumption prices meant rising awards from the Arbitration Court and rising labour costs. The Tariff Board is well described by Finlay Crisp as one of the characteristically Australian 'shelter institutions' which governments have interposed between themselves and sectional pressures;[1] but it has not been able to act effectively as a permanent revising Court, and at times there have been suspicions that it was not as independent of official trade policy as it might be. Meanwhile the linked spiral of tariff and arbitration awards seems a permanent and awkward feature of the economy.

Arbitration indeed was the rock on which the Bruce-Page government split, or perhaps the jungle in which it lost its way. Generally speaking, distrust between government and unions was at its height in the 'twenties (except for the really bitter strikes of 1916–17). The unions were embittered that very little (beyond linking the basic wage to quarterly cost of living indexes) had been done to meet the very awkward findings of a 1919 Royal Commission that, even taking a rather restricted view of the Higgins criteria, the basic wage was seriously inadequate; and not till the end of the Bruce-Page régime was an effort made to bring forward a comprehensive scheme of social security; this lapsed with the fall of the

[1] *Australian National Government* (Longmans, 1965), pp. 88–89.

government and the depression. From the government's business-man point of view, the unions were at best an unco-operative brake on development – they were cagey about migration schemes, a main feature of government policy – and at worst (and more usually) quite irresponsible in failing to cope with their left-wing activists. As a result, what might have been straight machinery measures to tidy up a mess were loaded with provisions to discipline the unions, and so had no chance of consideration on the merits.

The handling of the arbitration issue seems extraordinarily inept, though one must sympathise with the desperate resolve, born of frustration, to take an axe to the whole tangle of Gordian knots. The position was extremely complex, not least because of the union habit of shopping round between State and Federal Courts for tactical advantages; but even apart from this it was clear that any large dispute, and many small ones, would be likely to have inter-State implications. In an endeavour to bring some order into the confusion, Bruce attempted to secure paramountcy for the Federal Court. Defeated by referendum in 1926, in 1929 he tried the opposite tack: the Commonwealth should withdraw altogether, except for maritime industries which almost by definition were inter-State.

At this point the old Adam awoke in Hughes, who had never forgiven Bruce for his 'betrayal' of 1922 (it is fair to say a compelled betrayal), and was still conscientiously convinced that arbitration was the palladium of Australian industrial relations. The House, since 1928, was narrowly divided. His motion for a referendum or a general election was carried by one, and Bruce resigned.

There had been signs that not all was well; State development programmes had got out of hand; the tariff-arbitration imbroglio was ever more apparent; and perhaps also *l'Australie s'ennuie* – a political factor often overlooked. At all events, the Australian Labor Party under James Scullin came to power with 46 members of the House against 14 Nationalists, 10 Country Party, and 5 independents.

At that time wool and wheat together amounted to over 60 per cent by value of all exports. The average prices per pound of wool in 1928–29, 1929–30, and 1930–31 were 16.44, 10.29 and 8.60 pence; of wheat per bushel 57.50, 51.50, and 28.25 pence; wool exports were halved. Labor and the great depression came in together.

Chapter 5

Depression, War, Reappraisal, Reconstruction

T HE LABOR GOVERNMENT called upon to cope with unprecedented economic disaster was singularly unfitted for the task.
Perhaps more than any other group in Australia, Labor
incarnated the euphoria which foresaw only a self-sustaining progress based on continental resources, neglecting the nasty fact that
their development depended on outside markets and money. Labor
of the day – and this is still largely true – could neither wholly
accept nor wholly reject the limiting conditions set by conservative
capitalism, which was strongly entrenched in the Commonwealth
Bank and in the Senate, where the ministry was very vulnerable to
obstruction. The Hughes split and the long years in the wilderness
had deprived the party of experienced Federal leadership. In retro-
spect, it seems astonishing that Scullin managed to carry on for two
years in such a sea of troubles; there must have been some toughness in the man which does not appear in the record. Hindsight
suggests that a double dissolution should have been sought; even an
earlier defeat would have avoided much of the wild factionalism
which produced and followed Scullin's fall. But at the time there
seemed good tactical reasons against this – not only the desire for
office, but that of safeguarding the workers' interests, for example
by Trade Union preference, although the area in which this could
be effective was narrow.

Scullin himself tended to be obscured by strong personalities off-
centre. On-centre was the Treasurer, E. G. Theodore, who had both
toughness and intellectual grasp; but at a critical period, when
Scullin was in England, Theodore was in effect under suspension
following adroitly timed charges of corrupt practices while Queensland Premier. Far left of centre was J. T. Lang, Premier of New
South Wales in the crucial years 1930–32, and so tumultuously and
arrogantly demagogic as to be worse than an embarrassment. Right
of centre was Joseph Lyons, who was to be the Ramsay MacDonald

of a government even more ill-starred than its Labour contemporary in Britain.

Governments, Banks, and people

The first moves were conventional enough: minor economies such as the abandonment (in part ideological) of compulsory military training; curtailment of assisted immigration (more people left Australia than came); restriction of imports by tariffs and even prohibition – measures less effectual than the collapse of purchasing power with unemployment. More positively, the government attempted to secure wheat prices by a compulsory marketing pool, but this was vetoed by the Senate and wheat-growing remained a depressed industry long after general recovery.

By early 1930 the overseas payments position was really acute, and the visit of Sir Otto Niemeyer of the Bank of England powerfully reinforced the demand from conservative circles, including the Commonwealth Bank, for severe deflation. By the same token, this blank negativism powerfully exacerbated Labor opinion, much of which hailed Lang as the champion of the little people against the bondholders. Much of Lang's argument was sheer demagoguery – State developmental loans from Britain were equated with war debt, and the preceding State government having increased hours and cut salaries, this should simply be reversed and unemployment relief works financed by deficit borrowing; this when there was nobody to lend, but presumably on the calculation that a Labor Federal government would be forced to come to the rescue. 'The bankers and economists might think what they liked about this interesting programme; the result of the State election was an overwhelming victory for Lang',[1] with repercussions federally.

Matters came to a head in January 1931. On the one hand the Commonwealth Bank was pressing for deflation and yet more deflation, refusing credits to cover deficits until these demands were met. On the other, Scullin's re-establishment of Theodore as Treasurer, the Queensland charges being still uncleared, led to the resignation of Lyons, acting Treasurer, and Fenton, acting Prime Minister in Scullin's absence. Theodore seems to have been the only person in a responsible position with a coherent programme, other than one of purely negative economies, though there were of course

[1] P. H. Partridge, in G. Greenwood (ed.), *Australia: a Social and Political History* (Angus and Robertson, Sydney, 1955), p. 353.

any number of 'plans' floating about; this he probably owed to R. F. Irvine, a former Professor of Economics at Sydney whose thinking followed on from J. A. Hobson's and to some extent foreshadowed that of Keynes. Briefly, Theodore proposed reductions in interest rates, devaluation of the pound, and restoration of prices through central bank credit. Co-operation was refused by the Commonwealth and other banks except on strictly deflationary terms: budgets, State and Federal, must be balanced before all else. Simultaneously Lang was bidding strongly for general Labor support with an essentially repudiatory policy. It could legitimately be pointed out that while the Arbitration Court had cut wages by 10 per cent, rentiers were still largely unscathed.

The ministry endeavoured to meet the *non possumus* attitude of the bankers by legislation which seemed to have aspects both of inflation – a fiduciary issue of £18 million for unemployment relief and aid to wheat growers – and of political interference with private finance by proposing a central reserve bank and reconstruction of the Commonwealth Bank; the germs of the post-war Curtin-Chifley policy. In these post-Keynesian days, it is generally conceded that Theodore had the theoretical best of the argument with the bankers; at the time and in practice, with a hostile Senate and the mounting distrust of all right-thinking people, the policy could not succeed.

By mid-1931 the government had no option but to accept the 'Economists' Plan', worked out by a Loan Council committee of four.[1] This provided basically for a 20 per cent cut in all adjustable government expenditure, increased taxation, some loosening of bank credit, and a 22.5 per cent reduction, by conversion, of interest on internal (but only internal) borrowings. With considerable ingenuity, faces were saved all round: the lowering of interest made the plan acceptable to moderate Labor, the reduction of expenditure (most of which had already been 'adjusted' anyhow) met the main conservative demand. As the 'Premiers' Plan', the programme was accepted even by Lang, though probably not without mental reservation; though the Lang group of five in the House (and eleven other Labor members) voted against the cuts in salaries and social services, the necessary legislation was passed by grace of the opposition. But the days of the ministry were numbered: in November 1931 it was defeated by a snap vote on an intra-Labor squabble.

[1] Two of them, incidentally, became the first two Vice-Chancellors of the Australian National University.

Labor fractionalism was now indeed at its height. The right had been shed, but the entire New South Wales executive under Lang was expelled from the Australian Labor Party, while in Victoria and South Australia the local executives expelled parliamentary leaders who had supported the Premiers' Plan. In May 1931 Lyons and his supporters joined the Nationalists to form the United Australia Party; with Scullin and Lang men fighting each other in New South Wales, the result of the November election was a foregone conclusion. Theodore himself was beaten by a Langite. Lyons became Prime Minister, for the first three years without Country Party support.

Entrenched in New South Wales, Lang was still a problem. In April 1931 he had practically repudiated his State's overseas debt to enforce a reduction of interest to 3 per cent; the Commonwealth paid up and sued to recover in the High Court. So far Lang's gamble had succeeded, at the price of suspension by the State Savings Bank after the Commonwealth Bank had refused support; at the price also of the expulsion of his whole executive. In February 1932 it became evident that Lang had made little or no effort to act under the Premiers' Plan, and the Loan Council refused help to meet overseas payments. Once more the Federal government paid; but this time, under Lyons, it legislated to secure powers opened to it by the financial agreement of 1928, and directed that certain New South Wales revenues and bank moneys should be paid to the Commonwealth. Lang's counter-measures, which included suspending income tax assessments, led to his dismissal by the State Governor: whether or not this was a constitutional use of the Crown's reserve powers, the action was supported in the State election of July. Henceforth Lang was no longer a thorn in the side of the Commonwealth, though for some years he remained as irritant a nuisance as ever to the Australian Labor Party.

The depression had struck wide and very deep; at one time one-third of the workforce was out of work. It had wrecked the Federal Labor Party, and in New South Wales, where two Labor Parties fought each other bitterly, there were threats of civil violence from a grouping of young business-men and old soldiers, the 'New Guard'; though the only sword they actually unsheathed was that with which Major de Groot slashed the silk ribbon at the opening of Sydney Harbour Bridge, just ahead of Lang's scissors. Far more important, in a negative sense, is the fact that many of the

Australian Labor Party's executives, State and Federal, of the
'fifties and 'sixties had been the young unionists of the 'thirties, and
their personal experience of unemployment deeply coloured their
thinking – more deeply than with their opposite numbers in Britain;
perhaps because the depression was itself more catastrophic in the
less diversified Australian economy, perhaps because its effect was
worst during and not after a Labor régime. Whatever the reason,
this personal suffering lies at the bottom of the stand-pat attitude
of the unionist executives of Labor to-day, an attitude so distressing
to moderate social democratic intellectuals. The defection of Lyons
once more accentuated the distrust of the leader too adaptable to
parliamentary ways or to give-and-take: after Cook, Hughes,
Holman, Lyons, it is natural enough that the rank and file should
distrust the man who mixes too readily with the other side, and
yet in the absence of a revolution it is difficult to run a country
effectively without a good deal of such mixing. It is an impressive
tribute to the character of John Curtin that by patient effort he
rebuilt the unity of the party and brought it once more not only to a
central place in the counsels of the nation, but actually to guide
Australia through a war far more directly perilous than that of
1914–18.

As P. H. Partridge points out, while no party had any really
coherent policy to cope with catastrophe, the conservatives had at
least 'their orthodoxies ready-made'; Labor, being in power, had to
do its thinking on its feet and inevitably appeared far more inco-
herent, quite apart from its own factionalism.[1] Until Theodore was
given his head, Labor had no programme convincing even to itself.
By then it was too late; Lang was cutting the ground from under
official Labor's feet, while at the same time serving as a provocation
and rallying point for anti-Labor. But Lang's intransigence was
well-matched by that of the 'sound elements', and in course of time
this was recognised. Under Curtin, Labor's serious rethinking
culminated in Chifley's post-war banking programme, which has
exercised a strong influence on Australian polity even under conservative governments. It seems safe to say that neither the wild
gestures of Lang nor the hide-bound obscurantism of the Commonwealth Bank of his day are likely to be seen again, and no future
Prime Minister is likely to find himself so fatally hampered as was
Scullin through lack of power to make his government's financial

[1] *Op. cit.*, p. 362.

will prevail. From this aspect, the depression has had positive as well as negative effects.

The Lyons interlude

Lyons was as lucky in his timing as Scullin had been unlucky. The economic tide was turning, faintly enough at first; the conversion loans were successful, and by 1934 there was again a Federal budget surplus. Wool improved, though wheat remained a problem industry; manufacturing was assisted by the devaluation to £A125 = £100 sterling. There was some easing of tariffs, partly in response to the Ottawa agreements of 1932. A Grants Commission put federal subsidies to the 'claimant States' (Tasmania, Western Australia, and South Australia) on a more rational footing, but the problem of central banking was faced gingerly. Theodore, Lang, Sir Otto Niemeyer, and Sir Robert Gibson, Governor of the Commonwealth Bank, had between them assured at least that banking remained on the agenda: a Royal Commission of 1937 on the whole strengthened the case for central banking and greater Treasury control over fiscal policy, although nothing serious was done before war overtook the hesitant policy of the first Menzies ministry.

Lyons' difficulty was not the paucity but the plethora of ministerial experience, and claims, in his government. After the 1934 election he had to accept the Country Party in coalition, but the United Australian Party wing was strengthened by the re-enlistment of Hughes (soon dropped, however) and the recruitment of Robert Gordon Menzies and Richard Gardner Casey. With these, the first two of whom were prima donnaesque, and the pressures of Earle Page's Country Party henchmen, the task of securing Cabinet cohesion was no sinecure; Lyons was relieved of it by his sudden death in April 1937. Page, as Deputy, took over temporarily, and the United Australia Party was never less united: the faction fight was as fierce as, and perhaps more purely personal than, those to which Labor was habituated. When Menzies emerged a narrow winner, Page yielded with exceedingly bad grace, taking his party out of the coalition, though some dissidents continued to support the government. The times were inauspicious: Menzies was by no means too popular in his own party, a recession had set in, and the international atmosphere was darkening fast.

Reappraisal: from isolationism to total involvement

Australia in the 'twenties seemed to have settled back into a comfortable unawareness of world affairs. The ruling conservative coalition was on the whole content to follow Britain's lead; it was acquiescent rather than initiatory in Empire affairs, claiming a voice in the determination of policy (at least as regards the Pacific – little else counted) but showing little inclination for the more autonomous stance of Canada or South Africa. As for Labor and its leaders, 'they were apt and knowledgeable in Australian home affairs and in the daily traffic of politics but were inclined to lump world affairs under bold and convenient danger signs such as "imperialism"'.[1]

Nevertheless the changed position in the Pacific, if nothing else, dented this complacency. The Germans in New Guinea had been very close to Australia, but they were only a tiny handful, and their metropolitan base was on the other side of the world. Now the Japanese had supplanted them in Micronesia, and Tokyo was only 2,000 miles from their advanced base at Truk, itself only 900 miles from the main port of New Guinea, Rabaul. In the 'thirties matters were becoming complicated: the Japanese action in Manchuria was comfortably in the opposite direction, but together with the Abyssinian sanctions crisis it both showed up the weakness of the League of Nations and cast some doubt on the easy theory that Britain knew best. As early as November 1936 Curtin, the new leader of Labor, was envisaging the possibility that in the event of a European war Britain might be unable or unwilling to underwrite Australia's position *vis-à-vis* Japan – perhaps the germ of his dramatic turn, five years later, towards the United States.

Attitudes remained confused and ambivalent, especially perhaps on the Labor side, where they ranged all the way from a negative anti-imperialist isolationism, through League idealism, to support for strengthening naval and air forces, but exclusively as local defence against the risk of limited though perhaps heavy raids on some part of the long and exposed coastline. This was simply a tooling-up of the old Labor concept, going back to Fisher's day, of a citizen militia. Even the Spanish Civil War, though a source of spiritual anguish to many on the Left, had hardly the cataclysmic shock effect which it had in Europe; the strength of Catholicism in

[1] Paul Hasluck, *The Government and the People 1939–1941* (Australian War Memorial, Canberra, 1952), p. 30.

the Australian Labor Party may have inhibited any general whole-hearted reaction to the totalitarian threat so obvious to European labour. To the conservatives, this was merely a local ideological quarrel and here, at least, Neville Chamberlain might know best; an attitude shaken by, but surviving, Munich.

When war came the Menzies government, true to the form of the 'twenties, accepted with a minimum of consultation that Britain being at war, so was Australia; there was none of the deliberation of Canada, let alone South Africa. The usual machinery of war government was set up, with much less of haphazard scramble than in 1914: after all, Australia was a much more sophisticated and better-tooled nation now, and even had a War Book ready. 'Business as usual' prevailed to an extent that now looks rather shocking, and that certainly shocked Menzies when he returned in April 1941 from a visit to Britain. Debate was mainly on two themes: externally, how best to help Britain – and as regards the supply of wool and food-stuffs, this was the justification of 'business as usual'; internally, the need for unity, to be given body by an all-party national government.

One lesson at least was learnt from the first war: there was no toying with overseas conscription, the one issue in which all Labor's ambivalences were resolved. Labor objected to but accepted com-pulsory home defence service, and volunteers sufficed for a sizeable overseas force; but where best to help Britain? Not without soul-searching, the Menzies government accepted the British view that this was in the Mediterranean; for three-quarters of a century Suez had been the vital link between Australia and 'Home'. But as the Japanese showed every disposition to take advantage of the pre-carious or desperate position of Britain, France, and the Nether-lands in Europe, the Far East (Australia's 'Near North') inevitably began to loom larger than the Middle East. Till the last moment, Australian counsels were for playing for safety with Japan, and the swaying fortunes of war in the Mediterranean, of diplomacy in south-east Asia, were reflected in the all-party War Advisory Council; Curtin's pressure for more weight to be given to the local menace was resisted, but with increasing misgiving, by Menzies in the interest of an all-Empire concept of strategy.

By the course of events, not by any dereliction of duty on Menzies' part, the confusion as to where the main Australian strength should be committed was left to be resolved by the angry exchanges between Curtin and Churchill over the latter's attempted

diversion of Australian troops to Burma, where they would certainly have been lost. By that time, from an Australian point of
view, there was no option whatsoever: with Pearl Harbor, the
fantasy of so many sensational articles and cartoons became a frightful reality. The Near North was terrifyingly close; the Yellow Peril
was incarnate in arms.

For the existing ministry the pressure for a national government
became really urgent – a question of sharing office or no office,
though there were far more respectable arguments – when the 1940
election returned government and Labor (including four Langites)
with 36 seats each; two independents, a wheat farmer with Labor
leanings, a Melbourne business-man with conservative leanings,
held the balance. Curtin's attitude was one of impeccable democratic theory: during the imbroglio after Lyons' death he had met
feelers for coalition with the words 'any government, even if it has
the best policies, would do far better service to the nation if there
were arrayed against it in Parliament an Opposition courageous,
intelligent, and patriotic'. To that classic statement he adhered,
accepting only the all-party Advisory War Council. For once,
impeccable adherence to theoretic democratic virtue was also
tactically sound, for the government was breaking up through sheer
factionalism and shoddy intrigue.

Arthur Fadden, who was himself leader of the Country Party
merely because the factions backing the other leaders cancelled
out, took advantage of Menzies' absence overseas to engineer a
Cabinet *coup*, relying on personal popularity with parliamentarians
resentful of Menzies' air (justified enough on intellectual grounds)
of being made of superior clay. With admirable nerve, Curtin held
his hand, despite pressures to move in from his own party, notably
from the ambitious H. V. Evatt; anti-Labor must work out its own
doom. Fadden's ministry lasted forty days before being defeated on
quite minor budget matters: but the final vote was perhaps the
most moving and dramatic division ever made in the Australian
House of Representatives. All depended on the independents, two
undistinguished men who by the chance of the ballot stood for the
Australian people. Motivated by desire for a stable government for
the honest and efficient prosecution of the war, they voted with
Labor, thus making up for them the minds of four million evenly
divided people: a strange but impressive example of, and tribute to,
the workings of representative democracy.

This was on 7 October 1941: just two months before Pearl Harbor. It was providential, and it was high time. As Grattan puts it, 'In an atmosphere of high risk, people would take from a Labor administration what they would not take from a conservative administration in an atmosphere of low risk'; and it is anybody's guess as to whether the sudden heightening of the risk would have overcome the distrust engendered by the politicking, intolerably irresponsible in such perilous times, of the last months of Menzies (himself more sinned against than sinning) and the forty days of Fadden. Perhaps the odds would have been much the same as that government and people in Britain could have nerved themselves under Chamberlain as they did under Churchill. At all events, this was clearly Curtin's own calculation; it was at once put to bitter test. He had one grim satisfaction. Australia did not wait to find herself at war by the fact of Britain being at war. By deliberate intent, the Australian declaration of war against Japan preceded the British by twenty minutes.

Hands across which sea?

Prince of Wales and *Repulse*, whose arrival was to have put teeth into the empty jaws of Singapore, were sunk on the second day of war; by the end of January 1942 Rabaul had fallen; in February Darwin was heavily bombed; within six months the Japanese had become masters from Burma to the Solomons, a land area of over 1,500,000 square miles, a population of over 150,000,000. In his New Year message Curtin's reappraisal was dramatic, if grimly realistic: 'Without inhibitions of any kind, I make it quite clear that Australia looks to America, free of any pang as to our traditional links or kinship with the United Kingdom ... Australia can go and Britain can still hold on. We are determined that Australia shall not go.' There was some exaggeration in this; it was not meant as a repudiation of the Empire connection, but as a reinsurance. Pangs and inhibitions remain to this day; nevertheless the statement marks a watershed, though on the face of it it was in no sense a declaration of independence, nor could it be.

What it did repudiate – and this was an obvious necessity – was the complete subordination of Australia's view of her strategic interests to the British imperial grand strategy: this was the core of the Curtin-Churchill quarrel. Faced with the facts of January 1942, a Menzies administration would itself have grasped the point, but it would hardly have been so whole-hearted about it. Externally as well as internally, it was high time that Australia should have a new voice, if only to disengage herself, in American eyes, from an archaic, suspect, ill-visualised 'Empire'. The 'Europe first' policy held both in Washington and in London was doubtless correct enough globally. The Japanese onrush over-extended itself and received its first checks, at sea from the Americans in the Coral Sea and at Midway in May and June 1942, in New Guinea from the Australians at Milne Bay and on the Kokoda Trail (a bare thirty-five miles from the capital, Port Moresby) in August. Despite her unparalleled conquest in spatial terms, or perhaps because of it, Japan was the weaker partner and could wait. But it would have been disastrous had the priority been too rigid, and unloved as Douglas Macarthur became to the Australian land forces under him, from an Australian point of view it was fortunate that he and Admirals Nimitz and Halsey were not men to accept too readily that the tasks with which they had identified themselves were secondary.

On the home front, the Curtin government accepted with Churchillian vigour the implications of total war: rationing, even of foodstuffs normally exported, compulsory direction of labour. Under the immediate threat, the unions were abnormally amenable – after all, this was direction by their own side and in their own cause of White Australia. Even on conscription, compromise was possible. Compulsion for narrowly defined home militia service was not too far out of accord with Labor tradition, and in the heightened crisis of 1942–43 it was possible to extend the concept of 'home defence' to a reasonable approximation with military logic: conscripts could serve up to the Equator and within longitudes which included the Solomons, New Guinea, and half Indonesia; although by the time this could become effective the immediate threat was over. The wisdom of Curtin's earlier insistence on retaining his party's independence uncompromised by coalition was now apparent; it is unlikely that such a striking erosion of deeply-felt traditional attitudes could have been secured by a conservative or even a national government. Labor could demand far more on its own than as a party involved with the old régime.

This applied in other directions. Financial policy was taxation first, then domestic borrowing; the fact that under Labor the rich were soaked first made taxation easier to take for the lower income groups. The most important innovation was the introduction of uniform income tax, the States being required to vacate this field, against Commonwealth grants. This of course was only one, but perhaps the most striking, of many steps in the expansion of Federal *via-à-vis* State powers inevitably called forth by war needs, a centralisation in general accord with the Australian Labor Party tradition. So also was a much increased emphasis on social services of a Welfare State type, and reconstruction planning with a stress on full employment. Very untraditional for Labor was the launching of a massive immigration scheme as soon as the war was over. All these have become permanent features of the Australian scene.

Reconstruction abroad and at home: Evatt and Chifley

The urgent need for reappraisal became strikingly obvious as the high tide of Japanese advance receded, leaving behind in Asia the wrecked sea-walls of the old empires, and in Australia a Commonwealth whose powers and resources had been inevitably, and greatly, enhanced by the tasks of war. The chief architects of reconstruction were J. B. Chifley, who ever since the 1937 Banking Commission had been Labor's fiscal expert, had served as Curtin's Treasurer, and succeeded him as Prime Minister after his death in July 1945; and H. V. Evatt, a distinguished and ambitious lawyer who left the High Court Bench for politics in 1940 and was Attorney-General and Minister for External Affairs throughout the Labor régime. To them may be added Arthur Calwell, who sponsored the immigrations scheme, and J. J. Dedman, Minister for Post-War Reconstruction.

As the pressures for unity relaxed with the Japanese retreat, it was inevitable that policy should become more political rather than national. Labor deserved its landslide victory of 1943 and maintained its position with little loss in 1946, and its post-war record was by no means unfruitful. But its peace effort was less distinguished than its war effort, at least as regards Evatt's foreign policy; neither then nor since has Labor, or indeed Australia, been able either wholly to reject or wholly to accept the hard facts of world power in a revolutionary age. This is no discredit when we reflect that even such giants as the United States and the Soviet Union so often show themselves divided, uncertain, and nervous about their own policies.

Evatt's fundamental concern was to assert the independent rights of a rising but small power, both within the British Commonwealth and in the counsels of the world, and he extended this to a championship of the rights of small powers in general. But even with this rider, he laid himself open to the reproach of over-assertion in relation to Australia's very limited real strength. Some steps were unexceptionable, for instance the extension of Australian diplomatic representation, which had been initiated in April 1939 by the Menzies government; for others, such as the 1944 Australian-New Zealand Treaty (the first between two Dominions, and somewhat aggressive in tone) there was provocation in the inadequate measure of British consultation with Pacific Dominions on Pacific war and peace. This aspect of Evatt's policy was bitterly criticised by Menzies and other Liberal leaders as weakening the British Commonwealth.

The high point of Evatt's policy and career was his leadership of the smaller powers at the San Francisco conference to formulate the United Nations charter. On the main issue – the struggle to reject or greatly limit the big power veto in the Security Council – he failed; but in other matters Australian influence was considerable. Far more than at Versailles, Australia emerged as a nation in her own right, with an independent contribution to the shaping of the world's future organisation. Yet this was largely illusory, and in the not so long run solved nothing; in the first phases of the Cold War, Australia was little more than a helpless looker-on.

The major dilemma remained: of its own strength, Australia could be little more than an influential client; but whose, Britain's or America's? Ironically, the more the succeeding Menzies régime talked of the bonds with Britain, the more it fell (or rushed) into the American orbit. Beyond this dilemma is a more fundamental crux: 'Australia is a part of Asia' – a befogging cliché found in the mental equipment of people ranging all the way from conservative ministers to crypto-Communists – but how can a White Australia be part of Asia? Such problems have bedevilled the Menzies and Holt ministries; one cannot see that Evatt's principles would have exorcised them. The ambivalences remain, irrespective of which party is in power, and inevitably so, since Australia is too small to count for a great deal in world power terms, too large to discount herself.

Internally, there was a rare and refreshing measure of bipartisan (or, strictly, tripartisan) agreement in some fields. Long-term, probably the most important of these was the launching of a really big immigration scheme – a startling departure from Labor tradition. In 1946–50 the net gain from migration was over 353,000, and over 400,000 in each of the next two five-year periods. Even more subversive of tradition – this time general tradition – was the composition of this great influx, which included large numbers of displaced persons from eastern Europe. In 1947 under 10 per cent of the 7,580,000 population were born outside Australia or New Zealand, and of this tenth the only sizeable group not born in the British Isles was the 34,000 from Italy, followed by Germans and Greeks with 12–15,000 each. By 1961 nearly 17 per cent of 10,508,000 people were non-Australasian by birth; the British Isles component of immigrants, over three-quarters in 1947, was not much over two-fifths. The Italian-born now numbered 228,000, German 109,000, Polish 60,000, Dutch 102,000, Greek 77,000, Maltese 39,000. The stresses of assimilation, both moral and material, were great, on the whole surmounted certainly not without friction but with surprisingly little. At the same time, there was no weakening on White Australia; Calwell, to whom much of the general credit was due, applied the policy, with a rigidity which seems heartless, to groups too tiny to make any difference, for instance Japanese wives of Australian servicemen.

Despite much dispute on detail, there was general support for the Commonwealth's direct venture into development (in conjunction with Victoria and New South Wales) through the Snowy Mountain hydro-electricity and irrigation project; its initiative in setting up the South Pacific Commission to co-ordinate research and welfare work in the scattered dependencies of six powers in that area; its general encouragement of scientific and technical advance through the Commonwealth Scientific and Industrial Research Organisation and other agencies, and the foundation of the Australian National University.[1]

So far the government was riding the crest: crests topple. Much encouragement – too much – was found in the unwonted success of a referendum in 1946; this was to enlarge Commonwealth activity in social services, and as Geoffrey Sawer says 'is explicable on the simple principle that not even when voting in a constitutional referendum will the Australian voter readily shoot Santa Claus'.

[1] Dedman, who piloted this and other projects through the House, had later the singular distinction of receiving an honorary LL.D. from the university one year before he took its B.A. – in Political Science! – at the age of 70.

But the euphoria of this victory blinded the government to the fact that in 1944 a more significant referendum, for a much wider extension of powers for economic reconstruction not tied to social services, had been defeated; the electoral mandate of 1943 did not extend to a complete recasting of Commonwealth economic powers. The area of agreement was rapidly narrowing, and banking policy, the primary source of Chifley's reputation, was also a main source of his government's defeat.

Chifley's banking legislation, bitterly resisted by the opposition, had three major elements: subordination of the private banks to the Commonwealth Bank by a special deposit system and power to direct their general policy on advances; active Commonwealth Bank competition at all levels of banking; the reserve power of the Commonwealth Treasurer to direct the general financial policy of the Commonwealth Bank, and hence indirectly of all banks. The High Court declared unconstitutional a provision that all government accounts – including those of States and municipalities – should be held in the Commonwealth Bank. On the face of it, this provision was certainly stretching Federal powers, but was not in itself essential. The Court's judgement might or might not have heralded further adverse decisions whittling away more essential parts of the policy; too mindful that attack is the best form of defence, and over-confident of his mandate, in August 1947 Chifley abruptly announced, with surprising pique and lack of judgement, that the government would simply nationalise all private banking.

At once the depression battle was joined again; and indeed it seems that to some extent Chifley, and Labor generally, were still living in that past – a past not so remote psychologically, as well as temporally, as it is to-day when even the middle-aged can barely 'remember the depression'. The broad powers sought by the 1944 referendum had given rise to apprehension of a 'creeping socialism' through nationalisation of airlines and broadcasting, non- or only quasi-contributory medical and unemployment insurance, and so on. Taken with Dedman's somewhat doctrinaire socialist stance, this was just what the opposition wanted.

Bank nationalisation was eventually taken to the Privy Council; its adverse decision was formally on legalistic technical grounds, but in supplementary argument a strict construction of Section 92 ('trade, commerce and intercourse among the States ... shall be absolutely free') was developed. Since nationalisation at the Federal level would obviously be by definition inter- or supra-State, this clearly set limits to any Commonwealth programme of socialisation. The banking policy, however, was watered down rather than repudiated by subsequent Liberal-Country Party governments; despite promises or threats, the Menzies-Fadden ministries did not repeal its central provisions, and Holt, for example, showed no reluctance as Treasurer to enforcing Treasury's will in the 1960 'credit squeeze', an ironic vindication of the Labor line.

The Privy Council's findings were published in October 1949. By that time there were other troubles. A great Communist-inspired strike on the New South Wales coalfields in mid-winter of that year had led to much unemployment and privation; Chifley met it with firmness, even sending troops to work opencast mines; but non-Labor opinion was outraged to the point of describing the admittedly severe discomforts as 'Australians agonising in their Gethsemane'. This was blasphemous nonsense, even if it was uttered by a professor; but it was also a danger signal. More ephemeral matters – petrol rationing, social service details – played their part; but essentially Labor was mistaking enthusiasm for this or that benefit for a blanket commendation. Labor had done great things in war under Curtin, and the momentum carried it on to do great things in peace under Chifley; but it had by now lost touch with the central mass of opinion – a mistake which Menzies avoided, at least (with the possible and partial exception of 1961) in an election year.

In the 1949 election, to a House enlarged in accordance with the rapid recent increase in population, the Liberal Party (successor to the United Australia Party) secured 55 seats and the Country Party 19, against 48 for Labor. Robert Gordon Menzies entered on his reign of sixteen years, over double the length of Bruce's record, from which this time he retired voluntarily. The eight years of Curtin and Chifley had been a creative period recalling the best days of Deakin and Fisher. The Menzies era, twice as long, was to be marked indeed by great advances on the road to a sophisticated modern nationhood, but these were the work of the economy and the society rather than of the administration. Government's role was to be not merely negative but yet, on the whole and with some important exceptions, one of consolidation and co-ordination rather than of innovation and creation.

Part Two
ECONOMY

Chapter 6

The Central Problem of Centralisation

HE POPULAR overseas image of Australia is that of a 'sunburnt country' of vast empty spaces – which it certainly is – and of Australians as lanky or sturdy sunburnt bushmen, which few of them are. The average Australian is much more likely to be an office or factory worker. The fundamental demographic fact about the country is its high degree of metropolitan concentration; the six State capitals have over 60 per cent of the population, and radii of fifty miles around Sydney and Melbourne, enclosing about 0.34 per cent of the total area, also enclose over 43 per cent of the people.

This concentration is inherent partly in the history – to the normal colonial concentration in the port-capital was added, in New South Wales and Tasmania, the centralisation due to the rigid authoritarian control of a penal headquarters; partly in the geography, with its absence of deep indentations and large coastal plains in the better-watered areas, or of anything really corresponding to the American Middle West, the Murray-Darling providing only a much attenuated version of the Mississippi-Missouri. The historical working-out of these factors has been touched on in the conclusion to Chapter 2; we need only mention here the effect of the rail-nets focused on the capitals, sometimes with discriminatory freight-rates which favoured the concentration of manufacturing, and the fact that in many areas closer settlement coincided with the introduction of the telegraph, in itself a powerful centralising factor.

The cities . . .

On a broad view, taking capitals and provincial towns together, Australia is one of the most urbanised countries in the world, with the rural fraction rapidly diminishing – nearly a third in 1947, under a fifth in 1961. When we subtract the metropolitan component, the picture is different; nothing is more striking than the paucity of sizeable and truly autonomous regional centres. Only Newcastle, Wollongong, and Geelong have over 100,000 inhabitants and perhaps none of these is sufficiently distant from Sydney or Melbourne, or sufficiently detached economically, to be considered really non-metropolitan. There are only seven cities in the 40,000 to 60,000 class; one of these, Gold Coast, is merely a seaside satellite of Brisbane. Further down, in the 15,000 to 25,000 group, some 'cities' are simply aggregations of small towns with common interests, such as Yallourn-Moe on the lignite fields of Victoria, or the 'City of Blue Mountains', a chain of resorts along the main western rail and road route from Sydney, more mountainous (and not so very mountainous) than urban. Some, such as Broken Hill and Kalgoorlie, are mining towns with hardly any organic connection with the surrounding emptiness; on the other hand, much smaller isolated centres like Alice Springs do serve as regional co-ordinators.

The most astonishing imbalance is in South Australia; in 1961, 60.66 per cent of the people were in Adelaide, and *one-fifth* of the remaining urban population in Elizabeth (32,000), held up as a shining example of decentralisation but separated from Adelaide by some eight miles of more or less open country. More realistically, the 1966 Census included Elizabeth in the metropolitan area, which now had 70.7 per cent of the population; the next town, Port Pirie, had 13,947 people, a ratio to the capital of 1:66.

The implications of this pattern are far-reaching. At least three out of every five Australians live in vast sprawling suburbias. The cores of the capitals are indeed individualised to a surprising degree, seeing that they are so much of an age: all but Sydney and Hobart were founded within the twelve years 1824 to 1836. But in each case the city's heart beats to its own tempo, since the truly formative periods vary more than the dates of foundation. By countless subtle touches they express the geographical personalities of their States: the note of sub-tropical gaiety in Brisbane; the delightful archaism of Hobart; the new look of the Westralian boom superposed on an old-fashioned provincialism in Perth; the slightly too self-conscious dignity of Adelaide, city of churches; the Victorian exuberance (tempered by a Victorian Sabbath) of Melbourne; the brash virility of Sydney, in patches aggressively cosmopolitan and yet capable of transforming itself (especially when aided by an evening light) into an almost feminine charm. Yet they all share a firm and unmistakable Australianism, and this individuality holds only for each small nuclear core.

Around each nucleus spreads a vast penumbra of brick and tile, weather-board and corrugated iron – suburbs which, with a handful of exceptions, lack character because they have never had any autonomous prehistory, have never been anything else than suburbs, the dwelling-places of Barry Humphries' Mrs Norm Everage, whose personality is adequately displayed in her name. Contemplating these amorphous immensities from the air or on the ground, one is reminded of Robert Graves's devastating line: 'the suburbs of itself is Hell'. It is not quite fair: despite their formidable sprawl, they are pleasant enough places for the mechanics of living. But obscurely one feels that something is missing in these agglomerations of roads and houses in simple juxtaposition; that the garden and the sports oval, the beach and the pub, are scarcely enough for the full development of the art, as distinct from the standard, of living. Nor is it quite true that there are no slums in Australia.

The great cities have of course their full share of the diseconomies of metropolitan life: inflated land values, commuting rush hours, traffic congestions. Though urban public transport is far from reaching the American state of virtual collapse, it is in constant difficulty through the competition of the one-person car, with its concomitant parking problem.[1] Things are not helped by the absence of any overall governing authority, except in Brisbane where it has not been conspicuously successful; it is as if the Boroughs of London had no Greater London Council, though there are any number of overlapping agencies for planning and essential services. Hence vested interests proliferate and interfere with a more rational organisation of metropolitan space.

... and the bush

The impression of cultural uniformity persists in the small towns; all but a few are either in a standard rectangular grid-pattern, or else street-villages with a simple functional layout: motor service stations at each end, hotel and shops in the middle. Everywhere is the feeling of ample space: any Australian town covers three or four times the area of an English town of similar population, with

[1] 'It has been argued that the traffic delay and inconvenience caused by the breakdown of a single car during the busy period on the Sydney Harbour Bridge is so great that it would pay to heave the car overboard and compensate the owner. But ... the social costs are widely distributed, while the car is an individual possession.' J. B. Condliffe, *The Development of Australia* (Ure Smith, Sydney, 1964), pp. 63–64.

wide main streets (originally probably determined by the turning-circle of a dray with several yokes of bullocks), streets so wide in fact that for due proportion they demand to be flanked by Renaissance palaces. In the absence of Renaissance princes, buildings of a sufficiently grand scale could be erected only by wealthy corporations, and there are simply not enough government offices, courts, banks, or even pubs to go round. Allied with this, except in some old and some recently prosperous towns, is a lack of solidity, for which the general dominance, in most rural areas, of weatherboard and fibro is responsible; and there is still some tendency, in really small places, for some home-owners to be literally home-builders. Nevertheless, the last fifteen years have seen a general improvement in neatness, colour (often, unfortunately, in the way of clashing pinks and mauves), and general civic amenity and pride. The very rapid spread of the motel has contributed to this.

Distances between larger centres are usually too great, and the population too sparse, for bus services to be economic, except for some tourism; and they are inhibited also by the wide ownership of private cars, which are indeed essential for running the farm or station. Small service centres in wide areas of dispersed population have no near competitors in the form of large towns, and may have a bigger development of specialised services than their European equivalents: the climax is perhaps reached by Wyuna in Victoria, which has a total of eight buildings, three of them churches and not one simply a residence. This is extreme; but it may be said that if the big cities are getting too big – much too big in Sydney and Melbourne – for an easy art of living, the small towns are too small to support the full range of amenities that this needs. It is not simply a matter of missing libraries and art galleries; it is often extremely difficult to attract and maintain the bare minimum of legal and especially medical services.

The gradient between city, or at least suburb, and bush township is thus steep. Only some thirty-five miles from central Sydney one can look across the Hawkesbury valley (closely settled by Australian standards, empty enough to European eyes) to the Blue Mountain scarp, forested from foot to crest and even now fretted by settlement only along the edges, still a frontier. Elsewhere the frontier is 'hollow'; the pioneer fringe has moved on, leaving behind it empty pockets, or patches of relative (sometimes absolute) decline and depopulation, little ghost towns, groves of cypresses where homesteads once stood. This uniquely sharp contrast between city and bush forms the setting for a salient feature of Australian life: the inevitable weakness of local government, over against the dynamic of metropolitan concentration.

Local government in theory and fact

The practical consequences of this imbalance are serious. While it is probably true that few local authorities anywhere in the world, outside large cities, can 'live of their own', in much of Australia local government units may hold more square miles than people; resources are so disproportionate to needs that 'local government' becomes merely the administration of central regulation. The extremes are in Western Australia, where two 'Shires' are together twice the size of Great Britain (81,000 square miles) and have a combined population of under 500. Even in New South Wales, setting aside the vast emptiness west of the Darling, the Shires – the rural units – have an average size of 1,420 square miles and population around 9,130; and this includes the largest contiguous areas of 'closer settlement' in Australia. On the opposite tack, we may exclude the metropolitan areas around Sydney, Newcastle, and Wollongong, and the isolated mining town of Broken Hill: the average population of Municipalities – the *urban* units – is about 6,175. The standard of services which could be provided from local revenues is not likely to be high.

'Such a structure is local government in name only, and merely relieves the central government from the care of minor domestic matters.' One may add that the centre does not always desire such relief; the conscientious zeal of one Department of Local Government has extended to the precise siting of a bus-shelter in a town 175 miles from the capital. Yet, though there may be only a few thousand people, and while nobody expects the full range of libraries, clinics, or even the more valued swimming-pools, some things are essential: there must be hospitals and schools not too far away, erosion control may be needed no matter how empty the land may appear, and of course roads. If say 3,500 people are scattered over 1,500 square miles in three or four hamlets of up to 300 people and a lot of isolated homesteads – and this is a common pattern – the road-net needed for efficient circulation will still be much the same as for eight or ten times as many people; more roads are needed than can be afforded. Again, the few children of school age must come long distances, perhaps to a one-room one-teacher bush school. At every turn the paucity of people enforces unduly high overheads in the running of the country.

There has been no lack of attempts to foster local government; with one exception they came from the top. The first effort began with some panache in 1842, when instructions came from Whitehall to divide New South Wales into districts as nearly as possible 100 miles square and bounded by rivers and ranges, each to be sub-divided into 100 parishes, with elected councils for districts with over 10,000 inhabitants. As the total white population of the colony was about 130,000, a quarter of it in Sydney, the machinery was not notably realistic.

The one movement from below began with the formation of a joint committee by local units in the Northern Rivers region of New South Wales, to fight the water hyacinth which was infesting their streams. Its fate was characteristic: the Department of Local Government seized upon the idea to form federative committees for all sorts of things, electricity, airfields, water supply, weed control, many with oddly overlapping jurisdictions and odd combinations of functions. These statutory authorities for special purposes are quaintly named County Councils, though with one exception they have no relation whatever to the pre-existing Counties, which are simply land registration areas, mere names on the map and on files in the Lands Department. There is no bureaucracy so empirical as that of Australia (which may indeed be seen as one of its strengths), and little guarantee that name and purpose coincide. The apparent expenditure on rural roads in Victoria, for instance, is inflated by the fact that the Country Roads Board and not the Metropolitan Board of Works is responsible for the main Melbourne arteries – after all, they were country roads once! This fact only came prominently to public notice with the scramble to disclaim respon-sibility for a main city bridge which had to be closed to traffic within a few months of its opening.

So it has come about that even England, the classic land of administrative lack of uniformity, has not produced in 1100 years a structure so heterogeneous as Australia has evolved in about a tenth of that time. The local government areas, whatever their titles (which vary from State to State), possess fine schedules of powers and duties. In practice, despite the work of many able and devoted people, the major concern of at least the more outback authorities is the upkeep of the local roads; and their condition bears incisive witness to the poverty of local resources. In the more settled areas, there is at least a fair standard of competence, and since the war an increase in amenity and civic pride is very noticeable; but such things as main roads and education are State not local responsibilities. Even in such areas, it is likely that any serious devolution of control, as distinct from day-to-day administration, would lead to a lowering of standards, and this despite such existing disadvantages as the rigidity and uniformity of State educational systems.

All this amounts, in a classic phrase, to 'apoplexy at the centre, anaemia at the extremities'. Suggested cures, or rather palliatives – the situation is probably beyond cure – are three: New States, regionalism, and an omnibus decentralisation. There is no high probability of any of these being adopted on a scale large enough to make any substantial change.

Regionalism and decentralisation

The philosophy of the New States movement is perhaps better treated with Federal-State relations (Chapter 10). It may be remarked here, however, that while a better-balanced federation might have resulted if various nineteenth-century separatist proposals had given the Commonwealth more foundation members, it by no means follows that after fifty (or a hundred and fifty) years of evolution the unscrambling of the existing structure into three or four times as many units would produce any positive effect. More likely the Commonwealth, faced with so much weaker components (which would have lost the intangible but real strength of historic tradition possessed by the present States), would become even more centralised; unless indeed something like the sectional blocs of American States had developed.

The striking absence of any such sectionalism is probably associated with the small number and large size of the Australian States, and the concentration of so much of their economic and political power in their capitals. The great wool/wheat belt in the southeast, or the pastoral and mining north, could supply the economic and cultural base for a section in the American manner; but they are split up between three or four States, and yet not dominant in any one. This is probably a main factor in the failure of the Australian Senate to act, as it was expected to act, as a States' House: with only six units, the possibilities of bloc-making are limited.

Regionalism has a certain following, and at one time the Australian Labor Party toyed with a plan for a more unitary central government with some devolution of powers to provinces smaller than the existing States. Academically, there is much to be said for such a structure; practically, while the plank has never been repudiated and while Labor is still regarded as the centralising party, the vested interests of its State machines inhibit any action.

In the passion for reconstruction which possessed Australia, like the rest of the world, around the end of the second World War, several States set up regional planning commissions. These, with Commonwealth agencies, did a good deal of delimiting reasonable economic regions and publishing regional surveys: useful as far as it went, but that is as far as it got. Thanks to the activities of local regional leagues, there is for example some tendency for towns along the Murray to look along and across the Murray instead of over their shoulders and across the Highlands to Sydney and Melbourne; but this has not found any concrete expression. Such intra-State devolution as has taken place is by way of regional offices to facilitate central administration, with no hint of the essence of regionalism – local autonomy and initiative in development. So the regions on the planning maps remain merely filing-cases for facts and figures; useful for Professors of Geography, but a little expensive if that is all they are to be used for.

Decentralisation has been aptly described as 'a topic of constant comment, much promise, and little achievement'; more picturesquely, as a cargo cult as crude as any New Guinean attempt to find a magic short-cut to the white man's affluence. There is incessant incantation of the magic word; meanwhile the centres continue to grow unchecked, and seemingly uncheckable.

The basic reason for this is quite simple: while practically everybody pays lip-service to decentralisation in principle, when it comes to hard entrepreneurial decisions the advantages of the metropolis in market, labour, warehousing, supply of spares, repair facilities, managerial and commercial services, are real and obvious, and individually garnered; the social costs may be just as real but are not nearly so obvious, and they are widely diffused. Decentralisation is fine for one's competitors.

The facts are striking. In every mainland State, the metropolitan percentage share of manufacturing, whether measured by employment or by value of production, materially exceeds even the metropolitan concentration of population. In Victoria, Western Australia, and South Australia this share is over 80 per cent on either measure; in New South Wales about 75 per cent; in Queensland, Brisbane with 47 per cent of the people has 60 per cent of the manufacturing. There is an apparently greater rate of increase in factory employment in non-metropolitan than in metropolitan areas; but as in New South Wales and Victoria, which account for three-quarters of the factory workforce, this is almost totally due to expansion in para-metropolitan Newcastle, Wollongong, and Geelong, this trend is much more apparent than real. It cannot be regarded as evidence of decentralisation at work.

During the 1939–45 war, the obvious security risks of piling up the great bulk of Australia's major manufacturing industries in half a dozen seaports led to the establishment of some munition and other essential plants away from the capitals, and after the war these installations became available for private enterprise. In the eastern mainland States, there has been a good deal of effort to foster decentralisation by such measures as concessional rates on rail carriage and power and water supplies, aid to housing, and direct grants or cheap loans. But these have not been very effective; for one thing, it is politically essential to avoid accusations of favouritism towards this or that town or industry, and hence aid tends to be spread too thinly. The Commonwealth itself could in theory assist by instituting regional differences in company, payroll, and sales taxes, as it does with income tax to a very limited extent in the north and in undeveloped south-western Tasmania. But it doubtless feels itself hampered, or at least can excuse itself, by similar political considerations. For decentralisation to be a reality, considerable effort would have to be concentrated on a very few favourably located towns; and however objective the criteria used to choose them, it is not to be supposed that politicians would risk the baffled fury of the more numerous centres not selected.

It is indeed not very likely that any very vigorous programme on a State basis could be pushed through when, despite some gerrymandering, half or more of the voting strength is in the State capitals and naturally allergic to paying heavily for the creation of opportunities elsewhere; economists sometimes fail to notice that man is a political animal. Really effective decentralisation would almost certainly involve far-reaching planning and direct controls, including the direction both of capital and of labour, and probably by the Commonwealth rather than the States. This would meet with serious constitutional difficulties, and there is no effective demand for it anywhere, as is shown by the uniformly negative votes in referenda for the extension of Commonwealth economic powers. Meanwhile, any metropolitan satellite is likely to be passed off as successful decentralisation: the innocent overseas reader of hand-outs might imagine that Elizabeth, Kwinana twenty miles from Perth, war-time St Mary's thirty miles from the heart of Sydney, were all deep in the bush.

Despite, then, all the talk of decentralisation, the existing pattern of demographic and economic distribution is not changing its shape, only accentuating its present features. The metropolitan percentage of population has risen steadily since the war: 53.94 in 1947, 54.21 in 1954, 56.12 in 1961; or, on a more realistic calculation of metro-politan areas, from 59.9 in 1961 to 61.5 in 1966. Of the 1961–66 intercensal increase of a little over 1,000,000, three-quarters went to the State capitals, and 10 per cent to para-metropolitan New-castle, Wollongong, and Geelong, with the minor capitals of Canberra and Darwin.

When we look not at locational but at occupational distributions, the imbalances are even more striking. In the sixteen years 1948–49 to 1963–64, wool alone was never below 30 per cent of export values, and in the first ten of these years only twice fell below 45 per cent; all rural products combined accounted for 80 to 90 per cent of exports for the first post-war decade, 75 to 80 per cent for the second; manufactures (excluding processed primary products) to only 12 per cent. Rural industries thus remain the essential export base; but they play a shrinking role in the economy generally. The net added value of manufacturing is nearly twice the net value of primary production, and while the primary share in gross national product fell between 1949 and 1962 from 21.3 to 12.6 per cent, that of manufacturing rose from 26.3 to 28.2 per cent. The implied great increase in the tertiary services component is itself an evidence of increasing urbanisation.

This paradox is compounded by consideration of the workforce. The large primary share of exports, never less than two-thirds and sometimes over four-fifths, is produced by 9 per cent of the work-force, and the number of people directly engaged in primary pro-duction is declining absolutely – from a peak of 596,000 in 1933 by over 23 per cent to 457,000 in 1966; and this army of occupation of under half a million is spread out over at least two million square miles. It is true that over the next decade mineral exports will take a much greater share of exports, and may indeed outrank rural primary products; but they too are produced by a small workforce, and the general lines of the argument are unchanged.

In itself this reliance on primary exports produced by so few people speaks to a high pitch of labour and capital intensitivity which makes it possible, and the rise in the secondary (manufacturing) and tertiary employment sectors is a world-wide trend; rarely accompanied, however, by such a dominance of primary exports. And it brings its stresses: the fixation of developing 'our vast empty spaces', sometimes to the disregard of rational economics; the concentration of economic power in a few centres (the core of truth in the agrarian New States propaganda); *per contra*, the ruthless sectionalism of groups such as the dairy farmers and the persistent appeals of the powerful Country Party for electoral redistribution which, however speciously disguised, would amount to gerrymandering; the high cost of essential services, especially transport, in the outback; the continuing difficulty of running the countryside effectively; a certain moral unease, amounting at times to a guilt feeling, at the shift from the old Australianism of the bush, the decline of the agrarian virtues (mythical as these may have been, they are still a mythos); 'apoplexy at the centre, anaemia at the extremities'. All these are complexly interwoven and are very largely functions of Australia's extraordinary population distribution; a distribution, however, which has arisen quite naturally from the country's history and from the hard facts of its geography, and by processes likely to prove irreversible.

Chapter 7

Resources and Transport

USTRALIA'S ENDOWMENT in the three really basic resources, water, soil, and minerals, is extremely ill-balanced. In relation to area, the continent is really rich only in minerals; even here there are deficiencies, though except for oil these are not sufficiently serious to be major inhibiting factors in development. More important is the maldistribution of the power minerals, including water as a source of energy. Soils, as we saw in Chapter 1, are in general rather poor; but soil is amenable to treatment and in itself soil poverty is probably the least limiting factor. A more serious limitation is the paucity and maldistribution of water resources.

Water and the lack of it

The general aridity of Australia can be gauged by a few simple comparisons. The world has fifteen rivers each of which has an annual average discharge greater than that of all Australian streams combined; the Mississippi-Missouri and the St Lawrence together have three times as much. If we take ten and twenty inches of rain a year as critical figures agriculturally, then the United States (almost exactly the same area) has five times as much temperate land with over twenty inches as Australia has; the proportions are reversed for land with under ten inches.

High variability of rainfall usually goes with low amount, and together with the high to extreme evaporation rates over some two-thirds of the continent, this leads to extreme variability of run-off. To take only two examples – both from the wetter eastern margins – the annual discharge of the Fitzroy River in Queensland has varied from 3 to 503 per cent of its annual average, while for the Murrumbidgee, partly snow-fed and one of Australia's largest and most stable rivers, the figures are 17 and 350 per cent. These are figures for a full year; the Murrumbidgee's absolute minimum discharge at one point of time has been 2 per cent of the average, the absolute maximum 4,600 per cent. It will be obvious that to make such rivers reliably useful demands expensive engineering.

The great western plateaus, covering at least a third of the continent, are without defined drainage channels and have rarely much water to drain. Leaving these aside, the rest of the continent has a total annual run-off of under three inches per square mile, against nine for the entire United States. Run-off is very unequally distributed indeed; nearly 13 per cent is in Tasmania (0.9 per cent of total area), and over three-fifths in tropical Australia, which has other limitations. There is a strong aversion to allowing water to 'run to waste', but in many areas not much can be done about it. For decades projectors have suggested impounding such streams as Coopers Creek and the Diamantina, which drain – when in flood, and only then – to Lake Eyre, or even diverting coastal rivers into them; but it never rains but it pours, and rainfall in their upper basins tends to come in short but violent spells, when great floods spread out over the 'Channel Country' – a maze of braided streambeds hardly sunk below the general flatness. But dam sites are few or absent, vast barrages and training walls would be needed, and unless underground reservoirs could be constructed by nuclear explosions, or even if they could, evaporation rates are so high that it is unlikely that any benefit would result even faintly proportionate to crippling expenditures. As it is, with a general flood every three to five years, a 'catch crop' of pasture probably represents the best development, very likely the only one possible. More modest storages, using chemical films to reduce evaporation, may in time be practicable.

There are, however, large reserves of underground water; the Great Artesian Basin, mainly in Queensland, covers 670,000 square miles, and there are smaller basins in every mainland State. The Great Artesian Basin supports nearly all of Queensland's 24,000,000 sheep; but there are limitations to the use of artesian water. To begin with it is not inexhaustible, as was once hoped; nearly a third of the 2,700 bores put down in the Great Artesian Basin have run dry, though falling underground water pressure around many bores has allowed new water to enter more readily, and yields now seem to have settled down at a safe level. More important is the fact that artesian water is usually saline, often highly so, and can be used only, if at all, for watering stock. This may in time be overcome by new chemical techniques, perhaps to a considerable extent, and there is also promise in the use of solar distillation to desalinise bore water for domestic use; one such plant has already been installed in South Australia. But as a source for agricultural irrigation on any substantial scale, artesian water can be discounted.

Irrigation itself is discussed in Chapter 8; but it must be borne in mind that in the settled south-east urban demands are already pressing on possibilities. Well over half of the 8,000,000 or so people in the three States which share the Murray basin are in the last resort dependent on that river. There is already opposition from irrigation interests to diversion of water from the Goulburn, a tributary of the Murray, for Melbourne;[1] the fast-growing Adelaide conurbation already draws nearly half of its water (half of which again is dissipated through garden hoses) from the Murray. Existing, authorised, and planned commitments already account for thirteen of the possible twenty million acre-feet available in the Murray-Darling basin.

It is natural that there should be considerable interest in the possibilities of artificial rain-making by seeding of clouds for the pastoral inland, of desalinisation of sea-water for the coastal cities. For new towns on the iron-fields of arid Western Australia, one can see little alternative to the high initial cost of desalinisation (started in a small way) other than the long-term cost of shipping water in; and if city growth in the south-east continues at anything like the current rate, desalinisation may be necessary for survival there in the not too distant future. Beyond this, there are such pipe-dreams as the perennial flooding of Lake Eyre by desalinised sea-water, using nuclear power. If a tenth of the money spent on conquering space were spent on conquering the earth, this would certainly seem a likely technical possibility. But such projectioneering leaves too much out of the reckoning: assuming – a large assumption – that the climatic effects did enable a large increase in sheep numbers, for benefits to be anything like proportionate to costs we must forget about synthetics and see nothing but ever-rising wool prices. And such visions seem always tacitly to assume that better-favoured countries will self-sacrificingly refrain from harnessing nuclear power on their own account. For countries with limited energy resources and an intractable environment, nuclear

---

[1] Proposed closure of catchments for Melbourne's water supply may also interfere very seriously with desirable timber exploitation.

power may hold much promise for specific projects; it may lead to some levelling-up of world disparities; it will not abolish comparative costs. It is significant that the Australian Atomic Energy Commission itself, while calling for the speedier introduction of nuclear energy, places South Australia (where fuel costs are high) first in its priorities for the 'seventies; Queensland and Western Australia last.

The mineral boom

A good deal of Australian development in the last century was triggered off, or at least facilitated, by selective mineral exploitation, of which the gold rushes are only the most striking examples. The first quarter of this century saw a few important finds, but the second was a period of quiescence, the main exception being the copper development at Mount Isa in central Queensland. The last fifteen years, however, have seen a dramatic expansion both in exploration and exploitation. Between 1953 and 1963 the estimated reserves of copper, tin, and lignite ('brown coal') doubled, those of bauxite soared from 33 to 2,500 million tons, of iron ore from 350 to 15,000 million; and the first significant finds of oil and natural gas followed this decade. New reserves are constantly being found, and the end is presumably not yet in sight. Nickel reserves, for example, were regarded as negligible in 1965; discoveries near Kalgoorlie now give the prospect of substantial exports.

In summary, reserves are adequate for domestic demand plus exports in practically all the basic metals, black coal, atomic mineral sands and uranium, and salt; adequate for domestic demand in brown coal, limestones, and most clays, minerals which in any case rarely enter into exports anywhere. Major deficiencies are in the important alloy metals manganese, cobalt, chromite, and vanadium, industrial diamonds, the chemical minerals sulphur (which could be produced from sulphides at greater cost than imports), phosphate, borates, and nitrates; and, despite the recent strikes, oil. Recent finds in Queensland suggest that the phosphate deficiency may be overcome; this has been particularly serious in view of Australia's fertiliser needs and the limited expectation of life of the deposits on Nauru Island, Australia's major supplier as well as a perennially nagging problem at the United Nations. Some other minerals are undeveloped because they cannot compete in price and/or quality with imports, for example fluorspar; for others, such as magnesite, there is insufficient processing capacity. But on the whole the balance sheet and the prospects are favourable.

This is an impressive list of strengths, and Australian metallurgical (and to a lesser extent chemical) industries are in a general sense very well-found as regards basic raw materials. When we look at accessibility and other factors bearing on exploitation, the picture is a little different. A very large proportion of the recent discoveries is in the tropical north: this presents the difficulty of inaccessibility and a consequent lack of the technical and human infrastructure for exploitation, but on the other hand it presents a challenge and an opportunity, and if anything can provide the take-off platform for 'Northern Development', it is probably mining. It would be wearisome to attempt a catalogue, which in any case would be out of date before it was printed, but besides oil and gas two developments call for special mention: iron and bauxite.

Between the wars the Broken Hill Proprietary Company, originally based on the copper-lead-zinc of that town, built up a virtual monopoly, strongly integrated both vertically and horizontally, producing at remarkably low cost a wide range of iron and steel products. BHP had steel works at Newcastle and Port Kembla south of Sydney; a blast furnace and shipyards at Whyalla in South Australia, based on a whole hierarchy of solid haematite hills – Iron Knob, Iron Monarch, Iron Prince, Iron Duke, Iron Baron; more iron mines at Yampi Sound in the north-west and Koolyannobbing in south-west Western Australia; its own collieries, limestone quarries, and fleet, not to mention a subsidiary empire of rolling mills and manufacturing plants. Until about 1960, further development was inhibited by nervousness about the extent of reserves, which led to an embargo on ore exports. Five years of exploration, mainly in Western Australia, have revolutionised the situation; that State alone could meet current world demand for twenty years with ores of high quality (50–60 per cent Fe), much of it mined open-cast. But there is some feeling that an opportunity for building up firm export markets may have been missed, in that ore prices may decline as supply outstrips steel-making demand, which is increasingly for pelletised iron.

Be that as it may, immediate developments are exciting, though not without problems. In view of BHP's existing manufacturing capacity, further expansion will be mainly for export; this will involve new railways and two or three new ports, with pelletising plants and so on, in the extremely arid region which lies between Port Hedland and the Hamersley-Ophthalmia Ranges. In view of the virtual absence of other potential, the multiplier effect of the new settlements is likely to be small in relation to their high over-heads. Perhaps more serious, long-term, is the degree of dependence on overseas capital, American and Japanese; as it was put by the Country Party Minister of Trade, too much of such development might leave Australia simply with big holes in the ground. This is a special case of one of Australia's most pressing general problems.

Much the same applies to bauxite. Large deposits are being exploited by Alcoa and Australian interests in the Darling Range behind Perth, and at Gove in Arnhem Land by a consortium of Swiss Aluminium (50 per cent), Colonial Sugar Refining (27.5 per cent), and a number of other firms. At Weipa on the Cape York Peninsula really vast reserves are in the hands of Comalco, which is capitalised half by the American Kaiser interests and half by Conzinc Rio Tinto of Australia, which however is itself 85 per cent foreign-owned. Both Gove and Weipa are in aboriginal reserves, so styled; except at Gove, which is in Commonwealth territory, it is far from clear that aboriginal interests have been accorded much respect, but then the aborigines, unlike the Nauruans, have no access to the United Nations.

The processing side is complex. There are alumina plants at Kwinana near Perth and Gladstone in Queensland, and one is pro-posed for Gove; existing aluminium smelters are at Bell Bay in Tasmania, Point Henry near Geelong, and one is proposed at Kurri Kurri near Newcastle, while Weipa bauxite will also go to New Zealand. There has been a trend away from hydroelectricity for smelting; Point Henry will use brown coal and Kurri Kurri black, both mined locally. The Bell Bay plant (which originally also pro-duced alumina) which came into operation in 1955, was built and worked jointly by the Commonwealth and Tasmanian governments, but since 1961 has been owned by Comalco except for a minority Tasmanian State holding.

Energy resources: coal, oil and gas

Bituminous coal was the first mineral, apart from building materials exploited by Europeans in Australia. The first working at Newcastle goes back to 1801, and in the nineteenth century there was a small Pacific export trade as well as bunkering. Black coal reserves are adequate to meet foreseeable needs, but are poorly distributed: there are coal-fields in all States, but only in New South Wales and Queensland are the deposits really large, and the open-cut mines of the latter are being developed, with the aid of Japanese and American capital, largely for export to Japan. South Australia, with its rapid industrialisation and with no hydroelectric potential, has only limited sub-bituminous deposits with an expected life of perhaps two decades. Victoria also has very little bituminous coal, but makes up for this by enormous reserves of lignite, easily mined open-cut, the basis for the new towns of Yallourn, Morwell, and Moe, and for the State electric grid which was the greatest work of the first World War soldier Sir John Monash.

The bituminous fields in the Hunter valley behind Newcastle include some of the thickest and most easily worked seams in the world, and at least until the 'twenties of this century working methods, largely bord-and-pillar with wide unhewn barriers at the boundaries of holdings, were incredibly wasteful, more inefficient perhaps than in any country except India. By the 'fifties, largely as a result of government assistance, the mines were sufficiently modernised to seek export markets again; by this time oil fuels and Victorian lignite were eating into the home market.

Mineral oils indeed bulk largely in the import list, averaging almost 10 per cent by value, and apart from the security aspect of complete dependence on imports and their actual cost, in the modern world the possession of oil fields is something of a status symbol. In consequence a considerable, and as some think a dispro-portionate, investment has been made in the search for oil, both in Australia and in New Guinea.[1] No oil has yet been found in Australian New Guinea, but for some years the search there repre-sented the only considerable inflow of private capital.

In Australia itself, the first strike was made in 1954 at Exmouth Gulf in the arid western bulge of Western Australia, and was promptly headlined as 'The Most Important Oil Strike since 1854' when Pennsylvania began. Its later history has been that of other finds: whispers, headlines, whispers, silence. However, in the early 'sixties several strikes were made in southern Queensland, one of

---

[1] The complicated, and often irrational, policies of search subsidies and protective devices are critically analysed by Alex Hunter, 'Investment in Petroleum Exploration in Australia', *Economic Record*, Melbourne, Vol. 42 (1966), pp. 353–83.

which, Moonie (about 230 miles west of Brisbane), is already in commercial operation. Production is also beginning at Barrow Island north of Exmouth Gulf.[1] There are undoubtedly good prospects in other sedimentary basins. Very important strikes have been made offshore in Bass Strait, and it is reasonably certain that Australia will soon be producing a significant fraction of her needs. Prospects of anything like self-sufficiency, however, are much more doubtful, so doubtful as to be illusory, and costs of locally produced oils are likely to be high in relation to the costs of refining imported crude oil. However, the strategic importance of home production may well be held to warrant some added costs; but the politics of oil are likely to be as smelly in Australia as elsewhere.

The search for oil has produced a bonus in the form of natural gas. The richest areas seem to be those associated with the oil basins of south-central Queensland, and offshore in Bass Straits, but there have been finds in all mainland States. Those in Western Australia are conveniently placed north of Perth; Palm Valley, near Alice Springs, is as yet remote, but South Australia has a field at Gidgealpa in the extreme north-east and a share in the offshore shelf. The cost of pipelines and the conversion of metropolitan gas-burning installations is not likely to stand in the way of development; but there has been a good deal of inter-State haggling over distribution and even over offshore rights. Victoria, where the State Electricity Commission had built up a vested interest in lignite briquettes, is finding that this unexpected *embarras de richesses* presents complicated problems of adjustment between existing and new interests, internal and external.

Both gas and oil raise once more the question of overseas investment. Something like 45 per cent of the private capital in oil search has come from abroad, and rights have been signed away, on easy terms, to areas covering a very large part of Australia; particularly in Western Australia, many of the tenements are so large as to provide little incentive to really thorough exploitation.

Hydroelectricity

Like the rainfall and relief on which it depends, Australian hydro-electric potential is very unequally distributed. South Australia has

---

[1] As one of the few surviving breeding places of the green turtle, Barrow Island is (or was) a first-class nature reserve; but neither nature nor aborigines can stand in the way of progress.

none, Western Australia little, and that little is in the north where, given developmental demand, power may ultimately be generated by harnessing the very high tidal ranges of the gulfs which fret the Kimberleys coast. Tasmania has over half the total potential – and already develops over 750,000 kilowatts of its own potential of 2.4 million; here alone decentralisation has proved no problem, following *pari passu* with a (mainly light) industrial revolution which has transformed a previously rather backward and rustic poor relation of a State. The potential of coastal Queensland is unknown but very probably large, though here hydroelectric development, unless it can be integrated with irrigation (a large question), must reckon with the competition of coal, oil, and gas.

The show-piece is undoubtedly the Snowy Mountain scheme: Australia's Damodar or Tennessee Valley. Simply as engineering, it is a magnificent concept magnificently executed: a network of dams, tunnels, and power stations, diverting water across the main Kosciusko massif from the Snowy into the Murray-Murrumbidgee system. Already some 660,000 kilowatts are installed and 760,000 under construction towards the full potential of over 2.5 million; and something like two million acre-feet of irrigation water will be delivered west of the mountains. There are ambivalences: some hold that it has never been proven that similar benefits could not have been attained from less spectacular schemes, costing much less than the $900 million or so of the completed Snowy. In particular, it is very far from proven that the returns from irrigation will be at all comparable to the irrigation component of the cost; and yet in times of drought irrigation interests have expressed strong resentment at the priority given to power. The Snowy Mountain Authority, set up in 1949, is a joint Commonwealth-Victoria-New South Wales venture, and the irrigation water is not charged for in itself; but the works needed for its effective use, as distinct from its diversion across the ranges, would fall to the States or to individuals, and when these costs are counted the economics may look a little dubious.

On the power side, the Snowy already plays a most important role in the New South Wales and Victorian grids, providing large-scale regional integration of loadings; and anyone who remembers the almost constant winter blackouts from over-loaded installations in the early 'fifties will be impressed by this. As a side effect, it has opened up a large area of great beauty to tourism and winter sports.

It may be to some extent a status symbol, rushed into in the euphoric mood of post-war reconstruction; it is of course (as India knows well, or too well) easier to carry nation and Treasury along with one grandly conceived project than with a multitude of schemes, perhaps in aggregate not less wealth-producing but individually minor and dull. The Snowy is more worthwhile than most status symbols.

With the Authority approaching completion of its major work, there were demands that it should be retained and retooled for the very different task of Northern Development; its Chairman himself spoke of six Snowies in the north, without indicating where the six Murrumbidgees are. There may be room for one or two such developments in the east-central Queensland highlands; but on the power side there is the availability of thermal resources on a large scale, on the irrigation side many unresolved problems of economics. We need a great deal more cost-benefit analysis before blithely adventuring into the north.

Forest resources

Mineral and power resources, though often poorly located and expensively difficult of access, provide a sound physical basis for Australian development; the same may be said, with lesser qualification, of such essentials as wool and leather, not to mention the raw materials of food-processing industries, and without too much effort the country could become self-sufficient in cotton; oilseeds also offer considerable opportunity. Despite some recent improvement, such as the growth of an export of frozen crayfish, fishery resources are poorly utilised, being left for the most part to undercapitalised small producers, largely Italian; the fishing fleet is astonishingly antiquated. But there is one conspicuous deficiency in an essential raw material: timber, and especially soft-woods.

The total area of reserved or controlled forest is only 124,000 square miles, 4 per cent of total area – an extraordinarily low figure. On another estimate, which the official Year Book tacitly admits is highly unrealistic, the total 'forest' area is about 800,000 square miles; but, like India's 'culturable waste' one has only to drive through it to see that this is a bad joke: at least four-fifths of this area is either open woody grassland or savannah, or scrub completely useless except to provide ground cover and so limit rapid run-off.

Especially since the war there has been an active planting policy, mainly of *Pinus radiata* (Monterey pine), and something over 10 per cent of the annual cut is now from coniferous plantations; fortunately the Tasmanian paper industry can use quick-growing eucalypts, though a good deal of pulp must still be imported. Management in the State forests (which provide three-fifths of the annual cut) is good, but there is room for some uneasiness about logging methods by private contractors. A quarter to a third of annual timber consumption is imported – for soft-woods, 70 per cent – and unless there is a large-scale turn to expensive substitute building materials, the rate of plantation should be at least doubled if this large import is to be reduced without completely ruinous devastation of Australia's very limited timber reserves. Reckless clearing and ring-barking for pastoral occupation has already brought a heavy toll in erosion, silting, and flooding, and the need for conservation is by no means universally appreciated.

Transport and its problems

It is obvious that much of the potential wealth of Australia, particularly the newly-discovered mineral wealth of the great but arid western plateaus, is most inconveniently located in relation to the major centres of population and economic activity. It is inconvenient also that Sydney, Brisbane, and to some degree Melbourne, are backed by country rugged and in itself poor, while the islands of good land around Perth and Adelaide are quite limited in extent. In marked contrast to all other continents (with the partial exception of Africa), not one of the ports, small or great, is on a navigable river reaching far inland, for there are no such rivers. Inland water transport is now non-existent, and even when it did exist on the Murray-Darling, land portages to the sea were still necessary, for the shallow lake through which the system debouches is quite useless. With an economy historically dependent on the export of bulky primary products – wool, wheat, metals – produced in the interior, the physical problems and the costs of transport have always been a heavy first charge on energy and finance; transport, storage, and communications employ one out of every eleven workers.

The rail-net, or rather nets, of Australia developed in relation to this pattern, each focusing on the colonial port-capital, except in so far as Queensland's geography was better served by long fingers reaching inland from Brisbane, Rockhampton, and Townsville, themselves not completely linked by rail along the coast until 1924. This separatist concentration on a few outlets was reinforced by the fact that Victoria and South Australia were the only adjacent States with a common gauge, the broad gauge which in fact is not common to all of South Australia, since it used 3 ft. 6 in. lines in Eyre Peninsula, and is now traversed by the Commonwealth standard gauge of the Trans-Continental line.

Only in four places was there any trespassing across the borders, and then in response to geographical factors so obvious that not even a colonial parliament could decently defy them. Broken Hill ships to Port Pirie on a South Australian 3 ft. 6 in. line – now being converted to standard gauge – and at three points Victorian lines cross the Murray, though in two of these cases New South Wales lines carefully keep at a distance from their rail-heads.[1] Within the States, the metropolitan concentration may have been affected by political pressures to the detriment of minor ports; there may not have been much to this in actual routing, but rating certainly favoured the capitals in some cases; for instance, the trifling extra cost of taking Tamworth wheat through Newcastle to Sydney was far outweighed by the commercial conveniences (brokerage, warehousing, and so on) of the latter port.

The mixture of gauges has certainly meant a heavy toll in time and transhipment costs, and there has long been a demand for unification. Yet for huge and thinly populated primary producers like Queensland and Western Australia, the limitations in speed and haulage capacity on their narrow gauge tracks are quite acceptable (the notorious discomforts on Queensland lines are not inherent in the gauge) and indeed offset by the much lower capital and maintenance costs compared with broad or standard gauge. The cost of a general rationalisation would be fantastic – the 202 miles of standard gauge from Albury (NSW) to Melbourne cost $32 million – and in the face of road and air competition, it is very unlikely that it would now be economic. There have been extensions of the New South Wales standard gauge to Brisbane (1930) and Melbourne (1962), and the standard Trans-Continental to Kalgoorlie should be extended to Perth by 1968, giving through running from Sydney.

[1] It is reputed that it took the threat of separation in the Riverina to make the New South Wales legislature see limited reason.

Despite the increasing road competition, which has led to a fall from 27,000 route miles in 1941 to 25,000 to-day, the railways are still essential for many long bulk hauls and in 1960–61 accounted for about a fifth of internal freight in ton-miles, against just under half by coastal shipping and 30 per cent by road. Although only 500 miles of suburban lines are electrified, strenuous efforts have been made to modernise by the introduction of Diesels and 'piggyback' loading, and State haulage taxes and licensing practices protect the iron against the bitumen road as much as possible. Nevertheless, most of the State railways, once their major revenue-producers, now run at a loss; suburban services, with their un-avoidable component of rolling stock used only at peak hours, are increasingly difficult to maintain efficiently, and yet without them metropolitan traffic congestion, bad enough already, would be catastrophically augmented. Railroading has by no means reached the pass it has in the United States, with its feather-bedding and its reputation as an 'old man's business'; but it is tending that way. Nevertheless there is still some need for rail expansion – mineral lines in Western Australia, and perhaps a line, primarily for the beef industry, linking the Barkly Tableland to the Queensland railheads and providing quicker routes to the Brisbane meat-packeries.

There may still be one or two elderly drovers logging with bullock-teams in the deep Queensland bush, and in the north an occasional camel may be picturesquely posed next to a light air-craft; but as economic factors bullocks and camels became extinct shortly after the first World War. Australian motor registrations number over 3.8 million, nearly one for every three persons, and are over 2 per cent of world registrations for an almost infinitesimal fraction of world population: 'Scratch an Australian and you find a motor mechanic', though often a 'she'll do' one. Road haulage accounts for over three-quarters of domestic freight in tons, four times as much as goes by rail; the railways' better showing in ton-miles is of course due to long bulk hauls.

This great army of vehicles must move on an inadequate road system; Australian cars and drivers are and must be tough. The inadequacy is inevitable, given the sparseness of people over nine-tenths of the country: perhaps 15 per cent of the 570,000 miles of road are bitumen or concrete, but this figure is devalued when we realise that it includes city streets. At least a third of the road mile-age is not even gravel but either 'formed' – which means the occasional passage of a scraper – or simply cleared tracks. Given the resources, perhaps nothing more is possible, and certainly over the last fifteen years the replacement of gravel by bitumen on main eastern routes has been notable. Unfortunately, while Australia welcomes improvements on the vehicle side with open arms, standards of road design lag: there is only one road, from Sydney to Newcastle, being constructed on the American toll freeway pattern. While the Australian temperament probably contributes to the sickeningly high rate of mortality on the roads (one for every 4,000 of the population in 1964), bad roads must contribute at least as much.

Australia has a long and honourable record in aviation, from the box-kite experiments of Lawrence Hargraves around 1890, through the first large-scale use of aircraft to move heavy equipment (including disassembled dredgers) to the Wau goldfield in New Guinea in the early 'thirties, to the rise of Qantas from an outback 'milk run' service into one of the world's great airlines. The contribution of aircraft to the outback is essential: seeding and fertilising of improved pastures, flying doctors and flying parsons, are only the most striking of the services, themselves serviced by the bush radio linking isolated stations on the equivalent of the multi-party telephone line. Australians probably fly more *per capita* than any other people, with at least one flight annually for one out of every three persons. The safety record is perhaps the best in the world – here, mercifully, is one sphere where 'she'll do' won't do.

The organisation is bizarre. There are some intra-State lines, but most of these are subsidiary to the giants, Trans-Australia Airlines and Ansett-Australian National Airlines. Before 1946, ANA was the only large-scale operator, itself subsidiary to overseas shipping interests; the Chifley government attempted to nationalise, basing itself partly on defence arguments and on the substantial government contribution in the provision of airports and directional services. Nationalisation was ruled out by the High Court, and the government then set up TAA to compete. Partly because of mail contracts and priority in official passage warrants, but also because of more efficient management in building its fleet, TAA had soon a marked lead, while ANA was weakened by rate-cutting on a smaller but very vigorous line run by the self-made Mr Reg Ansett. By 1949 ANA was seeking a merger with TAA; with the fall of the Labor government, this lapsed, and in 1952 the new 'free enterprise' régime revivified competition – of a sort – by subsidising both

TAA and ANA to modernise their fleets, sharing the mails between them equally, and leaving warrants open to be used on either line, while services and rates were rationalised. By 1957 ANA was again in difficulties and suggested a holding company to control both lines; the Liberal government most virtuously declined to promote monopoly, and ANA sold out to Ansett.

At present, although specific decisions have often favoured Ansett-ANA (perhaps unduly), business is shared out with pedantic rigidity – fleets must be similar almost to identity, and the sharing of services means that there is almost a superfluity of flights at peak hours and nothing in between, so that while it is easier to fly to the next capital for a day than it was ten years ago, it is more difficult – with faster planes – to do one's business in half a day; while the efforts of a responsible private firm to compete in a big way with TAA and Ansett-ANA in air freight have met with a reception difficult for an outside observer to distinguish from wilful obstruction.

A more paradoxical comment on 'socialism without doctrines' and free enterprise without competition would be difficult to imagine; but it is all very much the Australian way. It remains to be seen how this strange two-headed organism will react to the challenge of supersonic jets, for which few, if any, Australian airports are really adequate.

Shipping has a somewhat similar but more complicated story. Australian-owned shipping is a negligible fraction of the world fleet – some 650,000 dead weight tons, about equal to India's marine – and is almost confined to the coastwise trade, where it has a legalised preferential position. It is, however, of great significance to the economy, accounting for a steady 5 per cent of domestic freight in tons and just under 50 per cent in ton-miles; once more, long bulk hauls, such as iron ore and coal for BHP operations, petroleum, and bauxite, account for this disparity. The size of ships is increasing and modernisation is reasonably active.

Overseas shipping is a different matter: its rates and services are not subject to Australian control, and the various conferences which do control them seem to adhere with unalloyed enthusiasm to the old philosophy of charging what the traffic will bear. The Vernon Committee of Economic Enquiry was moved to a cautious but pertinent suggestion: 'We think it important to stress the need for continuous examination and enquiry into the reasons why the rates on Australian exports are at times higher per mile, and even absolutely higher, than those charged Australia's competitors operating at greater distances from markets ... with so much of the gross export returns at stake, we do not think that governments can be indifferent to factors which raise costs.'

In both World Wars, necessity impelled the Commonwealth government to supplement private shipping; after the second war the Australian National Line had the largest fleet on the coast. Its management, however, was never as efficient as that of TAA, and despite favourable provisions such as tax remission and a low statutory return on depreciated assets it never achieved the hegemony that Labor had hoped for. With these advantages it was able to have some effect in keeping rates down, but most of its ships were in bulk trade (where BHP looked after its own), and most general cargo remained to private lines. The Liberal government tried to sell the line, but failed, and fell back on whittling down its special privileges. It is possible that the increasing tightness of shipping, rising rates, and the demands of Vietnam, may compel some revision of this policy even under a Liberal government; it is almost certain that a Labor government would try to put to sea in a big way again, and there is some politically independent support for a national overseas line. Meanwhile, the Liberal government's far from enthusiastic response to private efforts to introduce Australian-owned large tankers, though not so negative as its attitude to competition in air freight, provides another ironic comment on devotion to free enterprise.

Australian port facilities are in general adequate, though the adoption of the most up-to-date methods of bulk loading is slow, partly owing to the vested interests of wharf labour – until recently the most militant section of Australian unionism – but partly to the general technological lag in older industries. Ship-building, however, though on a small scale except at the Whyalla yards, is reasonably expansive; Whyalla has launched bulk loaders of up to 55,000 tons.

The problem of conservation

The very emptiness of the Australian continent seems to have induced a certain recklessness in its development: there was so much of everything except water that there seemed little point in taking the trouble to conserve. All that is changing now, but there is still a certain euphoria of vastness, and the recognition of the need for conservation of resources grows too slowly. It is inevitable that the exploitation of some resources means the destruction of others; the trouble is that the immediate material gains of commercialism are usually more obvious than the long-term intangibles of conservation.

As regards water and soil, the lesson on the whole has been learnt: when after heavy rain some water from the Onkaparinga south of Adelaide actually reached the sea, the Chief Engineer concerned issued a statement implying that the little river had been severely spoken to and it wouldn't happen again. The States maintain conservation services which are technically efficient; soil erosion by water and wind is still a serious problem in many areas, and with the alternations of drought and excessively intensive rainfalls probably can never be wholly overcome, but there has certainly been a great improvement in attitudes and measures over the last three or four decades. Nevertheless much of Australia still bears the indelible scars of past recklessness, and even now individual neglect or over-exploitation is locally damaging. There is a certain fatalism before natural calamity such as bushfire and flood; every few years, for example, heavy material damage is done by large-scale flooding on the New South Wales coastal rivers, and it certainly seems that more sustained attention, and more financial support, are needed for bushfire warning and combat services and for river control. Forestry services again are technically competent, and commercial lumbering is subject to official restrictions, but much fine forest has been devastated or destroyed, and even now there is room for disquiet in the application of control, which at times seems unduly relaxed.

Most of the more spectacular recent mineral discoveries are in country not likely to be useful for any other type of development, and rehabilitation of mined ground is not a great problem here; it is otherwise with the extraction of rutile, ilmenite, and zircon from beachsands on the New South Wales-Queensland border and the extreme south-west of Western Australia. This is a special case of the need for coastal preservation. The eastern shores of Australia must provide one of the most continuous and varied successions of scenic beauty to be found anywhere in the world; access to them is an essential part of the way of life in the great cities. It is deplorable, though in the circumstances of Australian society very natural, that their development for tourist and residential purposes has been very haphazard and has much too often resulted in squalor. Coastal Shires and Municipalities have been slow to realise that natural beauty is an asset which requires careful maintenance like any other asset; they are beginning to do so, and on reaches remote from the greater cities it is not too late for preservation which would permit access but prevent spoliation.

If, in the developed south-east, the coasts are not inexhaustible, neither is space itself. Australian cities grew up with a reaction against the cramped terrace housing of Britain; land seemed illimitable, and while in the last twenty years there has been a tendency towards higher-density housing and flat life, the Australian ideal is still the one-family house, set in a garden which is often sadly cramped, or more rarely so large as to become an unmanageable drain on energy and family resources. There was little check on the enormous expansion of suburbia, and the still increasing sprawl around the capitals makes it difficult to maintain zoning plans designed to secure a reasonable minimum of open space. Fortunately, the large areas of sterile Hawkesbury Sandstone around Sydney made it possible to preserve two great lungs, Kuringai Chase to the north and the Royal National Park (reserved as early as 1886) to the south.

These, however, point up the perennial dichotomy between conservation in the strict sense and holiday access. It is perhaps naive and priggish, or even a little callous, to insist too rigidly on the limitation of what one might call an all-year Bank Holiday atmosphere in these tracts on the doorstep of a conurbation of two and a half millions. However, in more remote areas there is a real need for a much more positive National Parks policy: many areas of great natural beauty are indeed reserved, but sometimes on a tenure which may become precarious when threatened by commercial interests, and the Parks do not have the financial resources to develop into great open-air museums like those of the United States. Similarly, the preservation of historical buildings on National Trust lines is in its infancy and hampered by lack of money, and often of interest too.

Most urgent of all is the problem of wild life preservation. It is incredible and appalling to reflect that before the first World War the koala, now protected and hardly seen outside small sanctuaries near the cities, was slaughtered for its fur in scores or even hundreds of thousands. The magnificent wedge-tailed eagle is still fairly common, but subject to constant attrition by farmers who cannot be convinced that as regards lambs its predatory activities are limited to sickly runts which would not survive anyhow. The extent to which the greater kangaroos are really competitors with sheep for scarce fodder is still a matter of research; but at present their slaughter is practically indiscriminate, and often carried out with revolting brutality; and if their commercial value for fur and meat is indeed an economic essential, it could probably be better realised in the long-term by systematic preservation. If the present unregulated massacre continues, the greater kangaroos may meet the fate of the American buffaloes, which also were numbered in their millions – indeed, probably many more millions. So much of the better image of Australia is bound up with its unique fauna (and to a less extent flora) that the wanton destruction of this aesthetic and scientific asset cannot be faced with equanimity. But this is only a special case of the general problem of conservation, which needs a much more sustained educational and legislative effort than it has received.

Chapter 8

The Economic Structure

As we have seen, the economic structure of Australia is paradoxical in that there is a striking disproportion between the shares of primary and of manufacturing industry in the workforce and in export contribution. The percentage of the workforce in manufacturing is about two and a half times as great as that in rural industries, and approximates to that of Canada, the United States, France, and Japan, that is between 25 and 30 per cent. But it contributes only 10 to 13 per cent of export values, and this is about the same percentage of its own output.[1] Both proportions are rising, but not at the same rate as manufacturing employment.

This has some political significance, in that the export dominance of what are sometimes called the 'basic industries' (that is, the rural ones) provides warrant for the continued existence of the Country Party, which has much of the nuisance value but not so much of the independence of a balancing third party in a two-party system. Economically it is in the long run a source of insecurity. Primary products are traditionally vulnerable to external price fluctuations – 'Year by year movements of up to 30 per cent in export proceeds are not uncommon' – and to internal calamity such as drought, and in either case a severe falling-off of demand is likely to have a strong deflationary effect throughout the economy. The 1965–66 drought in south-eastern Australia, for example, perhaps the most severe general drought in the century, was certainly one factor in a marked decrease of demand for motor vehicles, a sensitive indicator. Motor engineering is an important segment of secondary industry, and in fact 1966 could be called a year of near-recession.

Australian economic growth, past and future, must be seen against a background of rapid population growth, 2.35 per cent per

---

[1] In 1949 and 1962, the percentages of raw primary products to total exports were respectively 59 and 63; processed primary products, 35 and 22; manufactures other than such products, 5 and 13.

annum between 1950 and 1960 – actually a higher rate than that of India. A large component, some two-fifths, is due to immigration, but in 1963 the rate of *natural* increase, although below those of the United States and Canada, was slightly higher than those of Poland, Yugoslavia, Spain, and Portugal, and considerably higher than those of most western European countries.

The very high intake of migrants in the early 'fifties imposed severe temporary stresses, especially in housing; but without it economic growth would have been much slower, since the abnormally low birthrates of the depression and the war meant an abnormally low native entry into employment: from 1947 to 1961 immigration accounted for nearly three-quarters of the increase in the workforce. The position in the 'sixties, after the post-war 'baby boom', is very different. Nearly a third of the population is under fifteen years old, a higher proportion than at any time since 1921; conversely, nearly one-tenth is over sixty-five, and this is higher than ever before. The proportion of workforce to total population has been declining, a trend accentuated by an increasing tendency to prolonging full-time education. Female participation in the workforce has increased, but is still limited, partly by a feeling against married women working, partly by sex discrimination in pay and conditions – not until 1966, for example, did the Commonwealth make it possible for married women to have permanent appointments in the Public Service. Women are much less prominent in the professions (except perhaps medicine) and in business than in most Western countries; even in the universities there is only a handful of women with full professorships, and any addition makes the headlines. There is here a serious wastage of trained talent.

Balancing these and other factors, the Vernon Committee of Economic Enquiry (1965) envisaged a likely increase of the workforce in the ensuing decade of 2.57 per cent per annum (against 1.91 in the preceding decade); this with a net immigration of 100,000 a year, which is more than that in recent years and would represent about two-fifths of the increased workforce.

On any assumption, if growth is to be sustained at a reasonable rate the economy will need not only expansion but diversification. Both, but especially the latter, will be difficult to attain in the land industries which are still the dominant source of export values.

The rural sector

Little less striking and no less important than the high proportion of rural production in total exports is the high proportion of output exported, probably over half and ranging up to 95 per cent for wool and 65 to 75 per cent for wheat, sugar, and dried fruits. Although the physical handicaps to expansion are serious, it seems likely that market opportunity, or the lack of it, could be even more of a limiting factor.

Despite the drift from the land, expansion of production has in fact been substantial since the war. The use of fertiliser and machinery has doubled, and the aerial seeding of improved pastures and spraying of crops have increased unit yields. Wheat yields are still low per acre – though high per man – by world standards; but superphosphate, improved strains, and the substitution of leguminous fodders for fallow in the great wheat/sheep belt have increased them from twelve bushels pre-war to nearly twenty, and further improvement is possible. In wool, the rise in the weight of fleece seems almost to have flattened out, but carrying capacity has been much improved by sown pastures, trace minerals such as cobalt to offset local nutritional deficiencies responsible for sheep diseases, and myxomatosis, which at least temporarily routed the rabbit. Before the set-back of the 1965–66 drought sheep numbers had increased since 1950 by about half, to 165 million. Sugar-growing by individual farmers under the aegis of the Colonial Sugar Refining Company, the monopoly processor, is technically highly efficient and could expand given new markets, which are of course subject to international agreement. Horticulture is not very expansive areally but is progressive technically, and here also further advance is likely.

Actual cropped area, which was rather higher before the war than in 1950, has risen since that year by about half, to 30 million acres, half of them under wheat. In some areas physical expansion has been remarkable: between 1945 and 1963 Western Australia added over 750,000 acres to its wheat area, doubled its total crop area, quadrupled its sown pastures, more than doubled its wool and nearly doubled its meat production. It is, however, not very likely that this pace can be maintained; and it is certain that further increases on any substantial scale will mean relatively much higher capital outlays. Achievements quite notable in themselves do not amount to a great deal in numbers on the land: the very well planned and successful pioneering schemes in the 'Ninety Mile Desert' of South Australia and behind Esperance in Western Australia will settle some 12,000 to 15,000 souls.

The problem of rural development in the tropical north is one of the most hotly debated current issues in Australia, and must be left for separate treatment (Chapter 9); but something may be said here about irrigation, which is often enough talked about as if it were a panacea. For the desert to blossom as a rose, however, there must be reasonably fresh water available *somewhere*; it is not as yet practicable to irrigate with dehydrated water.

The actual area irrigated in Australia is about 2,890,000 acres (1964–65), about twice as much as just after the war; New South Wales and Victoria account for all but about 500,000 of these acres. But it should be noted that something like three-quarters of the total area is under pasture, mainly in the Victorian Wimmera and the Riverina, and although one cannot deny this the name 'irrigation', it has obviously little in common with the general image derived from the classic irrigation cultures of Asia: it does not imply a dense population and intensive use.

Yet, owing to the great variability in stream flow, basic costs are high since storage must be large relative to area commanded, and this really means very big headworks, comparable to those of countries basically dependent on irrigation but for much smaller command areas: the Australian figure for acre-feet of impounded water per acre irrigated is 6.5, nearly twenty-two times the Indian figure. High installation costs thus go with low intensity of use; it is true that use might be made more intensive by a more thorough integration of dry and wet farming, but this would call for some quite radical reorganisation, and yet would hardly alter the basic situation.[1]

An informed estimate, yet one admittedly 'by speculative assessment', from a source certainly not hostile to irrigation development, puts the ultimate Australian potential at 10 to 12 million acres,

---

[1] An ironic comment on irrigationist claims was provided in March 1965, when drought rendered the supply from the important Wyangala Dam inadequate for both the arable farmers and horticulturalists on the upper Lachlan (one of the major Murrumbidgee tributaries) and the down-river pastoralists. The local tensions split the Lachlan Development League. By October 1966, however, the upper reaches were being devastated not by drought but by flood.

three or four times the present area.[1] There is relatively little scope for expansion in the Murray-Darling, and in fact some 70 per cent of the potential would be in tropical or sub-tropical Australia. Its development 'would be sufficient to provide post-war expansion rates for over a hundred years' – in itself an illuminating comment on irrigation as a dramatic short-term solution to the northern problem.

It is difficult to resist the conclusion that much of the motivation behind demands for more irrigation rests more on a traditional hankering for the rustic virtues believed to be associated with closer settlement than on an objective estimate of what Australia stands to gain from irrigation expenditure. As a matter of fact, the striking recent increases in rural output – 50 per cent in the twelve years before 1963 – were accomplished by a stable or declining workforce; this is clearly a function of increased capitalisation and improved technology. While the closer-settled irrigation areas certainly contributed their share, even here it would be very difficult to disentangle the strictly irrigation component from that, probably larger, due to other advances in farming technique.

Of course other than strictly cost factors are involved, and in specific cases expenditure not warranted in narrowly economic terms may be socially desirable; quite a few of Australia's capital assets might never have been secured had cost-benefit analysis been the only criterion.[2] But one can well understand the Vernon Committee's scepticism to the Wool and Meat Producers' claim that 'it becomes obvious that investment in irrigation shows magnificent returns to government' and 'hence should be paid for by the community at large'. The Committee dryly agreed that 'to assess accurately the cumulative value of all the benefits would be a major economic exercise', but in fact many of the minor exercises are yet to be done. Scientific cost-benefit analysis has begun, but has not as yet made any considerable impact on public thinking. In any case, water charges to farmers, far from rapidly recouping the major costs, usually meet only reticulation and maintenance expenses.

Admitting non-economic desiderata in some special cases, the conclusion seems clear that a good deal more solid arithmetic is needed before any dramatic expansion of irrigation could reasonably

[1] F. B. Haigh (Queensland Irrigation Commissioner), in *Water Resources, Use and Management* (Melbourne University Press, 1964), p. 21.
[2] In 1858 the young Stanley Jevons, then an assayer in the Sydney Mint, elegantly demonstrated that public railway construction in Australia would be an offence to Political Economy.

be accepted as a high priority for the available resources. More expenditure on the less spectacular task of covering the innumerable small bores and dams, or otherwise checking evaporation, might be more in order.

'The community at large' does in fact make a substantial contribution in support of rural industry. While 'protection' in the ordinary sense of tariffs cannot apply to commodities basically for, and basic to, the country's exports, there is a very considerable amount of government assistance. Typically this takes the form of price-support linked with organised marketing. Wool is the only major commodity – admittedly a very major one – not so supported, and that is due to conflicting interests among the growers themselves. In general organised marketing contributes to a high domestic price, but this is not invariable; a notable exception is wheat, which in the early 'fifties was locally available at about half the export price; since most was exported, this to the growers was an acceptable sacrifice. Essentially the objective is to flatten out, or compensate for, the fluctuations of external prices, and this seems to have been generally achieved: including wool, not so backed up, only about three-sevenths of the 1952–62 fall in export prices actually impinged on the rural producers; excluding wool, their index of prices received actually rose by 22.6 per cent against a fall of 13.4 per cent in the export price index.

The justification for this policy is of course quite simple, that it keeps graziers and farmers in trade, and as they have hitherto supplied all but a small fraction of exports, it keeps Australia in trade. It is often, though not always, a tax on the home consumer and hence, through wage levels adjusted to the cost of living, an added cost to other industries; but the alternative of severe and unpredictable drops in purchasing power all round seems worse. On the other hand, it does contribute to an undue rigidity in land use, by keeping in production groups only marginally efficient, if that; the classic case is the dairy industry, to the Country Party a sacred cow but from a wider view, to use an Australian phrase, in some regions a fair cow.[1]

---

[1] Derogatory phrase applied to any untoward 'person, situation, or turn of events' (S. J. Baker, *The Drum*, Currawong, Sydney, 1959); may be applied e.g. to a black horse which is favourite but unplaced. The Country Party dairy interest secured the withdrawal of a Department of Health pamphlet on diet which suggested, mildly, that in some ways margarine was nearly as good as butter.

On the whole, it does seem more important to keep the dominant export industries exporting than to look too narrowly at the domestic price anomalies involved. This was the view of the Vernon Committee, which gave a rather tepid blessing to the system (if anything so *ad hoc* may be so styled) and, correctly, was rather more enthusiastic about subsidies for fertilisers and legume seeds, research, and a more forthcoming attitude to rural credit – measures less direct in the short-term, but likely to be of more lasting productive effect. Perhaps – the Committee seems to hint this – a general revision of these complex supporting structures is needed; but general revising is not the Australian way. Faithful to the old tradition, she prefers to proceed by the piecemeal solution of pragmatic problems, one at a time, as they arise. *Solvitur ambulando =* she'll do.

Scope for rural expansion undoubtedly exists; with increasing population, and with the spur of competition for markets, it will come about, and the technological tradition is good. But limitations must be recognised. First of all, probably, must come the realisation that the old individual pioneering will not do, will not aggregate to a total which makes a real economic impact. 'Closer settlement' must be interpreted in a way appropriate to the scale and intractability of the Australian environment; this was indeed foreshadowed in the rural 'Socialism without doctrines' and irrigation schemes around the turn of the century (above, pp. 47–48). The small intensive farmer on his own is up against the fact that the things he is good at – dairying, horticulture, truck farming – are just those in which overseas markets are most difficult of access, while local markets are restricted, except around the capitals where there are already plenty of incumbents. With increasing urbanisation, this may change to some extent; but the really fertile and well-watered areas are small, and to carry on this sort of farming far away from the market calls for an infrastructure which so far is lacking or rudimentary.[1] To succeed demands a degree of capitalisation beyond the resources of most individual farmers. 'Closer settlement' will probably expand, and become more technically intensified,

[1] 'The example of California, which grows a variety of fruit and vegetables for the national market in the United States ... is not relevant to northern Australia which lacks the road and rail connections with distant centres of dense population.' J. B. Condliffe, *The Development of Australia* (Ure Smith, Sydney, 1964), p. 53. It also lacks a consuming centre of the size of Pasadena, let alone Los Angeles as a whole, to give take-off.

in areas with access to big local markets; it is unlikely that it will make serious conquests beyond the existing fairly settled areas, except perhaps locally (and probably temporarily) in response to mining development.

There will be exceptions to this generalisation, but they will be collective rather than individual, by way of holdings from large organisations which will meet the capital costs of installation (apart perhaps from housing and so on) and will naturally exercise some control. These organisations may be governmental or private; three of the most successful post-war developments have been those initiated by the Australian Mutual Provident Society in the Ninety Mile Desert, by the Esperance Land and Development Company (a subsidiary of American Factors Limited), and by the South Australian government in the mallee scrub of Kangaroo Island. Such sponsorship is no guarantee of success; there has been no more abject failure than the American-backed Territory Rice project at Humpty Doo. The moral is plain: careful planning followed by large-scale and expensive preliminary development, before there is any return, will be essential to success; and no remarkable rural population increases are likely. Projects resulting in substantial productive gains are likely to be far more capital- than labour-intensive.

The agrarian dream still has a strong hold on many Australians, at least on many outside the capitals; lip-service is paid to it by politicians; it is in some sense still the *raison d'être* of the Country Party, and – on ideological grounds more applicable to Portugal or Italy than to Australia – it is a main strand in Democratic Labor Party policy. But it must surely fade before the facts of life in a century of mechanisation and a continent built and watered as Australia is.

The drift from the land is the more notable in that wage rates in rural industry are actually *higher* than in manufacturing; although the 1958 ratio of 113:100 in favour of rural rates is inflated by the good awards obtained by the unions for skilled pastoral workers such as shearers, it is still probably unique. Agricultural employment leads nowhere; credit facilities for setting up small farms are difficult to secure except in phases of enthusiasm, generally ill-judged and short-lived, for 'soldier settlement'. The Vernon Committee reported that taxpayers in rural industry – not labourers but people with 'substantial capital invested in their farms'—who earned less than $1400 a year actual income were a quarter of the whole; a third if wool and wool/wheat growers are excluded. A tenth actually earned less than $800, a truly miserable figure for Australia. And it is almost certainly just those who most nearly conform to the Democratic Labor ideal of a peasant proprietary – the dairy farmers and the small truck farmers near the capitals – who also must conform most closely to this harsh un-Australian level of reality. Australia remains 'a big man's frontier'.

Manufacturing industry

The Australian definition of 'manufacturing' is a wide one, including oil refining and iron and steel at one end of the scale, motor repairing and even dyers, cleaners, and shoemenders at the other. (This of course is one factor in the poor showing of exports relative to value of production.) It is thus not surprising that out of a total (1963–64) of 59,000 'factories', nearly 43,000 employed up to ten persons; many of these would be, for example, one-man-and-a-boy country garages.

The impression of dispersion is misleading: if the giants are few – only eighty-one plants employed over 1,000 workers each – there is in fact a high degree of concentration in the more important industries. When we turn from the factory to the firm, we find that actual monopoly is significant in basic steel and such essentials as steel sheets and wire, sugar, glass, explosives, cement, base metal extraction, and paper; it will be seen that these are mainly producer industries. Indeed, the analysis by Karmel and Brunt suggests that monopoly or tight oligopoly is at least twice as strong in Australia as in the United States.

At a lower level, despite Section 92 of the constitution (inter-State trade 'shall be absolutely free'), the national market for many consumption goods is in fact segmented by factors either geographical (distances between small densely-settled State cores) or historical (differing State industrial policies), or by a combination of both (capital-focused rail-nets on different gauges). There is thus some tendency to local quasi-monopolies. This imperfection of competition has perhaps a bearing on the fact that Australian small and medium business, despite an increasing addiction to Public Relations gimmicks, has often a somewhat dated and provincial air. By and large, also, protection, while its role in fostering initial industrial growth has been undeniable and in many cases doubtless essential, has not fostered industrial dynamism once growth had attained a level of viability.

This is very apparent in the prevalence of restrictive practices and the acceptance, with very little question, of monopoly: after all Broken Hill Proprietary, Colonial Sugar Refining, the Collins House metals group have always been there. Many restrictive practices can of course be laid to Labor's door; jobs may be held up by questions of union delimitation taken to a point which suggests an Indian sub-caste, and one sometimes suspects that the only point of a forty-hour week is to work another ten hours at double rates. On the entrepreneurial side, 'While just about every restrictive practice known to man is used in Australia ... price agreements, both vertical and horizontal, are by far the most common.'[1] These are more than just nuisances. In the aggregate, they seriously restrict effective purchasing power and reduce potential investment saving; as so often, a splendid economy for the individual entrepreneur is a very false economy on the national scale. Collusive tendering is rampant; 'whenever tenders were called' the Western Australian Government Railways received identical quotations for forty-six articles, ranging from cement and cables to fly-screens and toilet paper.

The eminent lawyer Sir Garfield Barwick as Attorney-General achieved one ambition and contributed to the domestic happiness of thousands of Australians by putting through the first Federal divorce law; he was less successful in his second mission, which might have advantaged many more thousands, of carrying comprehensive legislation against restrictive practices. He was promoted (briefly) to be Minister of External Affairs, and his legislation was temporarily withdrawn for further advisement with business interests. It emerged onto the Statute Book some six or seven years later, its teeth perhaps not entirely drawn, but certainly blunted.

The most important single group of industries is 'Industrial metals, machines, and conveyances', which has between 40 and 50 per cent on almost all indices – number of plants; employment; values of land, buildings, plant, output; net added value of production. This group also provides the bulk of manufactured exports. It is followed, at a long interval, by the clothing and food processing trades, which are rather older and have shown only a slow

[1] P. H. Karmel and M. Brunt, *The Structure of the Australian Economy* (Cheshire, Melbourne, 1962), p. 95.

rate of expansion (in terms of employment) since the war, though improved technology has led to increases of production. Apart from petroleum refining and iron and steel, the really big increases since the war have been in consumer durables – plastics, electrical gear, motor vehicles, rubber and paper products.

With full employment at a high standard of living, these consumer durables are a particularly important sector of Australian industry: the ratios to population of cars, refrigerators, washing machines, motor mowers, tape recorders, and TV sets are high. In the early 'fifties, indeed, private investment in the immediately profitable provision of household electrical gear added to the amenities of life by outstripping the electrical generation provided by public investment, the balance being restored by frequent black-outs. This concentration on quick returns with neglect of the infra-structure was aptly characterised as a 'milk-bar economy': all amenity and little substance. The situation has now changed, and indeed about 1960 there was a degree of saturation in the consumer durable market. But there are more permanent stresses in the structure.

In the first place, while the small numerical size of the market is to some extent offset by individual high purchasing power, it still is not a mass market in the American or West European sense. To counter this, firms may be less specialised while at the same time not covering all stages in the production of some of their specific lines. A good deal of Australian manufacturing is indeed assembling and, because of the small scale of the market, essential components must still be imported. It is amusing that ignition keys for 'Australia's own car', the Holden, are made in Milwaukee, and indeed the car itself, while designed and almost wholly built in Australia, is produced by a subsidiary of General Motors.

The problem of foreign capital

The degree of dependence of Australian manufacturing on over-seas association is indeed disturbing, though largely inevitable. The tariff-protected market is big enough to be worth getting into, not big enough for full economies of scale all the way. It is not that a country which can design aircraft cannot cut ignition keys; but the 100,000 or so keys a year are a spill-over, even with freight almost a give-away, from the millions produced in America. There is thus a strong incentive to the setting up of subsidiaries of overseas firms, naturally very often in association with existing Australian interests in the same line. Short-term this has considerable advantages for Australian industrialists: know-how both technical and managerial, finance, the goodwill of a great international name, are available on easy terms. Long-term, in the interest of national industry rather than that of the individual industrial enterprise, the price is higher, perhaps too high. Franchises often apply to the Australian market only: 'Of the more than 1,000 such agreements known to exist, the great majority (over 80 per cent) either give no right to export or limit exports to neighbouring territories. Over 75 per cent exclude south-east Asia.'[1] How serious this is can be seen by comparing the very considerable increase in volume and value of manufactures over the fifteen years before 1965 with the almost static percentage of manufactured exports in the same period.

Again, there is little incentive to research. Admitting that the scale of Australian resources for research and of the market profits to be gained from it are such that basic research on the scale of a great American or European firm would be impracticable, still much more could and should be done; but why do any when one can borrow its results on easy terms? Some of the big monopolies such as Broken Hill and Colonial Sugar are honourable exceptions, but as a general rule Australian industry carries out very little techno-logical and hardly any basic scientific research. Even the inexpen-sive market and managerial research lines are laggard. There seems to be a preference for diplomate technicians rather than graduates – they cost less and are less likely to have upsetting ideas. As a result Australia exports, if not manufactures, then at least first-class applied scientists whose talents and training are lost to the nation – if indeed their achievements are not bought back at enhanced cost.

Quantitatively, the actual capital investment from overseas is the least of the problem; it was calculated to have been under 10 per cent of total investment during the 'fifties, though the rate has probably since increased. Its strategic emplacement is another matter. In the 'fifties, a large proportion was in consumer durables, and here relatively small initial investments with high plough-back have enabled overseas interests to secure a disproportionate degree of ownership and control; perhaps a third of manufacturing indus-try is really foreign-owned, 40 per cent effectively foreign con-trolled. The big quasi-monopolies already mentioned are effectively

[1] Condliffe, *op. cit.*, p. 186.

Australian-owned: steel, paper, cement, glass, sugar; and outside interests are minor in pharmaceuticals, agricultural machinery, and a good deal of industrial equipment – the last two after all follow on from the steel monopoly. Food processing, traditionally independent, now seems increasingly a field for take-overs. But overseas interests are very strong in rubber, oil refining, aluminium, radio, and TV equipment; overwhelming in motor vehicles, heavy chemicals, electronics, tobacco – and all these are in effect key basic industries, except tobacco which is a key consumption industry.

In the 'sixties, overseas investment has moved into the new mining developments on a massive scale. This is probably inevitable given the enormous outlay needed before any returns come in; but it brings with it a new dimension, since the States control their own mineral wealth, and it is already apparent – most notably in respect of the oil and gas of the continental shelf along the South Australian-Victorian coast – that the temptation of a State government to steal a march on its neighbours may lead to most embarrassing complications in a field where a unified Commonwealth approach is obviously desirable. All that one can say is that in the last resort, as many smaller countries than Australia have seized upon, actual physical possession of the stock in trade is nine points of the law; but not if one State is playing its own hand against rivals or the Commonwealth.

The general problem of overseas investment is indeed too serious to be faced either with the businessman's euphoria of 'vast prospects and little interference' or with Labor lamentations at the sell-out to Wall Street or Texas. As we have seen, it is not the amount but the deployment that is the crux. Australian investment tends to go into the safe channels of public services – water and electricity supply and so on – or into the more exciting, but more perilous, streams which offer quick returns – consumption goods, hire-purchase, speculation. It is very difficult to mobilise Australian capital for really big but long-maturing enterprise. To some extent this is due to lack of experience and confidence, though the successes of Broken Hill Proprietary, Colonial Sugar Refining, and the local component, more brains than money, in Conzinc Rio Tinto show what can be done. What is needed is a greater degree of interdigitation of Australian and overseas capital, a more equitable sharing of risks and rewards. Diversification of source would also be desirable; there is at present too much leaning on America as fairy godmother. It must be admitted, however, that of the likely suppliers, the Japanese are rather too devoted to 'giving too little and asking too much', and Hong Kong capitalists to going for quick returns and speculative empire. A solution is being sought through a National Development Fund or Bank which it is hoped will deploy Australian corporate investment as well as overseas capital into long-term developmental undertakings in the north and elsewhere.

With all this, there remains the risk of an insidious colonialism. As Condliffe sums up, 'What is lacking is risk-taking entrepreneurship rather than capital.' One must qualify this: there has been no lack either of capital or of risk-taking (with other people's money) in the get-rich-quick sector of the 'milk-bar economy', in speculative building and finance companies, lush hotels, hire-purchase financing and so on: the discreditable number of spectacular and disreputable crashes in the early 'sixties is all too ample evidence of this. It must be admitted that there are difficulties in the mobilisation of the massive sums for long-term developments in which a huge preliminary investment is needed; and hence the temptation to enlist large-scale overseas capital for such projects, in which moreover know-how is as important as money and even less likely to be locally available. Much overseas investment will be necessary and unexceptionable; yet, unless more effective steps to secure Australian equities are taken, this may be mortgaging the future.

The tertiary sector

'Tertiary industry' is a residual term covering a wide range of activities: gas, water, and electricity supply and sanitary services; building and construction; transport and communication; banking and insurance; commerce wholesale and retail; professional and domestic services; education; hotels, catering, and entertainment; and, cutting across most of these categories, direct government employment whether Commonwealth, State, or local. As in most advanced countries, the tertiary component of the workforce has increased markedly in the last two or three decades, and now stands at about 60 per cent. Differences of classification make such statements merely general indices, but this is just below the figures for the United States and Canada, just above those for the United Kingdom and the Netherlands. The direct contribution to productivity of many tertiary groups, such as the professions and public authority, is difficult to evaluate, but the total contribution aggre-

1   Outback: a mob of sheep coming to water at a bore. This might be anywhere in the drier sheep country.

2   Closer in: Aberdeen Angus herd on the Hunter, eastern New South Wales.

3   The arid heart: pastoral country in the Centre.

4   The humid margins: tree ferns in Yarra Valley 50 miles from Melbourne.

5 Glaciated terrain near the summit of Mount Kosciusko, New South Wales.

6 Feral buffaloes, descended from those brought from Malaya 125 years ago, in the Adelaide River swamps, Northern Territory. The white flecks are brolgas, a type of crane.

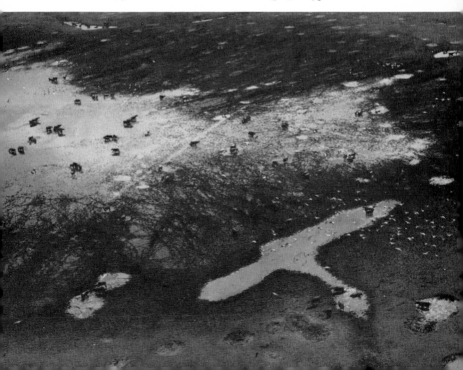

7   Port Kembla, south of Sydney, and its steel-works.

8   Mount Tom Price, the new iron-ore workings in the Kimberleys.

9 Port Arthur: the old convict settlement. Australia's most
impressive ruin.

10 Ballarat gold diggings in the 'fifties: police checking licences,
a typical pre-Eureka scene.

11 The hollow frontier: slab and shingle hut near Canberra, completely vanished in the last twelve years.

12 The hollow frontier: not World War I, but Sutton gold-field, fifteen miles from Canberra, last used by unemployed fossickers in the 1930 depression.

13   Tom Roberts' The Golden Fleece: a shearing shed of the
     'nineties.

14   An electrified shearing shed of today.

15 Sydney Cove, the earliest known picture, 1791.

16 Sydney Cove today, seen from under the Bridge.

17　Melbourne: Tom Roberts' impressionist painting of Bourke Street, c. 1890.

18　Melbourne: Bourke Street today.

19 The 'motor cavalcade' at the official founding of Canberra,
    12 March 1913.

20 Canberra and its Lake Burley Griffin today.

21 The white north: main street of Normanton, in the Queensland Gulf Country.

22 The black north: a government settlement in Arnhem Land.

23 Bigpela man taim bilong bipoa: a traditional tribal leader of Minj, Western Highlands of New Guinea.

24 Bigpela man taim bilong nau: Ninji, a local Government Councillor of Mount Hagen, Western Highlands, New Guinea.

gates to over half the Gross National Product; and the tertiary sector is also of the utmost importance as the great intake of consumption, especially of manufactures.

'Utilities' in Australia are mainly provided by governments, for historical reasons already discussed (pp. 48–49, 105–7); the main exceptions are gas in Victoria and Western Australia. Only in transport does private enterprise compete strongly, and here railways are entirely State-owned; communications, except for broadcasting and TV (where about two-thirds of the stations are commercial), are also entirely in the public sector. As everywhere, public comment fastens on the component of tertiary industry which is publicly employed – in 1961, 824,000 out of 2,536,000, or one-fifth of the total workforce. References to hordes of bureaucrats usually disregard the fact that the gross figures for government employees include teachers, postmen, and railwaymen; these three categories alone account for about 300,000 people, and of course there are many other 'blue collar' workers. The big increase in public employment took place during the war; more recently it has grown at little more than the rate for the workforce as a whole.

Australia's Domesday: the Vernon Report

For a general view of the problems facing the Australian economy now, and probably for the next couple of decades, the primary source is the massive two-volume Report of the Committee of Economic Enquiry set up in early 1963, and generally known as the Vernon Committee.[1]

The establishment of the Committee seems to have been meant as a sop to public discontents arising from the 'credit squeeze' of 1960 and nervousness about British relations to the European Common Market, which could obviously have a strong impact on Australian exports. A certain coy restraint was observable in the original announcement, but this was as nothing to the official

[1] The Chairman, Dr (now Sir) James Vernon, managing director of Colonial Sugar Refining, was originally an industrial chemist and had much stronger academic links than the generality of business executives. The other members were two economists, Sir John Crawford, formerly the dynamic Secretary of the Department of Trade and Commerce and now Vice-Chancellor of the Australian National University, and Professor Peter Karmel, who in the last five years has played a leading part in the foundation of new universities in Adelaide and New Guinea; and two businessmen, Messrs K. B. Myer and D. G. Molesworth, leading figures in retailing and meat-packing respectively.

reception of the Report presented to Sir Robert Menzies in May 1965 and to Parliament nearly six months later. The Commission had taken with unbecoming seriousness its directive to report on the bearing of numerous factors on the achievement of the government's avowed objectives – high rate of growth with full employment, cost and price stability, and other conventional goodies – and had recommended in effect a permanent projection of itself in the form of a high-level Advisory Council on Economic Growth, something like the Economic Council of Canada. To good Liberals, this looked horribly like Planning; Sir Robert's startled reaction resembled that of Frankenstein when his monster broke loose. In view of the three to two representation of 'practical men' on the Committee, this could hardly be brushed aside as an academic economists' nostrum; but it was firmly repudiated on the ground that Policy is the prerogative of politicians.[1] The episode is an instructive example of Australian pragmatism.

For all that, the Vernon Report remains as Australia's Domesday, 'the greatest inquest ever held into the Australian economy'. It may be regarded as an enormous gloss on a sentence of Condliffe's: 'the change from local markets sheltered by tariff protection and import restrictions to the ruthless competition of world markets requires a degree of sophistication still lacking in most enterprises'.

The Committee's initial approach was to project to 1974–75 recent trends in the growth of the workforce (with immigration held at 100,000 a year) and productivity. To maintain the desirable objectives listed in the terms of reference with the projections arrived at would mean a growth of 5 per cent per annum in Gross National Product; the central task was to examine ways and means, obstacles and opportunities, to the securing of this high rate of growth. It is clear from the start that this involves delicate questions of import-export relations, capital inflow and savings, protection and the balance of payments. The present writer is not too well equipped to discuss these matters, but some indication of the nature of the problem must be given.[2]

The rate of 5 per cent per annum is one-fifth higher than that of the preceding decade, and to attain it may demand 'a degree of

---

[1] Clemenceau's dictum on war – 'too serious to be left to soldiers' – applies.
[2] Indebtedness must be acknowledged to the special issue of *The Economic Record* (Vol. 42, No. 97, March 1966) published by Melbourne University Press for the Economic Society of Australia and New Zealand; this is an excellent guide. The Report itself has of course been used.

national exertion to which Australia is unaccustomed'. Yet in many respects the Committee's prognosis was cautious; in considering likely export demand for the rural sector, for example, it sets out very fairly the international factors liable to limit expansion – technological changes reducing the raw material component in manufactures, synthetics, agricultural protectionism, and the European Common Market. Nevertheless it holds that expansion is possible, and is perhaps a little optimistic about the chances of official policy guiding high-cost marginal producers into more rational land-use. On the other hand, the spectacular developments of the last few years suggest that it almost certainly under-projected the income accruing from mineral exports, and it may also have undervalued possible import replacement, not only in oil but in manufactures.

A high growth rate in an only partially tooled-up industrialising economy will call for an increase of imports, which if not delicately balanced might well be on such a scale as to become self-defeating. Even more likely is an increased demand for capital inflow, which may produce rapid short-term expansion but, through overseas control of enterprise and continuing interest charges, may compromise the future. The Committee showed itself keenly aware of such considerations. Immigration for example will certainly add to productivity in the long run, in some cases by bringing new skills and entrepreneurial activity, and more generally by the increased demand leading to economies of scale. But in the short run, its effect is rather to widen than to deepen investment – that is, to place a higher proportion of investment in the infrastructure of housing, schools, roads, public services, and amenities; the days are long past when, as in nineteenth-century America, immigrants would put up with anything, nor would Australian Labor put up with it if they would. Hence the recommendation that immigration should be held to 100,000 a year.

Much attention was given to the problem of overseas investment in Australia; while it is agreed on all hands that a good deal of such investment is necessary for devlopment, in some sectors it may have already grown to an unhealthy extent, and take-overs in particular often bring no real gain to the economy. Although the Committee accepted a continuation of new overseas investment at the recent level of $300 million a year, it was not without misgivings: long-term this might introduce a serious permanent debit in the balance of payments position, while leading to an increase in the proportion of Australian company assets owned abroad to around 46 per cent in 1974–75. This projection has been challenged, but even on the critic's revised estimate of 34 per cent, few would disagree with the Committee's conclusion that 'Australia should so order its affairs that it can become less dependent on capital inflow. We regard this as essential.' Yet to absorb even the present rate of inflow without becoming utterly dependent, and even irrespective of the long-term effect of inflow on the balance of payments, this means a regular expansion of exports; and in view of the difficulties of rural exports, it is important that the export share of manufactures should be increased.

To this end something can be done by governmental encouragements such as investment allowances or more generous depreciation provisions, but a higher rate of internal saving will also be essential. The Committee was sceptical of the chances of any substantial increase in personal saving; hence reliance on increased public saving – 'in effect, greater current surpluses' – will be needed. This really means 'removing funds from the private sector by taxation and ensuring that government expenditure is not increased on that account' (this may seem an astonishingly pious hope). To ensure diversion into investment, this involves using taxation to curtail consumption expenditure, which could of course react on investment in consumer goods production (and such goods are on the whole the most likely manufactured export possibilities). Hence the need for governmental encouragement to manufacturing.... The argument seems a trifle circular; but then the science of economics sometimes appears to be devoted to the enunciation, and occasionally the unravelling, of interlocking vicious circles.

The problem of protection

All this in a sense leads up to the crucial problem of protection. It has been estimated that about 650,000 employees – 60 per cent of factory workers, 15 per cent of the total workforce in the early 'sixties – are 'dependent in some sense on the tariff'.[1] The political dangers of tampering with the tariff are only too obvious; nothing could so unite Chambers of Manufacturers and Trade Unions in a spirit of a resistance to government as any official suggestion for a serious revision in a less protectionist direction. Yet the tariff

[1] W. M. Corden, in A. Hunter (ed.), *The Economics of Australian Industry* (Melbourne University Press, 1963), p. 174.

structure has its less obvious but built-in obstacles to growth – undue rigidities and over-high costs. Like arbitration, it has become an extremely complex and all-pervasive body of precedents, covering over 3,000 items with a variety of forms of duty; as Condliffe puts it, 'the protective net is spread so wide that it must be modified to allow the economy to function'. Modification is achieved, imperfectly, by allowing *ad valorem* duties or free import; but while technically the onus is on the industry concerned to make out its case for protection to the Tariff Board, politically speaking it often looks the other way round.

It was certainly high time that an effort should be made to reduce this agglomeration of specific vested interests into a body of general principle; and the Vernon Committee did indicate steps in this direction. It suggested reduction of tariff complexity, more frequent review by the Tariff Board of its own work, abandonment of the (strongly entrenched) notion that 'because an industry exists it automatically has the right to all the protection it needs' (or says it needs), and a clearer recognition of the distinction between temporary relief to meet an emergency and long-term protection – it should be clearly understood that 'temporary protection should be a holding operation only, pending review by the Board'. These proposals are sheer common sense; but in the general climate of Australian opinion, they are likely to remain aspirations.

To some academic economists, this seems meagre enough; but the Committee not unnaturally may have hedged, since advocacy of free trade, or even a too open suggestion of the desirability of a general lowering of tariff barriers, might well have prejudiced acceptance of any other recommendations, however innocuous. In the upshot, its main recommendation was in effect for a yardstick for the granting of protection – the concept of a general cost disability – that is, the excess of Australian costs over duty-free imports – of about 30 per cent as the desideratum for granting protection in any specific case. On the whole, the Report is 'firmly protectionist and yet moderate when compared with government policy or the views of most Australians'.[1]

Regulating the economy

For a general summing-up – which may seem to confirm our remark about vicious circles – it seems best to let the Committee

[1] W. M. Corden in *Economic Record*, *op. cit.*, p. 129.

speak for itself. After pointing out that the necessary expansion of exports may not be attainable, while considerable imports of production goods are in any event essential to development, it goes on to say that 'In these circumstances, Australia is in the position of having to husband its resources for growth.' Increased personal saving through policies restricting consumer demand would help, but 'if there is still a long-run tendency for imports to outrun exports and increased capital inflow is either not available or not desired', special steps to reduce imports would be necessary: a general tariff rise; import taxes; import licensing; devaluation. Any of these would mean increased pressure on home production and hence have inflationary consequences; drastic cutting of home demand (say through taxation for increased government surpluses) would be deflationary unless accompanied by import restriction. Hence

> a combination of measures would be required that would both reduce total demand and divert expenditure away from imports. Such a course would reduce demand for imports while maintaining the level of demand for domestic production. Whatever means might be adopted, some cutting back in the rate of growth of the economy would have to be expected, if only because of the need to economise on imported equipment and raw materials. The problem would be to minimise this effect. (Report, para. 17.65)

Devaluation would increase the incomes of exporters without greatly increasing exports; this would lead to demands for increases in money wages, hence inflation and a need for further devaluation – this quite apart from the effect on external credit of accepting the stigma of devaluation. Import licensing may be appropriate in emergencies but as a general policy 'implies a degree of control over economic decisions and of interference with the normal processes of economic growth which can lead to pronounced distortions in the economy and impair growth'; a general increase in the tariff (or import taxes) 'would be less objectionable but would lead to some increases in costs and pressures for higher wages'.

Finally

> A prime difficulty will always be to determine whether a fundamental long-term problem is developing or whether the situation is more likely to be a passing one. Growth would suffer unneces-

sarily if the periodic short-term balance of payments crises that are bound to arise were met with severe measures to restrain demand or to restrict imports. (Report, para. 17.66)

(There may be a backward glance here at the 1960 'credit squeeze'.) Such short-term difficulties can be met by the 'first line of defence', drawing on overseas reserves or the International Monetary Reserve, and some domestic restraints. If 'a long-term imbalance, such as might be caused by a chronic deterioration in the terms of trade', were to loom over the horizon, the more drastic remedies outlined above would come into play.

An essential task of the proposed Advisory Council on Economic Growth – a permanent Vernon Committee, bigger and with a better-found secretariat – would be precisely to scan the horizon for such long-term changes in the economic weather. We have seen the reception that this proposal met with; nevertheless, the Vernon Report will remain a basic document for the Australian economic agenda for some time to come: 'The debate will never be the same again.'

The paradoxical economy

To sum up this discussion, we may conclude that Australia is at least reasonably well endowed with natural resources, and with a population decently educated and energetic, or capable of energy. It has had an unusually high degree of political stability, and has always been firmly within the capitalist tradition, so that it has not had to face the traumatic experiences of older developing countries, torn between the demands of ancient custom and status as against new market and contract. On the other hand, though class conflict has certainly not been lacking, large-scale industrialism hardly preceded the era of 'social capitalism' and was early brought within the 'new province of law and order' – Australia's captains of industry may have been rugged individualists but never got the chance to be robber barons on the American scale; they were hardly more than bushrangers. The State has usually been a balancing force, and indeed directly responsible for some activities – railways, power – in which American capitalism was most aggressive and least social.

It is true that geographical factors impose limitations, expressed internally in that alternation of high concentration and extreme sparsity of population which imposes high overheads in the running of the country, the provision of a modern service infrastructure; externally, geographical distance from markets and suppliers imposes a constant added cost. The economy which has developed has its paradoxical aspect in its dependence on a narrow range of primary products, vulnerable to world price fluctuations, while yet being quite highly developed technologically and supporting a society in many ways affluent. Industrially, it started almost from scratch some seventy or eighty years ago and has always been very much dependent on imports both of capital and of know-how, and for an indefinite time it must remain a net importer of both. 'Balance of payments' is a recurrent, if not constant, nightmare.

There is thus some truth in the epigram that Australia is at once a developed 'have' country with a high standard of living and technology, and a developing 'have-not' country with an element of colonialism, perhaps quite a strong one, in its economy; one might say at the top of the one scale and the bottom of the other. At all events, enough has been said in this chapter to give some suggestion of stresses and strains which must give concern to thoughtful Australians. The problem may be summed up in Condliffe's words: 'Economic development is a question primarily of national will and secondarily of organisation.'

Chapter 9

The Problem of the North

<hr>

USTRALIA NORTH OF THE TROPIC comprises 39 per cent of the land area but carries only about 3 per cent of the people. The white population of the Northern Territory did indeed increase by 38 per cent in the five years 1961–66; but in absolute numbers this is only from 27,095 to 37,166, and of this increase over half is accounted for by the capital, Darwin. With 20,261 non-aborigines, Darwin follows the example of the greater capitals by possessing 54.5 per cent of the population; without it, the half-million square miles of the Northern Territory have a density of one person to thirty-one square miles.

Over against this emptiness lies Asia with its hundreds of millions, and it is no wonder that probably no internal problem is so consistently the subject of active, and often acrimonious, debate as 'Northern Development'.

Of the white population, about 60 per cent live in a strip about fifty miles wide, largely devoted to sugar, along the Queensland coast. As is so often claimed, this is indeed the most successful (perhaps the only) large-scale example of white settlement, doing all its own work, within the humid tropics. Leaving this region aside as relatively no problem, tropical Australia is by and large a most intractable land. It looks well-watered by Australian standards, with a large proportion receiving over twenty inches of rain annually. But average annual temperatures, even on the coast, are exceedingly high: Wyndham in Western Australia has an annual mean of 85°F, and Marble Bar, eighty miles inland, has exceeded 100° on 160 consecutive days. The rain falls almost entirely in the five hot-weather months, and largely in short intensive bursts, so that run-off is rapid. Evaporation rates are very high. Taking a five months' growing season as the minimum for non-irrigated cropping, only about 14 per cent of the area is suitable for agriculture without irrigation, and in about a quarter of this, where the five months of adequate moisture balance are not continuous, anything but improved pasture would be very hazardous. Much of the better-watered area is, except in patches, very poor in soil fertility – the laterites around Darwin, the sandstones of the Kimberleys, the sandy heaths of Cape York.

There is then very little counterpart to the great alluvial plains of monsoon Asia. On the most optimistic view, even with high capitalisation, agricultural potential is very severely restricted. On the other hand, the mineral wealth is incalculably great.

Motivations

The fundamental motivation for 'peopling the north' is an almost obsessional compound of guilt and fear: uneasiness amounting to guilt at the spectacle of this vast practically uninhabited land within the ring-fence of 'White Australia' while across the Timor Sea myriads of peasants wring a miserable existence from tiny fragmented fields; fear that Asia might someday do something about it – specifically, once Japan and now China. The inferences are drawn that the north must be populated so that it can be defended, and agriculturally developed so that Australia can legitimate its possession by feeding starving Asians. Apart from this, there is a romanticism of the frontier, a vision of pioneer achievement which looks – but very superficially – to the arid American south-west as its exemplar.

It is easy to see that objectively this is nonsense. Malays certainly, Chinese probably, knew North Australia long before any European 'set a bootprint on our shores', and had it been of any use to their economy, they would have left more than a few ephemeral fishermen's camps. The north may have a monsoon rainfall, but it has none of the other features of the monsoon lands which have made Asian populations possible – the great snow-fed rivers, the wide alluvial basins and deltas. Just conceivably it might be of more use to planned Chinese agricultural colonisation than the Mongolian margins or the deserts of Sinkiang, which are also blanks on the population map; but with all the capital and shipping imaginable, made available for a couple of decades, it is impossible to see more than ten or twenty million Asian peasants being settled in the north, on wretched dry farming, merely extending the world's poverty area; but that is only a year or two of population increase in India or China.

One cannot empty an ocean into a quart-pot, and that is what northern Australia amounts to as a relief for Australian population pressures; nor is there any reason to suppose that Asian leaders are unaware of this. Indeed, as Erle Cox's novel *Fool's Harvest* pointed out as long ago as 1938, should Australia fall to the onslaught of Asian hordes, they would be more likely to settle the south, leaving any surviving and unwanted Australians to 'people the north' or perish – probably the latter.

The defence argument is almost laughable. Select well-equipped bases are no doubt necessary, but beyond this it is unlikely that any-one really supposes, in his heart, that the population of the north will within the foreseeable future be numbered in millions.[1] Even if there were a million or so scattered there, with families as hostages to the fortunes of war, that in itself would not be enough to add very appreciably to defence capacity, but might be just enough to provide the necessary minimum of transport facilities that would make the path of the aggressor that much easier.

As for feeding Asia's millions, the inglorious history of Territory Rice Ltd (1956–60) at Humpty Doo is instructive. Widely publi-cised by its American backers as 'a rice bowl for our Asian neigh-bours', it was adequately capitalised but rushed into before all the technical problems had been worked out; CSIRO had done a great deal, but not enough. Despite the ballyhoo, nobody noticed, or cared to point out, that whatever the yields 500,000 acres could produce only a minuscule contribution by Asian standards, even were the project successful to the full extent of the uninhibited handouts. As it was, yields were quite inadequate in relation to costs, the crop was subject to depredation by pests (including uncontrollable wild ducks), and within five years Territory Rice was sold to mining interests – not for development but as an income tax deduction.

[1] It is true that John Yeoman, in *The Scarce Australians* (Longmans, 1967) cites estimates of population capacity going up to 480,000,000 (by the Viennese geographer Albrecht Penck) or 500,000,000 (including New Zealand and the Pacific Islands, by the economist Colin Clark). One can only say that to a modern geographer these are just fantasies. The 1949 estimate of Dr Joseph Gentilli (127,222,000, or, if a white population only, 96,250,000) is quoted by Yeoman out of context, ignoring Gentilli's clear warning of its speculative disregard of essential variables. Since Griffith Taylor was an anti-booster and made himself so unpopular by this attitude that he left Australia, his estimate of 62,000,000 is more to the point. Those who quote it omit his firm conviction – made around 1918 and so far confirmed by the event – that the future distribution of the population would be as it then was. This would then mean some two or three million in the north – and on Asian or general world standards it would st'll be empty.

Land of trial and error

The paucity of results so far should not discount the fact that Australia has made a long-continued, if not always strongly sustained, effort to develop the north. The Overland Telegraph from Adelaide to Darwin was put through in 1873, and the succeeding years saw many pastoral explorations and occupations. From 1863 until 1911 the Northern Territory was under South Australia, and despite the distance by sea from Adelaide to the 'Top End' efforts were made to promote agricultural settlement; in 1877 the colonial government even attempted to introduce Japanese colonists, but this foundered on Japanese objections.

The historical accident by which the north is split between two States and a Commonwealth Territory has inhibited co-ordination; State conflicts for Commonwealth aid are still strong. The Queensland coast apart, the problems of tropical Australia are common to all three political units, and there would be much to be said for a single latitudinal territory instead of the arbitrary longitudinal split.[1] This could have led, for example, to a better layout of transport feeders to the ports, giving the Territory an alternative to Darwin; as it is, a few hundred wharfies and other unionists at Darwin could strangle any policy of which they disapproved. There was little enough policy in any case, and the militants disapproved of what there was: in 1919 they riotously enforced the withdrawal of the Commonwealth Administrator, and virtually deported his successor, together with the Territory Judge and the Government Secretary, in a neat little reversal of the Rum Rebellion.[2] Such anarchy was the resultant of isolation and top-heavy remote control, in the best or worst colonialist manner and acting on a turbulent disfranchised proletariat; but it does not seem evident that fancy

[1] There would also be much to be said for a Ministry for the North instead of the administration of such wildly different areas as the Northern Territory, Papua and New Guinea, and an assortment of tiny islands, from the sub-Antarctic (Heard Island) to the Equator (Nauru), all under the one Minister for Territories. The objection to a more rational set-up is probably political: there is tactical advantage in keeping colonial Papua and the Trust Territory of New Guinea under one roof with the indefeasibly Australian Northern Territory.

[2] It is not easy, despite Royal Commission reports, to ascertain what actually happened in this *opera bouffe* revolution, and it is diverting to compare such completely antithetic accounts as those by a later Administrator, C. L. A. Abbott, in *Australia's Frontier Province* (Angus and Robertson, Sydney, 1959, pp. 53–55), and H. I. Jensen, 'The Darwin Rebellion', *Labour History*, No. 11 (Canberra, 1966), pp. 3–13.

schemes for carving up the north into half-a-dozen petty States (so that local community effort would be fostered) are anything but Utopian: their handfuls of citizens would become even more the neglected subjects of distant Canberra, and even more officials, Commonwealth and Statelet, would be spread over the land.

As in India and many another underdeveloped country, if the index of development were the same as the index of publishing activity, the picture would be bright indeed. Perhaps the most incisive and comprehensive of the numerous official publications was the Payne-Fletcher Report of 1937, which drew attention to the vital need for better transport and to the uneconomically large size of many cattle stations under absentee control. Both are still pressing problems. The Report, while noting that in many cases enormous land grants had been made on 'absurdly generous terms', noted also that in reaction 'the protection of future public interests tend[ed] to become an obsession', and sought a compromise solution in fifty-year development leases. This Report was made to the Lyons government, and something effective might have been done had not the war intervened. Much that was effective was done during the war, when Darwin was a base and on occasion a front (it was heavily bombed), but in the nature of things this was *ad hoc* and little of permanent value remained except the bitumen Stuart Highway from Alice Springs to Darwin.

The Curtin-Chifley régime set up the Northern Australia Development Committee, a move which, by associating the Queensland and Western Australian governments with the Commonwealth, sought to see and plan for the area as a whole. With the return to normalcy and relative *laissez faire*, this aspect seems to have withered away. The sense of mission of the Minister for Territories, Paul Hasluck, was undeniable and probably stemmed from his early interest in the aborigines of his own Western Australia; but it found its outlet mainly in the even more challenging problems of New Guinea, where the reign of Hasluck, practically coterminous with that of Menzies in the Commonwealth, was in truth and with all discounts made a dynamic epoch.

In effect, the most important contribution of the Menzies governments was probably in the extension and deepening of scientific research, not only in the Northern Territory. The well-organised and well-illustrated reports of CSIRO's Land Research Division are models of technique which have deservedly been followed or adapted in other underdeveloped countries; but without concomitant economic analyses their value must remain rather academic. It is not enough to know what can be grown, and where, in physical terms merely; the economic climate is quite as important as the meteorological. Sophisticated economic enquiry has not indeed been absent; the Commonwealth Bureau of Agricultural Economics, for instance, has devoted much attention to the beef industry. But until recently there seems to have been a marked lack of co-ordination between physical, technical, and economic research.

Possibly to some extent as a result of nervousness arising from the Indonesian take-over in West Irian, which seemed to bring Asia appreciably nearer, 'Northern Development' became one of the issues in the 1963 Federal election, with both sides, but especially Labor, promising to do something about it. The replacement of the Liberal Hasluck by a Country Party man whose concerns and aptitudes certainly seemed more northern than New Guinean might be taken as pointing to increased interest in the north. Instead of the ministry and the executive commission promised by Labor, however, the last Menzies government went no further, either in promise or performance, than a Northern Development Division in the Department of National Development. Whether this was much more than a diversion may be doubted: certainly its first Director felt sufficiently frustrated to resign within two years and to make history by winning for Labor a traditionally Country Party seat in Queensland, at a time when Labor fortunes were at a low ebb. Much was due to the candidate's obvious enthusiasm and technical expertise, much to a characteristic desire to 'give a fair go' to a man who had flouted the Canberra Establishment; but probably more to a wave of local enthusiasm and to some extent national concern with Northern Development. This was concurrently finding expression in such vigorously propagandist pressure groups as the Federal Inland Development Organisation (FIDO) and the Townsville-based People the North Committee. More than ever before, the north was on the map, and it will remain there; but it is still likely to remain as a blank on the population map.

Agricultural potentialities and problems

In a broad review of potentialities, mineral development may be taken as read (Chapter 7). There is no doubt at all that the next few years, to the end of the century and perhaps beyond, will see very active mineral exploitation. This will mean a big injection of capital (despite the hazards of overseas control) and, here and there, settlements big enough and stable enough to provide small local markets. It is questionable, however, whether these will be large enough to provide a take-off point for a significant development of more or less intensive agriculture. After all, Broken Hill has been a large town (by Australian inland standards) throughout this century; its effect on the surrounding country has been about nil, except as a shopping centre for a sparse pastoral population. Mount Isa, with its railway, has been cited as an example of the multiplier effect of a fairly large town (about 15,000); it is fair, however, to point out that this is hardly a really remote and undeveloped region, the railway to Cloncurry, only sixty miles away, dating back to 1908 while the near-by uranium settlement of Mary Kathleen has already lapsed into insignificance on a 'care and maintenance' basis. One factor often overlooked is that modern mining is increasingly mechanised or even automated, and the labour force needed is not likely to be absolutely large.

It is very difficult, at this stage, to form any assessment of the real agricultural potentiality of the north. As we have seen (p. 135), the Queensland Irrigation Commission speaks of several million irrigable acres – four million in the Queensland Pacific littoral, one and a half around the Gulf of Carpentaria, one in the Kimberleys. This is admittedly 'speculative', and seems as unrealistic as that word generally implies. J. H. Kelly, a northern man if ever there was one, talks of 400,000 acres excluding the Queensland east coast, adding that even the Ord River, with a three million acre-feet dam to command 200,000 acres, would hardly be economic by southern standards.

There remain the brute economics, which in 1965 were subjected to a devastating, almost microscopic, survey by Bruce Davidson in *The Northern Myth*. His analysis is rigorously and ruthlessly financial; he lays great stress, for instance, on the extremely high costs for necessary construction goods, machinery, fertilisers, and so on, as compared with those in the south. It might be cheaper to import duty-free from Japan, but that would strike at the heart of protectionism. This of course does not apply nearly so strongly to the Queensland littoral; less than 6 per cent of the State's arable land is irrigated, but this provides a quarter of the return from agriculture, and here multi-purpose development – that dreamt-of

northern Snowy, probably on the Fitzroy – may well seem reasonable. But the sugar coast is hardly the problem.

Rice, since Humpty Doo, is under a cloud, which may or may not
lift; interest now focuses on cotton and safflower. The Ord scheme
is the centre of the hottest controversy: the darling of Western
Australia, an embarrassing baby to the Commonwealth which is
expected to endow a child whose promise is debatable. Once more,
there is no doubt that cotton, safflower, and forage crops can be
grown on the Ord, and grown well, if not perhaps quite so well as
on special demonstration areas; but marketing is a different question. The Namoi Valley in northern New South Wales has already
a vigorous cotton-growing community, and there is little doubt that
all Australia's needs could be met more cheaply from the east.
Further development in the north-west would probably lead to the
old round of high subsidies or artificially bolstered internal prices
to make export competition possible. It is questionable if it is worth
it.

Apart from irrigation there are certain dry-farming possibilities,
especially in the less remote areas behind Darwin and in central
Queensland: millets, groundnuts, safflower. These come up against
vested interests: oilseeds extension in general must face the bitter
opposition of the dairy industry, which fights hard to maintain
margarine quotas; coastal Queensland has already a groundnuts
industry. More attention might be given to the possibility of dry-
farming groundnuts in the 'Top End' with local extraction of oil
(providing the desideratum of a secondary industry) and a local
market for the crushed meal as cattle-feed. The existing groundnut
production behind Darwin needs considerable technical improvement, but here if anywhere there seems to be a feasible agricultural
opening, which could be less highly subsidised than most. In fact, if
carried out on a sufficiently large scale for export, a subsidy might
not be necessary at all, the growing pains once over. Admittedly
this would be to some extent a gamble on world markets, but
although in general the ifs and buts tend to discount optimistic
assessments, this is the reverse case: Davidson's cautions about
Asian and African production seem distinctly hypothetical.

The beef industry

Minerals apart, it seems probable that the backbone of Northern
Development will remain beef: the one 'system of land use which

has proved its ability to survive in the uncertain physical and economic environment without subsidies because it relies on large-scale production with a high output per man'.[1] It is capable of considerable expansion – partly by overcoming deficiencies – but the last words of this quotation are significant; it is a highly extensive form of land use, and its development to its full capacity would not involve any dramatic 'peopling the north'.

The beef cattle industry accounts for 6 to 8 per cent of Australian exports, and its recent foray into the American hamburger market was significant enough for several states in the American West to clamour for restrictions. Over a third of Australia's fourteen million beef cattle are reared north of the Tropic, despite formidable natural difficulties – for instance, owing to the intense heat and consequent dehydration, a calf born at any time between dawn and late afternoon has very little chance of surviving the first day. Cattle numbers could probably be doubled. Australians eat much less beef per head than they did before the war – this probably reflects more sophisticated dietary habits – but with the growth of the population, and probably increased demand from overseas, market prospects seem reasonable.

Paradoxically, the unfitness of the land for anything else may even prove a safeguard, as other countries with growing populations may well turn to more intensive use of their grazing land, while Northern Australia remains a great pastoral reserve. Much effort, however, will be needed to achieve full capacity. The major problems fall into two groups: those on the cattle station and those on the way to market.

As regards the first, the great needs are more fences and more watering points. Fencing into smaller (but still very large) paddocks is essential not only to rotate the stock, but for adequate segregation by age, type, and sex; it has been neglected on the larger absentee-owned stations. With too few watering points, the cattle trample the areas around dams and artesian bores, to the destruction of the grass cover so that they have to move farther to find pasture; this puddling of the ground also greatly increases erosion and silting. Tick control and more breeding experience with such drought-resistant strains as Zebu crosses and Santa Gertrudis are also needed.

[1] Bruce Davidson, *The Northern Myth* (Melbourne Univ. Press, 1965), pp. 110–11.

A reform of land tenure is probably needed to ensure such investments being made and maintained. At present immense areas are held by absentee (and largely overseas) interests such as the Vesteys group, which under one company name or another controls over five million acres in the East Kimberleys and eighteen million in the Northern Territory, a total of over 40,000 square miles. With exceptions, these huge holdings are less carefully worked than smaller ones with resident holders, not managers; certainly their percentage turn-off of meat animals is less than that of smaller holdings in comparable country. The record of the larger companies, which in the Northern Territory were exempt from income tax from 1937 to 1952 under the legal fiction that they were resident there, hardly supports the view that tax exemption is a ready tool for developing the north, unless it is very selective; still less that all long leases should be converted to freehold. However, it is important not to be misled by the term 'closer settlement' into thinking that subdivision to provide more manageable units would mean a great increase in numbers of people: Kelly's careful estimate for an efficient productive unit varies from 400 square miles on the Barkly Tableland to 1,300 in the 'Top End'.

As important as on-station improvements is off-station transport. Traditionally, this was by droving on the great stock-routes, and the larger enterprises had holdings disposed along the tracks as way-stations where cattle could rest and recuperate. Droving is still important for relatively short movements, but on a few main highways cattle are transported by two-decker Diesel 'road trains', though the high hopes of using air transport to move stock to meatworks at the ports have proved fallacious. The proponents of 'air-beef' overstated their case grossly, and the last such scheme lapsed about 1960. Allowing for the inevitable loss of condition on long rail or road journeys, a great extension of beef roads is certainly essential, and less certainly desirable is a rail connection from the existing line south of Darwin, by the high-potential Barkly Table-land, to the Queensland railheads.

This could be linked with the current development of the brigalow country, an area of about 12 million acres, mostly south of the Tropic, in east-central Queensland. It is dominated by an acacia, difficult to clear since it regenerates by suckers; but once cleared the brigalow is good pastoral country, with more reliable rainfall than in the great pastoral lands to the north and west; it has even some wheat and millet potential. It would thus provide an admirable fattening area, and an active clearing and roading programme is under way.

All this does not amount to much in population terms, and in view of the stagnation or decline of the rural workforce this may be as well. There is one indigenous resource worthy of more attention than it has received: aboriginal labour. Especially in the remoter regions, the beef industry has depended heavily on the grossest exploitation of aborigines; Northern Territory stations employ about 1,200 aborigines, mainly stockmen, to about 300 whites. Until 1957 many received no more than five shillings a week plus rations; from 1957 their wages were regulated, but were only a quarter of those paid to a white man doing equivalent work.

There seems no doubt that given training and good working conditions, many aborigines make excellent stockmen, but the 1965 application by the unions to secure award rates for aborigines was sternly resisted by the cattlemen. They were very reluctantly brought to accede to a compromise by which award rates were to be payable in three years except to 'slow workers'. Who is to define 'slow' may be unclear – or only too clear; one may confidently expect the unions to keep a close eye on this wide loophole. It remains to be seen whether the threat to replace a third or a half of the aborigines by white workers can be made good; and it is significant that, for the first time, the aborigines did not take this lying down: by early 1967 strike action was at least beginning to dent the graziers' front.

Populate or develop?

The general dilemma remains: build on assured foundations, for known returns, in the south and accumulate the resources for a massive technological assault on tropical Australia later on; or accept an essentially political imperative and to hell with economics? These are the extreme approaches, and we need not, and surely should not, bet on all or nothing.

There can be hardly any doubt that any really substantial agricultural development is in the foreseeable future quite uneconomic, and that if the north does get off the ground, the impulse will be given by mining. Tax concessions, selective and carefully conditional, may be desirable, and adequate credit will be necessary – to include provision for the amenities which in the age of aircraft and airconditioning can take the nastier edges off pioneering, especially for the women. Something also will have to be done to offset the feeling, so strong in the north, of 'we-they', *they* being the south generally and Canberra in particular. The Northern Territory legislature, for instance, is beautifully old-style Crown Colonial: the appointed Administrator as President, six official, three nominated, and eight elected members, with assent to ordinances reserved to the Administrator, in effect to the Department of Territories at Canberra. This puts a white population, admittedly tiny but larger than those of Tasmania or Queensland when they became self-governing, far below New Guineans in political status. It must be admitted that Canberra puts up the money.

The common slogan 'populate or perish' puts the issue in false terms. To rural Australia, a town of 25,000 is a large city, and it is simply not noticed that whatever is done, the north will still look a blank on the map to Asian eyes. The Ord, the centre of the most ardent hopes, costing about $75 million (mostly from the Commonwealth) when and if fully developed, would mean an increase of population (families and non-farming population included) of say 20,000 people, and this is a liberal estimate. Kelly, who knows the north as well as anyone and is an advocate of 'closer settlement' (in rational northern terms), has estimated that at full development the white population of his 'remote regions'[1] would be tripled – to 300,000. Treble it to 900,000, and the north will still be empty; but it is not useless now, and it would be more useful then. The point is not to 'people the north', but to use it.

Kelly, more level-headed than many northern advocates, says very wisely:

> Because of the preponderance of emotional arguments in favour of northern development (in terms of a 'yellow peril' or of the undesirability of large cities) it is difficult to present an economic case which will be heeded by those who have become sceptical of the emotional case.[2]

Indeed, among the worst enemies of Northern Development are some of its most ardent protagonists. When we hear that Henry Lawson –

[1] Western Australia north of 26°S (*not* the Tropic), Northern Territory, all Queensland west of 144°E.

[2] *Struggle for the North* (Australasian Book Society, Sydney, 1966), p. 176.

a Sydneysider who in his heart loathed the bush – told us sixty years ago that 'We in Australia have the responsibility of developing a higher, a nobler form of civilisation concerned mainly with smaller self-supporting community towns' (no reference being given) – well, it is difficult to command the seriousness the question deserves. Over against this rhetoric we have the brute negativism of Bruce Davidson's balance sheets, technically correct enough (though this has been questioned) but making no allowance at all for the intangibles of a nation's life.

Of these intangibles, the moral issue imposed by the 'White Australia' ring-fence is the most serious. True enough, rationally considered, that the north would be useless for Asian colonisation on a scale to give any relief to Asian population pressures, and that Asian leaders know this; the irrational provocation is always there. It cannot be abolished by 'peopling the north', for however many people Australia eventually holds, it is almost certain that the broad distribution of population will not be substantially changed. With techniques which we can currently envisage, the north *cannot* be peopled in any sense which will look peopled by Asian standards. We must forget about expressing development in terms of human numbers, and concentrate on the more effective exploitation of area.

This will not in itself solve the problem, but at least it would make it a little easier to fend off the accusation of being mere dogs in the manger. (In this regard, Japanese participation in mineral development has its positive aspect.) We may set aside the vision – or the pipe-dream – of a great rural population in the north, but it still remains incumbent, morally and materially, that Australia should do what can be done to make it more productive. At best, that may not be very much on a world scale, and it will not be done by blindly rushing ahead with grandiose schemes; but given the intractability of this vast and harsh land, it may yet be a great achievement.

Part Three

POLITY

Chapter 10

The Structures of Government

THE POLITICAL SYSTEM of Australia is disconcerting alike to the British migrant and the American visitor. The former must live under a written constitution in which his long-accustomed 'sovereignty of Parliament' is vulnerable to the judicial review of the High Court; this may not greatly bother the average man, but living under two governments, State and Federal, does have noticeable effects on his daily life. He may well be annoyed at being compelled, on pain of fine, to vote at numerous elections, and baffled by the inconsequential results of preferential voting, while his chances of really effective participation in affairs through local government are less than in Britain. The American also might be puzzled by preferential voting, were he compelled to indulge in it; and while he might at first think himself at home in a federal system, he would perhaps be repelled to find that the Head of the State is neither democratically elected nor possessed of power, that the Executive is formally responsible to the Legislature, and that the Senate, despite appearances, is not a States' House. And he would almost certainly be perplexed by the relationship between the Commonwealth and the Crown.

The Crown in the Commonwealth

The Governor-General of the Commonwealth and the State Governors are pre-eminently the Australian incarnations of Bagehot's 'dignified element' in politics; some might say they are the only element of dignity. The Governor-General does not represent or act as agent for the British Government – that is a diplomatic function carried out by the British High Commissioner. His task is to perform the Sovereign's duties, which are rarely indeed of more than a symbolic order, and even so cannot be carried out except on the advice of the ministers he appoints, but appoints in accordance with the parliamentary situation. Since the adoption in 1942 of the Statute of Westminster, even the Governor-General's constitutional discretion to reserve for the royal pleasure laws which might conflict with Imperial[1] policy or treaties has become practically a dead letter.

The State Governors are not the Governor-General's subordinates, and in theory their position is rather different from his. In form, though not in practice, they are not appointed on the advice of ministers, and just conceivably they could be directed from London to dissolve Parliament or disallow legislation; in the past there have been conservative attempts to secure such action. In 1932 the Lang government was dismissed by the Governor of New South Wales on his own responsibility, and his action was confirmed at the polls; had it not been, his position would have been untenable.

As in Britain, the only time at which regal or vice-regal action can be of direct political significance is in parliamentary crises. Before 1910 Governors-General thrice refused requests for dissolution, but at that time there was effectively a three-party system and hence alternative governments could be formed without new elections. Nowadays the Governor-General's office rises to crucial significance only in the event of prolonged deadlock between the House of Representatives and the Senate, when he may accept or reject a ministerial request for double dissolution. The definition of 'prolonged' may be a nice one, and since the deadlock may plausibly appear to have been fostered deliberately either by the government, as in Cook's case in 1914, or by an obstructionist opposition majority in the Senate, as in Menzies' case in 1951, the Governor-General's discretion becomes a matter of some delicacy. These two are the only cases, in each the request was granted, and since it is generally agreed that the decisions were correct, it may be doubted whether much discretion to refuse is now left.[2]

The main point of controversy about the Governor-General is whether he should be an Australian or a man of distinction from elsewhere in the British Commonwealth (in practice, from Britain) and hence above any slightest suspicion of local bias. (Strangely enough, such doubts do not attach to the appointment of Australian politicians to the High Court, where the occasions for the decisive exercise of fallible judgement are far more numerous and just as momentous.) Thirteen of the fifteen Governors-General to 1965

[1] The word is *demodé*, but it is difficult to find a substitute.
[2] With poetic justice, the electorate defeated Cook and upheld Menzies.

were or became British peers, and the first Australian, Sir Isaac Isaacs, was appointed in 1930 only after a hard tussle at Buckingham Palace between Scullin and George V, who pointedly omitted the customary expression of royal pleasure. From the traditionalist point of view, worse was to come. Isaacs was at least a distinguished liberal Chief Justice of the High Court, but after the exalted incumbency of H.R.H. the Duke of Gloucester the Chifley government secured the appointment of Sir William McKell, a Labor politician not only still active but actually Premier of New South Wales. Menzies, then opposition leader, found this 'shocking and humiliating'; one hopes that these feelings did not survive McKell's grant to him of the 1951 double dissolution.

The appointment in 1965 of Richard Gardiner Casey, an Australian of distinction *and* a peer, was by no means the least example of Sir Robert Menzies' genius for making the best of both worlds. In one of Lord Casey's avatars, as Governor of Bengal, it is impossible that an Australian successor could be found; but now that even a Liberal government has seen the nationalist light, it is unlikely that in the future the rather undignified quinquennial excursion to comb the clubs and lobbies of the London Establishment will often be thought necessary.

The Parliament of the Commonwealth

Formally, the Commonwealth is a Federation with residual powers left to the States. There is a wide overlap of concurrent powers between those necessarily or desirably left to the Centre, such as foreign affairs and defence, Customs and external trade, currency, immigration, posts and telegraphs, and those clearly in the State province, such as education, hospitals, and land tenure; for instance, the States retained their own rail systems, but the Commonwealth is responsible for the Trans-Continental line from Port Augusta to Perth and the two sections of the incomplete line from Port Augusta to Darwin. Although the Centre has been inordinately slow in taking up some powers expressly open to it and in which continental uniformity is desirable, such as divorce and company legislation, the history of the Commonwealth (as of all countries in this century) has been one of continual expansion of central power. The need for rapid and decisive action on a continental scale in two world wars was of course a powerful factor in this trend, but it would have been inevitable in any event owing to the increasing complexity of national government and the power of the Federal purse.

This expansion, however, has come about with remarkably little formal constitutional change: only five of the twenty-six referenda proposals (to 1966) have been carried, and for much of its life the High Court has been on balance adverse to a liberal interpretation of the constitution, though less so than the Judicial Committee of the Privy Council, the ultimate appeal in some cases. Moreover, State government has certainly not withered away, even though many State activities depend on an elaborate system of Commonwealth grants. Despite the loss of income tax by the Uniform Tax agreement of 1942, the States retain taxing powers; they are essentially welfare and development agencies, and as such their activities have increased. Although the emphasis had shifted before the successful 1946 referendum gave public sanction to the Commonwealth's initiative in social services, in many respects the State powers are those which impinge most directly on daily life – after all, they regulate such vital things as schools, police, housing, betting, and the supply of water and of beer.

The Parliament of the Commonwealth consists of a Senate with ten members for each State and a House of Representatives, by the constitution twice the strength of the Senate, plus members for the Australian Capital Territory and the Northern Territory.[1] These are elected on different principles.

Senators hold office for six years, half retiring every three years, and are elected by proportional representation in single State-wide constituencies. The single State constituency, except in Tasmania far too large for personal contact, means that Party and not personality dominates; proportional representation that between 6 and 8 per cent of the (compelled) voters fail to master the complicated ballot paper. More seriously, it has led to Labor and non-Labor Senate strengths being usually nearly equal, and most seats are perfectly safe so long as the incumbent keeps in with his party machine.

The Senate may not initiate nor amend money bills, but it can reject or request, and persist in requesting, amendments to them; it has thus formally some power over Supply. Without forcing the

---

[1] Paradoxically, Tasmania has only five Representatives, its constitutional minimum. The 1967 'nexus' referendum to break the 2:1 ratio was very decisively defeated.

issue to the danger point of double dissolution, a hostile Senate (half of which may have been elected three years back) can seriously obstruct a government with a new majority in the House. But when both House and Senate are of the same complexion, the Senate may be treated with scant respect, kept hanging about for most of the session and then forced to scramble through the legislation.

The Senate has never really acted as a States' House, and has been ineffective as a house of review (distinguishing review from obstruction), nor has it often indulged in that open debate on general issues which sometimes lends a faded distinction to the House of Lords. Its best work has perhaps been through Select Committees – it initiated a very good joint Senate-House committee which at long last led to the recent purposeful development of the national capital – but even here it has not done a great deal. Although by convention some ministers are drawn from the Senate, most of the effective work is done in the House; and the high proportion of safe seats, rewards for men of no particular quality except long-enduring party orthodoxy, puts a premium on mediocrity. The Australian Senate has nothing like the power, nor consequently the prestige, of its American counterpart; and one may even wonder whether it earns its keep.

Nowadays the prestige of the House of Representatives is not what it was, and its effective power has been whittled down by the arts of Cabinet management. But it is livelier than the Senate, and on the whole its members do earn their keep. They are elected triennially from single-member constituencies by compulsory preferential voting. States are represented on a population basis (except for Tasmania), and in theory electorates should be roughly equal in population, with a 20 per cent tolerance; inter-censal population changes of course distort this theoretical division, and although there is provision for redistribution, this is not mandatory at fixed intervals. Some anomalies are unavoidable, but when at the 1966 elections the theoretical range was 40,000 to 60,000 electors per seat while the actual range in Victoria was 30,000 to 117,000, it is clear that 'one man, one vote' has become meaningless.

By and large, the 20 per cent variation has been operated to the advantage of rural areas, on the ground that the vast area of bush needed to secure numerical equivalence to a metropolitan seat would be quite unmanageable electorally. Even with air transport, there is still something in this, but not a great deal. A redistribution would benefit the Liberal Party, since population trends swell the new suburban areas which are a main source of its strength, while many of the undersize electorates are inner-suburb Labor strongholds. The Country Party favours interpretations of the Electoral Act which would amount to a gerrymander on a continental scale,[1] and moves for a redistribution in 1962 came to nothing as a result of a paradoxical tacit alliance between the Country Party, ever threatened by metropolitan concentration, and Labor, fearful for its pocket boroughs in the city cores.

To British eyes, the combination of compulsory and preferential voting is perhaps the strangest feature of political life. Compulsory voting was adopted in 1924, without a division, on a private member's bill; both sides wanted it – it saves so much electioneering trouble – but neither wished to appear to push for it. Since people not wanting to vote are likely to be either too stupid to value their democratic privilege or to understand the issues, or sufficiently intelligent to dislike a forced choice between two evils when a more effective protest would be mass abstention (in Britain, a clear warning to one or both parties to set the house in order), it is difficult to see how compulsory voting conduces to intelligent politics.[2]

Preferential voting is a different and more serious issue. Voters indicate their order of preference by placing 1, 2, 3 . . . against candidates' names; if nobody secures an absolute majority of first preferences, the one with the lowest total of firsts is eliminated and his seconds distributed to those so favoured, and so on until somebody has an absolute lead. A man who originally stood in second or third place may thus be elected, on the ground that if not the most favoured he is at least the least disfavoured by the voters. There are snags: position on the ballot counts – there is always some 'donkey voting' straight down the list, and until the order was settled by lot, rather than alphabetically, Aaronses and Adamses had an unfair start in the political stakes. As it is, the parties issue 'how to vote' cards instructing the faithful in the distribution of their preferences; even so, the results are occasionally bizarre. In 1961 the Menzies

[1] Though hardly so extreme as the iniquitous State gerrymanders which kept Queensland Labor and South Australian anti-Labor in office for decades at a stretch.

[2] It is a little hard when a reasoned decision to 'vote informal' equates one with the donkey vote.

government scraped home with a majority of two, one of whom was perhaps the most extreme right-winger in the House, and he was in effect elected by ninety-seven Communist donkeys who failed to follow the party line.

This is rare; results do not very often differ from the first count, though with only 122 members to be elected, even three or four reversals may be significant in a close election. On the whole, preferential voting probably tends to dampen down swings, except in crucial 'realignment' elections (1949, 1966), without leading to the fractionalism or the too-narrow majorities (in number of seats) associated with proportional representation, and without such extreme anomalies of 'first past the post' as the British 1931 election, when Labour had one-third of the votes and one-thirteenth of the seats. It has worked directly to the advantage of the Country Party, which can expand its influence beyond its safe sectional bailiwicks without risk of splitting the anti-Labor vote (since Liberal and Country preferences are normally exchanged), and indirectly to the advantage of the Liberals, since in some electorates their interest in itself would not win against Labor in a straight fight, but the Country Party can mobilise, against Labor, voters who would not give their first preferences to the Liberals. This is accepted by Labor as in the rules of the game, and in State elections preferential voting has on occasion enabled Labor to indulge in factionalism with safety, so long as the factions retained sufficient fraternal feeling not to leak preferences to the class enemy. Recently, however, the Democratic Labor Party (pp. 205–10) has upset this comfortable assumption.

Although their days of sitting are surprisingly few, sixty-odd a year, most MHRs are hard-working men and a fair proportion are men of ability. Yet the actual working of the House as a legislature is often clumsy and ineffective, and there can be no doubt that the prestige of the House has declined over the last two or three decades. Some of this decline is due to the diffusion of executive responsibility through delegation to all sorts of statutory authorities, many necessitated by the complexity of modern government, many set up to shelter governments from direct sectional pressures, all tending to draw attention away from Parliament itself. Some is due to the tendency of the Press to 'give the people what they want', which does not always run to adequate reporting and discussion of debates but does run to gossip about scenes, scandals, and so-called 'salary grabs'; this of course is the common lot of politicians, paid to do the distasteful work of politicking and then accused of lack of taste in doing it. But some of it does reflect failings in Parliament itself.

Not all of these failings are inevitable. Inevitable, in the modern age, is the tightening of the control of business by the Executive, which has a job to do and cannot tolerate too much talk about it and about. Not inevitable is the failure to publish bills well in advance, and to organise the time of the House so that technicalities are reserved to Standing Committees and major debate is consecutive. This failure means that much of the talk – a good deal of which is broadcast – is horribly trivial. Except in a haphazard way at Budget sessions, when there is virtually a free-for-all for any member who can get called (and that may depend largely on caucus or leadership decisions), the findings of important governmental enquiries may not receive any discussion at all; and yet major policy may be based on them.

Paradoxically, the smallness of the House is a factor in its ineffective conduct of business: there is less *apparent* need for devolution of the details into Committees; these are of course used, but not on anything like the British or American scale. Then again, the average government strength from 1949 to 1966 was seventy; from these had to be drawn the Speaker (not nearly so much withdrawn from vulgar Party as in Britain), a score of ministers, Whips, and a number of Committee chairmen; sometimes Assistant Ministers. Not only are the Front Benches numerically strong, but a higher proportion of backbenchers than in Britain may expect promotion if they stay good boys. The pressures against independence are strong and, though the Liberal and Country Parties make much self-righteous play of their freedom from the rigid caucus control of the ALP, in practice they are not so different. Backbenchers of any weight or general reputation in the country are a handful, and it has been said, perhaps with little exaggeration, that 'the party oligarchies find a wide measure of agreement in suppressing politics'.[1]

It is not surprising, then, that debate is stereotyped and Executive

[1] This Bellocian view is the theme of G. S. Reid's 'Parliament and the Executive: The Suppression of Politics', in H. Mayer (ed.), *Australian Politics* (Cheshire, Melbourne, 1966), pp. 378–97. It remains to be seen whether the considerable increase in parliamentarians, necessitated by population growth and the failure of the 1967 'nexus' referendum, will make much difference.

control often too strong for effective ventilation of very relevant views. Yet, despite the often distressingly low level of public discourse, sometimes degenerating to a ritual exchange of forced vulgarities which are considered wit, most MHRs do take their work very seriously. But, except for the Front Benches and likely aspirants thereto, it is in a sense their private work: they are indefatigable ombudsmen. This fits well with the Australian style: one gets the impression that few countries can be more hedged around with bureaucratic regulation, but in far fewer can the man or woman with a soundly-based hard-luck story be more readily assisted to find a way through or around the rules. Here at least Press and politicians are at one.

Constitutional checks: High Court and referenda

As we have seen, the Australian Parliament is not supreme. Any of its Acts may be invalidated by the High Court or by further appeal to the Judicial Committee of the Privy Council in London; in cases between Federal and State governments, such appeal can be made only by leave of the High Court itself.[1] The powers and prestige of the High Court and the American Supreme Court are thus much closer than are those of Senates in Canberra and Washington.

The influence of the Court, whose members are appointed by the Federal government, has on the whole been conservative, except from about 1920, when those stalwart liberals Isaac Isaacs and H. B. Higgins had risen by seniority to dominating positions, to 1942. In its first twenty years the Court included the Founding Fathers Barton, O'Connor, and Samuel Griffiths, who had obvious claims to interpret the spirit of the constitution's letter, and did so in the interest of a federal balance which leant towards States' Rights, apart from a war-time widening of Commonwealth defence powers. Since the second World War, the weight of decisions has been restrictive, as for example those on airline nationalisation and Chifley's bank nationalisation legislation, both held inconsistent with Section 92.

Yet the Court has never been as negative and obscurantist as the American Supreme Court was in the palmy days of Republican dominance after the Civil War. Within the limits set by its duty of interpreting a written constitution, it has endeavoured to move with

[1] This position is under review.

the times – perhaps with over-much legal caution, but then one can hardly blame judges for sticking to the law of the land, however awkward and annoying this may be in specific cases.[1] The dilemma is neatly illustrated by pronouncements by the liberal Higgins J and the conservative Latham CJ, each forced by the intractable facts to present a view opposed to his own personal philosophy. Higgins: 'not a section, not a word in this Constitution can be changed by the Federal Parliament, no matter how urgently the change may be required, and even though every member in each House of Parliament may vote for the change'. Latham: 'The distinction between inter-state and intra-state trade appeared more real in 1900 or 1901 than it does to-day. The distinction . . . is a distinction upon paper, and not in fact, as to how Federal and State powers in such a large subject-matter should be distributed. A new approach is needed to Section 92 . . . [Another section], on industrial powers, is legalistic in the extreme, and it turns on the most important element in modern life. . . . There is a great deal of necessary formalism . . . which might well be saved to industry and the community if amendments were made in this part of the Constitution. . . .'[2] It is not the responsibility of the Court, but of politicians and people, that changes were not made when the chance was there. The results of constitutional referenda have been disheartening to those who wish to see more flexible and dynamic government.

It is true that the conditions for success of a referendum are onerous: the proposal to hold one must first be passed by absolute majorities in both Houses, and it must then secure an overall majority of voters with majorities in over half of the States. Of the five successful proposals, two were minor matters of machinery, and the Federal/State Financial Agreement validated in 1928 was widely thought to be so, though it formed the basis for the Commonwealth's attachment of New South Wales revenues in 1932. The 1946 social services referendum was successful, but then one does not bite the hand that proposes to feed one; the success of that of

[1] As an instance of less than Solomonic judgement, the High Court held in 1965 that both Federal and State governments had power, on different bases, to control commercial flights between Sydney and Dubbo. Since the Commonwealth was backing an Ansett and New South Wales a TAA subsidiary, Dubbo remained for some time without an air service, Justice Kitto remarking 'A degree of public inconvenience will exist. While this may be regretted, it leads to no legal conclusion.'

[2] I owe these instances, and much else, to Professor L. F. Crisp's *Australian National Government* (Longmans, 1965).

1967, giving the Commonwealth powers to further aboriginal advancement throughout the continent, was a moral gesture. The reasons for this record are complex; it is not a small versus big State affair, since there is little consistency in State voting except in Western Australia, which oddly enough has been generally 'Yes' – oddly, since it has been the only State to make a serious move towards secession, in 1931.

Partly, no doubt, this negative attitude is simply directed at anything coming from Canberra, an amalgam of States' feeling and general distrust of remote control – although on one occasion Western Australians were adjured to vote 'Yes' to avert domination by Sydney and Melbourne. Another likely factor is that few referenda are on clear-cut simple proposals; the extreme was the fourteen items in Labor's package deal of 1944. The average voter may quite reasonably feel baffled by all this, or may simply think that complicated constitutional matters are above his head, and play for safety with a 'No'. He is very likely right about himself, so it is hardly fair to call this irresponsible; but with compulsory voting there may be resentment at the politicians, who are paid to settle such things, passing the buck, and hence a 'No' which is irresponsible.

Whatever general reflections this record may educe, the blunt fact remains: Australians are unadventurous in their political philosophy. Hence 'the referendum has turned out an essentially conservative device, and if the Federal government wants a change, it must look elsewhere for the means.'[1]

Unadventurous as they may be, Australians are nothing if not pragmatic, and despite High Court and negative referenda, Commonwealth powers have in fact expanded. While the existence of the High Court is a standing invitation to its use by those who wish to block change, there are many Commonwealth activities, not specifically granted to it by the constitution but generally desirable, which can be brought within the defence power or the right to appropriate moneys to 'incidental' purposes, and which have gone unchallenged. Canberra had indeed indulged in social services long before these were fully legitimated in 1946, and it would be difficult to find in the thirty-nine articles of Section 51 ('Powers of the Parliament') anything specifically authorising the creation of the Commonwealth Scientific and Industrial Research Organisation,

---

[1] J. D. B. Miller, *Australian Government and Politics* (Duckworth, London, 2nd ed. 1959), p. 152.

which is yet one of the most useful and widely-publicised Federal agencies, and one of the most legitimate sources of national pride. Or a possible constitutional objection may be forestalled by the arranged marriage of State powers with Federal money: the off-spring of one such union is another source of national pride, the Snowy Mountains Authority. 'She'll do.'

Public Services and administration

The administration of Australia employs (or Australian adminis-trations employ) one out of every five persons in the workforce: in the middle 'sixties, some 900,000 people. About a third are on Federal payrolls, and under a third of these are strictly members of the Public Service of the Commonwealth. Many or most of the army of nearly a million are not, of course, in any sense bureau-crats: the rank and file of the armed forces, the railways, and the post offices, teachers in State schools; nor is the Commonwealth Public Service itself a homogeneous body of bureaucrats. It is not so much a matter of 'The Bureaucracy' as of a host of special bureau-cracies surrounding the civil services proper in both Commonwealth and States.

These include on State level railway and electricity commissions, boards for marketing and irrigation; on Federal such statutory authorities as Trans-Australia Airlines, the Australian Broadcasting Commission, the Snowy Mountains Authority, and CSIRO. Apart from and yet a part of this proliferation of agencies carrying out delegated administration are State and Federal arbitration courts and commissions. This devolution of authority to agencies in the last resort under parliamentary control, but with varying degrees of autonomy in their normal workings, has been seen as 'perhaps the most distinctive characteristic of our political system', though it has of course many analogues in the modern world.

Its high degree of development in Australia is probably due at bottom to the fact that many of the functions of such agencies are essential to the development, welfare, or simply running of the country, and are beyond the resources or outside the interests of private enterprise, although their working has often a very material impact on private fortunes and to that extent becomes matter of politics. In a country where economic sectionalism is extremely strong and politics itself is largely the expression of the conflict of economic 'syndicates' or pressure groups, there nevertheless comes a point when even the doctrinaires of State or of private enterprise must see that if these functions are to be carried out at all, they must be allowed to do so largely under their own rules, perhaps run or backed by the State but normally removed from political interference and partisan appointments.

Conversely, such bodies are very useful to politicians as shielding them from the too importunate demands of vested interests, demands which can be neither accepted nor rejected without offending some body of voters. A superb example of this shelter effect is afforded by the action (if that is the right word) of the New South Wales government in the 'margarine war' of 1966. The rigorous enforcement of drastic quotas on margarine is an article of faith with the dairy farmers on whom the Country Party contingent of the government largely depended; on the other hand, the Liberal component drew its strength from city consumers, turning to cheaper margarine and denied the free choice which is one of the unalienable blessings of private enterprise. As this was just the sort of issue on which the previous Labor government had been defeated, the dilemma was a pretty one. In face of a massive free choice and free enterprise campaign by margarine interests, it was 'resolved' by referring the quota system to the Australian Agricultural Council, a joint Commonwealth-States body with merely advisory powers and not due to meet for some time. Nothing could be more in the Australian style.

All this does add up to 'Socialism without doctrines', and if nationalisation on a Federal scale is greatly impeded, or perhaps barred, by judicial interpretation of the constitution, this does not hold, or holds much more doubtfully, at State level. Anti-Labor governments tend to reduce, but rarely to liquidate, their commitments in spheres which might compete with private enterprise; even the Menzies governments have been decidedly ambivalent in this respect (cf. pp. 126–27). Arrangements differ widely from State to State and from time to time. With this multiplicity of quasi-autonomous agencies exercising wide delegated powers, and nothing much in the way of a co-ordinating body except the ministry itself, it is surprising that confusions and conflicts are not more frequent. They do occur, as when the Department of Health suddenly banned the import of non-pasteurised cheese[1] without bothering to inform

---

[1] The implication that Denmark is somehow less cleanly than Queensland is passing strange.

the Department of Trade, but their comparative mildness and rarity pay tribute to the Australian talent for bureaucracy tempered by empiricism. Though it sometimes appears a little odd, there is after all a good deal of common sense in the Australian style.

A 'shelter' motivation is also apparent in the surprisingly frequent recourse to Royal Commissions for enquiries which a British Parliament would probably conduct for itself by a Select Committee. An Australian Royal Commission is rarely a widely representative and rather awe-inspiring body, appointed to make a comprehensive review of large social issues; it is more often a short-term and strictly *ad hoc* assignment to solve a particular problem, for example the 1954 enquiry into the possible ramifications of the Petrov espionage case. It is usually manned from the judiciary, sometimes by a single judge; this too is intended to take the matter out of 'politics' to the advantage both of politicians and the public: the former are sheltered from inconvenient work and decisions, the latter reassured by the comfortable aura of impartiality which surrounds the Bench.

Apart from these minor bureaucracies, the Commonwealth Public Service itself has risen greatly since 1939 in numbers, technical competence, prestige and power. There was certainly room for improvement. In its early days, recruitment was almost entirely by competitive examination of school leavers – fourteen or fifteen year olds; very few posts, and then only those where some special technical competence was obviously and inescapably necessary, were filled by persons with some higher education. After the first World War, returned servicemen were given an almost complete monopoly of entry. It would be difficult to think of another civilised country content with such low educational standards in its administrators.[1] Only in 1933 was provision made for the regular recruitment of graduates – the depression had shown up the appalling lack of economic *nous* in even the higher echelons – and then it was restricted to 10 per cent of annual intake; in 1939 there were only forty-nine graduates in the whole Service. The older procedures put a high premium on seniority, and this was accentuated by the jealous importance attached by the Public Service associations to the provision for appeal by anyone who felt passed over at a specific

[1] 'Democratic sentiment applauds the sound argument that every office boy should have a chance to become a manager and perverts it into a practical rule that no one shall become a manager who has not been an office boy.' W. K. Hancock, *Australia* (1945 ed.), p. 120.

promotion. This obviously makes for routine correctness and little else.

The second World War broke down the barriers. When Chifley took over the Treasury, only one of his top six officials had a Bachelor's degree; by 1959, only one had not. Before 1939, it seems that the possession of a degree was at best no aid to advancement; since 1945, this position has been reversed. A main factor in the establishment of Canberra University College was to enable public servants to better themselves by part-time study, and until it became part of the National University in 1960 its students were mainly part-timers and there were no science courses.

On the difficult question of political activity by public servants, the Australian position is a moderate and reasonable one; the regulations, initially as rigid as the British ban, were modified (mainly under the Fisher and Chifley governments) to allow resignation to contest elections, with reinstatement if unsuccessful; of course with safeguards as to the use of official information. The line between using and being aware of inside knowledge is impossible to draw, but on the whole this liberality has not been abused. Public comment by technically qualified public servants on what seem to them ignorant political decisions within their special province of expertise is a more difficult problem, leading sometimes to demotion or resignation. While the Commonwealth and most State services have been remarkably free from even the vaguest accusations of serious corruption, there is room for uneasiness at the readiness of some officials to resign or retire into private employment which could be advantaged, if not by specific information, then at least by the skilled guidance of one who knows the ropes of relevant Departments.

The Public Service has deserved well of the Commonwealth. Even in the bad old days, its standards of industry and integrity, if not of information, were high; since the second war and reconstruction, it has provided not only that continuity of administration amidst governmental change which is the first task of a civil service, but (increasingly) an informed leadership, and this without noticeably overstepping the intangible bound which divides helpful assistance in policy-making from undue influence over a minister. In practice, those public servants whose position is sufficiently high to make their inescapable personal biases politically significant do seem to have filled successfully their difficult dual role, of being both servants to the enduring Commonwealth and helpmeets and counsellors to the passing ministry of the day.

Nevertheless, the world over the bureaucracy is the 'they' end of a popular 'we-they' dichotomy. In Australia this feeling is strong, but to some extent diffused since centralisation is as much a matter of the State capitals as of Canberra: the decisions which affect ordinary daily life are as likely to be taken in them as in the national capital. However, it is easy enough for State governments and the metropolitan Press to blame everything on the remote and aloof bureaucrats in Canberra; yet it could be argued that there is a positive advantage in having the central bureaucracy well removed from the daily pressures of vested interests in any one State capital – that indeed is why it is standard practice in federations to erect a neutral capital, often styled 'artificial' but in this aspect wholly natural. In any case, influential national organisations increasingly maintain offices in Canberra – the capitalists have very sensibly stolen a march on the unions in this, paradoxically since Labor is (ostensibly) more centralist in outlook than the other parties; and after all since in these days Canberra is fifty minutes from Sydney by air, and under two hours from Melbourne, it is difficult to see how it can be so very 'remote and aloof'. Moreover, though the headquarters of nearly all Commonwealth Departments are now in Canberra, many Federal public servants live and work around the continent.

Still, though the old egalitarian and anti-authoritarian tradition may be weakening, it dies hard, and it cannot be denied either that Australians by and large dislike and distrust élites, or that of necessity an élite of a few hundred people[1] is forming itself in Canberra. This élite has of course its sub-élites: Treasury and Trade do not always see eye to eye, External Affairs plumes itself, sometimes perhaps without too much warrant, on its esoteric diplomatic finesse. But increasingly this is the main centre of power in Australia; not of course invulnerable from other powers: Chambers of Commerce, of Manufactures, primary producers' groups, Trade Unions.

With the ever-increasing technical complexities of modern government, anything like democratic control is increasingly difficult to exercise; and as in all bureaucracies there is a tendency to shun the harsh light of publicity, except in the softer and more

---

[1] According to R. N. Spann (in H. Mayer, *op. cit.*, p. 439), 582 in June 1965, of whom two-thirds were graduates and one (1) a woman.

flattering radiance of 'Public Relations'. Publicity is often unfair, and yet without it administrative expedience so easily becomes Reason of State. Many members of the Public Service élite would be distinguished men in any country or calling, and by and large it has so far maintained a truly national collective view; but it is no denigration of its essential patriotism and devotion to recognise that there is some risk of oligarchical alienation. That eternal vigilance which is the price of liberty is still in order; unfortunately, the Parliament of the Commonwealth is subject to a Front Bench control of Business which is basically necessary to efficient working, but has been carried to an over-rigid extreme. Hence Parliament is not too well fitted to exercise this vigilance.

State governments

In our opening chapter we had some vision of pre-European Australia: a landscape not formless, indeed possessing not only variety but a pattern to that variety, the pattern of the practically desert core girdled successively by arid sparsely vegetated scrub and grasslands, savannah, and the marginal forests. But the frontiers of these belts were blurred, transitional zones rather than strict boundaries; there were no straight lines, and the handiwork of man was apparent only on a local, in fact a micro, scale. The Australia of to-day has been extensively worked over by human activity, over most of the continent except the desert core the original landscape has been modified and in many areas transformed. There are plenty of straight lines.

Of these none are more significant than those which form the boundaries of the mainland States, with but two exceptions: the major one of the Murray between Victoria and New South Wales, the minor one of the eastern part of that between New South Wales and Queensland. Within this framework, the greater part of the development of the continent has been done by agencies of the States. Despite all that has been said of 'the failure of federalism', the States remain cardinal factors in the society and politics of Australia, in its human and economic geography, and not only in the sense of statistical filing-boxes. They have personalities of their own.

The Commonwealth was created in one piece, and changes in form have been minimal; in contrast, the State governments have grown from colonial beginnings, their constitutions have been subject to substantial modification, and they cannot be regarded as miniatures of the Commonwealth. In all except Queensland (where it was abolished in 1922) there is an Upper House; only in Victoria is it elected by universal suffrage. The complicated election system of the New South Wales Upper House is as pretty a device as can be imagined for ensuring that changes of public opinion have no chance of becoming effective before they are forgotten in new changes. Only supply 'for ordinary services' cannot be vetoed by this Legislative Council;[1] the other Upper Houses can even reject money bills, and since in South Australia, Tasmania, and Western Australia they are elected on fancy restricted franchises, in political form these States are less democratic than Britain with its largely hereditary, but also powerless, House of Lords.

Nor do these oligarchical powers rust unused, especially perhaps in South Australia, which is paradoxical in view of its priority in introducing the ballot and votes for women. A recalcitrant Upper House cannot only frustrate by normal obstruction, but in extreme cases, by throwing out the budget, it can force a government to the polls without having to undergo that hazard itself. However, the pragmatic Labor leader finds his account in a ready-made cast-iron excuse for walking in moderate ways, and even more than the Federal Senate, the State Upper Houses provide very convenient rewards for consistent party virtue, whatever the party.

State Public Services tend to be rather more old-style than the Federal Service, and there is little exchange between them. In technical departments, such as soil and water conservation, marketing, and so on, standards of competence are high. Unfortunately, for some States – notably, in recent years, Victoria – this cannot be said of the vital matter of education; Tasmania, rather provincial in most aspects, is here an exception. Especially in the smaller States, administration as such is much less of a semi-autonomous on-going concern than it is at the Centre, and is much more affected by the flux of politics and ministerial personalities. In the early 'fifties, for example, one was conscious of a perceptible downwards bump in administrative standards as one drove from Victoria into New South Wales; but strangely enough the long Labor régime (1941–

---

[1] The Upper House cannot be restored in Queensland or abolished in NSW without a referendum; in the latter State it was a long time before Labor obtained a Council majority, and when it did enthusiasm for abolition magically waned. Obstruction can be worked both ways.

1965) in the latter State got better as it went along, and one now has the impression that administrative morale is riding high while Victoria is in the doldrums.

The weakness of local government has been discussed in Chapter 6; indeed, it is doubtful whether it is reasonable to consider it under the heading 'political structure'. Indicative of this is the fact that, although there have been notable exceptions such as Chifley, in Australia the politician who won his spurs in local government is a much rarer creature than in Britain. As in Britain, however, when politics do enter into local government, anti-Labor tends to mask itself as 'independent'. It is not likely that many voters are taken in.

Commonwealth and States: 'the failure of federalism'?

The Commonwealth of to-day is clearly a more activist and initiatory organism than the grand co-ordinator, with initially almost minimal powers, envisaged by most of the Founding Fathers. Almost alone, Deakin saw clearly that the power of the purse would inevitably aggrandise the Centre *vis-à-vis* the States (he may even have exaggerated this a little), and indeed his own policies, and those of the Fisher and Curtin-Chifley Labor régimes, contributed not a little to this evolution, the latter fostering the stereotype of Labor as a party of movement, over against the parties of resistance, which now seems quaintly outmoded.

'The failure of federalism' distresses traditionalists. Certainly Australia adopted federalism for the same reason as did the classic exemplars of modern federations, the United States and Canada: to enable a number of communities, basically agrarian and mercantile, to add to their strength by union (and save on the overheads of administration) while reserving to the units the autonomy necessitated by local problems and traditions; this in a vast area with small and scattered nuclei of population, and in a context of emerging from colonialism while retaining the metropolitan values of representative government. But the socio-economic cast of the Australia of to-day differs more from that of the Australia of 1900 than the latter did from the America of 1800, or at least 1840; and it would be highly unrealistic to expect that in an age of two world-embracing wars and of dizzy technological change, the balance appropriate to 1900 could be statically preserved. What we could reasonably expect, given the Australian pragmatic tradition, would be that whatever happened to formal constitutional checks and

balances, to cope with its increasingly complex tasks the actual
business of government would evolve flexible and workable compromises expressed in *ad hoc* instrumentalities; and this is just what
has happened.

There is a wide range of such co-ordinating agencies. Some are
by way of specific joint agreements, such as the Snowy Mountains
Authority; some are 'shelter' institutions designed to protect the
central government of the day from undue importunities and
allegations of bias by the States (as we have seen, this is a standard
feature of Australian administration). Thus in 1910–12 Western
Australia and Tasmania argued, plausibly, that protectionism disfavoured their essentially rural economies and that they needed
assistance to maintain services at the level of the richer States, and
hence secured annual Federal grants. South Australia also was a
'claimant State' from 1929 to 1959, and to introduce some order
into the process the Commonwealth Grants Commission was set up
in 1933 to advise on allocation.

The most important co-ordinating device is the annual meeting
of the Premiers' Conference and the Loan Council, which brings
together the State Premiers and their Treasurers with the Commonwealth Prime Minister and his, to survey the needs and demands of
the States. Conference and Council meet at the same time, the
former to allocate the proceeds of uniform taxation, the latter to
decide on loans and borrowing policy. Naturally this slicing of the
cake is a lively affair; 'asking too high and offering too low is as
familiar in federal finance as in any oriental bazaar'. To each
State, of course, its own needs and demands are moderate and
precisely equal; to the Centre, they must be balanced against supply
– and it is probably to the good of the economy that the Commonwealth has a double plus a casting vote on the Council.

This free-for-all haggling is often unedifying; the States are
sometimes ferocious in mutual criticism, irrespective of party colour
and to the advantage of the Centre. But it is at least open, and
without it accusations of bias – a Liberal Centre penalising a Labor
State or *vice versa* – would probably be far more common; strident
as they are in presenting their own demands, other States would be
quick to detect and resent any such dangerous precedent. Ideally,
it might at first sight seem better still if the Grants Commission
principle were applied, especially if (as is sometimes hinted)
Queensland and Victoria were to become claimant States and South

Australia to revert to that status. However, there are snags: the Commission deals with moneys indefeasibly in the Commonwealth's gift, while uniform taxation and subordination of borrowing powers represent material surrenders by the States, and the further surrender of equal participation in the actual process of allocation would make the States completely creatures of the Commonwealth they created. Moreover, there would no longer be a quota of non-claimant States by which to evaluate the needs and performances of the claimants, which is the essence of the Grants Commission procedure.

The system makes for political irresponsibility, since State governments purchase electoral support by grandiose programmes, and can ascribe their failure to execute them to the niggardly Commonwealth and the greedy other States. For this reason, while State Premiers sometimes go through the motions of demanding the return of income taxing rights, they would probably be horrified if given them. Like arbitration and much else, the Loan Council approach is constantly under attack by the academically tidy-minded and (often very loudly) by those affected by adverse decisions; but the former cut no ice, and for the latter there is always another time.[1] Bruce Miller has even suggested, very plausibly, that in effect Conference and Council jointly fulfil a main function of the American Senate: to be 'the means through which regional interests operate to assert their demands'.[2]

Meanwhile, in assessing the growth of Commonwealth versus State powers, it is important to distinguish between the theoretically possible and the actuality imposed by a common-sense view of political feasibility. No more than anyone else do Federal statesmen wish to buy unnecessary trouble, and that would be the certain result of playing the game too hard. So it comes about that while the Commonwealth provides half of State revenues, less than a third of this moiety has strings attached. The imposition of conditions is doubtless increasing, but for a long time yet, and to an unusual extent, the States can call a lot of the tunes without paying the piper.

'New States'

Australian conservatives often seem to wish to put the clock back to an idealised 1901, without giving any idea as to how they would

---

[1] One hesitates to quote 'She'll do' again, but really it seems irresistible.
[2] *Op. cit.*, p. 160; cf. R. J. May on 'Politics and Gamesmanship in Australian Federal Finance', in H. Mayer, *op. cit.*, pp. 127–28.

go about this Utopian task. The most interesting approach is by way of 'New States', which in some entirely undefined manner would 'restore the balance of the Constitution'. The constitution explicitly provides for their creation – but only with the consent of the old State(s) affected. This at once robs the solution of much of its plausibility by inhibiting tampering with existing boundaries unless both States concerned agree; and in some cases – notably in the Riverina and as between South Australia and Victoria – it is precisely the existing boundaries which prevent a more rational organisation of area. But the prospect of joint assent at a relevant time is obviously pure fantasy. In two areas, where this consideration does not apply, New States movements are of some significance: northern Queensland, and New England in northern New South Wales.

Separatism in northern Queensland has an obvious root in mere distance – Townsville, central on the coast, is 700 air miles from Brisbane. It was strongest when the sugar plantations depended on indentured 'kanaka' labour; in 1891, indeed, the legislature briefly accepted a division of the State into three, but this was a snap vote on a mere resolution. Federation and the change to white (largely Italian) labour ruled out the development, still conceivable in the 'nineties, of a region based on a socio-economic 'peculiar institution' like that of the American South, and utterly unlike that of the rest of Australia; and with this vanished the most solid reason for separation. However, the excessive excentricity of Brisbane does lend point to the distance-plus-neglect argument, and separatism revives intermittently.

The New England movement is more active and more serious, and points up some general attitudes in rural Australia. It has held embryonic constitutional conventions, and in 1954 induced a number of Shires and Municipalities to disregard the disapproval of the State Labor government and hold local polls which returned handsome majorities for a new State. At the same time, it seems a little naive to point with pride to a century of unsuccessful existence: it suggests that, like Social Democracy in Imperial Germany, New Englandism is a satisfying but escapist habit of mind: 'How beautiful was the Republic, under the Empire.'

The core of New England propaganda is neglect of the north by Sydney, and such germs of truth as there may be in this are displayed with a high degree of magnification. Antipathy to 'socialistic domination' by the metropolis is also a good cry – in fact, some pamphlets devote pages to the menace of Communism in Asia before beginning to hint that Australia's security lies in more States. This almost hysterical anti-Labor bias of some (not all) New England agitation is self-defeating: it ensures an absence of response from the capital and weakens unity in New England. In fact, the movement is to some extent wrapped up in a mystique of Jeffersonian agrarianism: all the virtues are bush virtues, and the city is wicked *per se*. While not all New England supporters are Country Party, the two do go together; but of course Country Party leaders who have climbed to power largely on this sectional appeal, such as Earle Page and Fadden, remember when they get to Canberra that this is not a Federal but a State matter, and States' Rights work in reverse.

New England could indeed be a very workable State on the Australian scale; with 64,000 square miles, say 750,000 people, and the coal and industry of the Hunter valley. There indeed lies the rub: some New Englanders have always preferred not to include Newcastle – which after all is redder than Sydney – and since Greater Newcastle already includes about a third of the population of the proposed New State, once it also was freed from the domination of Sydney, it is difficult to see how anything could stop it from rising in turn to metropolitan dominance, even if the new capital were well away on the Tablelands. However, the point is now academic. In 1967 the Liberal-Country State government held the long-awaited referendum in the entire New England area. New Staters seem to have anticipated the referendum confident that it would be successful. For years it had been talked of as the magic key to advance; although of course it was recognised that a further State-wide poll would be necessary, it was not thought possible that a solid New England could or would be coerced into unwilling union. Reasonably good, sometimes handsome, majorities for a New State were secured on the Tablelands and the north coast, both Country Party strongholds; but Newcastle and the lower Hunter would have none of it, by even more striking 'No' votes. The Jeffersonian anti-urban bias, the contempt of the city, rebounded. Nothing remained for the New Staters but to affirm that they would continue trying, on the more restricted basis which probably conforms to their real desires (but is also a much weaker proposition). But after such a set-back, it will be difficult to work up momentum again.

New England, with or even without Newcastle, is far and away the best-found of any projected New State, including those which straddle existing boundaries, and would be reasonably viable; it may even come about, a long time hence. But one cannot see that the addition of a seventh or an eighth State would make any substantial difference to the working of Australian federalism or quasi-federalism.

Unification?

Ideally, the most rational organisation of the Australian space would probably be that with which the ALP has (long ago) platonically flirted: a unitary state with provinces. This could mean a smoother machinery for continental problems, more real local participation in local problems, the emergence of sections in the American sense, corresponding to real and homogeneous regional interests and to some extent offsetting the prevailing and increasing cultural uniformity. The main difficulty – on a theoretical plane – is that the existing metropolises would not easily fit; both quantitatively and qualitatively, their resources and demands would be excessively different from those of the other units, and they could become in effect so many troublesome free cities. On a practical plane, there is no visible basis of support for such a recasting: it was an ALP idea, but an aberrant one, and anyone who can see that party's State machines yielding an iota of their power and patronage is a visionary indeed. The other parties are in like case, though the nationalist 'new look' of the Country Party, if it is more than window-dressing, would not be incompatible with such a development.

But all this is wishful thinking in the academic wilderness; the Australian way of life is just not adventurous in these matters, and probably nothing short of a really shattering crisis – say the discovery of a cheap synthetic which really was a substitute for wool – could work any really radical change; and in that event the change would not be likely to be democratic and high-minded. And the system, which in many respects looks cumbrous and illogical, does work reasonably well, in a fashion agreeable to the Australian political mode which at once moulds it and is moulded by it.

The States are there: they are historical entities incarnating strong and multiplex traditions and interests. It would be difficult to maintain that there is a comparable mystique of the Commonwealth. The sense of 'The State' as distinct from that of the various States seems weak; it is perhaps growing, but so far almost confined to restricted élites in the Commonwealth Public Service and the armed forces. This is not to say that people regard themselves as Tasmanians or Victorians or Queenslanders first and Australians only afterwards: far from it. They have an intense loyalty to Australia – as a continent and a culture, one might say as a social commonwealth – with a small c; a much milder loyalty to Australia as the political Commonwealth. Perhaps this is in part a reflection of geographical isolation; there are no international land frontiers in all the 3,000,000 square miles, no neighbour powers to compel the internal cohesion which comes from centuries of tradition of external differentiation and conflict. With the rising challenge of Asia and the concomitant 'part of Asia' mythos, this may well change, radically, before the end of this century.

Chapter 11

The Party Structure

USTRALIA PRESENTS the very peculiar feature of a two-party
system run by three parties. It is not a very happy *ménage
à trois.*

Only two governmental choices are possible, Liberal-Country
Party coalition or Labor, and yet the apparently logical conclusion
is not drawn: there is no prospect that the Country Party will
surrender its independence and merge with the Liberals. Entrenched
in its rural strongholds, it has been content to remain a sectional
rather than a national party and by consequence to be a perpetual
junior partner. Yet the electoral situations (p. 175) enable it to
demand a high price for its subordination, in the form of more than
its fair share of portfolios, and this in return reinforces its independence. While some Country leaders would be outstanding in any
political company, this principle of near-parity brings into Cabinet
some men of very moderate ability, and keeps them there. It is an
easy road to the top.

This faithfully reflects some characteristic traits of Australian
political life: opportunism, distrust of intellectually ordered system,
strong economic sectionalism. These things are as strong, or
stronger, on the other side of the House. In its origins, and to a
large extent in its organisation, the Australian Labor Party has been
avowedly based on economic sectionalism, that of the Trade Union
movement, although this sectional interest has been strong enough
numerically, and widely enough distributed, to make the party
essentially more national (though not more nationalist) than is the
Country Party.

The Australian Labor Party

There can be no simple description of the Australian Labor Party
and its workings; especially at State level, one gets the impression
that, even more than is normal in politics, the ALP is like an ice-
berg – only one-eighth is visible above the surface. (One might add

that in the recent past it has seemed subject to melting as it drifted into the warmer waters of affluence.) Basically, however, it seems fair to say that historically its strength has been founded on its close nexus with the Trade Unions. But to-day this by itself is just not good enough. If the ALP is not to drift into mere sectionalism, it must come to terms with the challenge of the new technology with its ever-increasing armies of white-collar employees; the current ethos of suburbia is not very susceptible to the old ideology, at times almost syndicalist in feeling, of solidarity and mateship in the class struggle. Affluence has brought the party to a crisis perhaps more fundamental than that of the great depression, though paradoxically one not altogether dissimilar, since the choice may once more lie between electorally expedient reformism and radicalisation.

The ALP machines vary in detail from State to State, but a common characteristic is the weakness of the electoral branches *vis-à-vis* the unions, a weakness which is built into some of the State constitutions. Branches are strikingly weaker, unions stronger, than in the British Labour Party, even of the pre-Wilson era. This is one factor in the very obvious lack of practising intellectuals in Labor politics, again a sharp contrast to Britain: there are plenty of intellectual fellow-travellers, but singularly few in the parliamentary parties, and still fewer in the Executives where power is concentrated. This has made for purity of doctrine, though not conspicuously for unity; but it has put the ALP at a great disadvantage in stating a case with general appeal. There have been no long-range reconnaissance groups like the Fabians and hence, since 1949, the ALP has most conspicuously failed to be the 'party of initiative' it was once believed to be. Like Mr Dooley's Democrats, it can only deplore and denounce; the other side has asserted and affirmed. Even within this defensive stance, in the last two decades the ALP has chased after new questions and caught up with them only when they have been settled by default, as with Vietnam conscription and State Aid for church schools.

Considering their importance not only in the ALP but in the national life, there seems singularly little academic attention paid to the Trade Unions, except historically.[1] There are about 350

[1] It is passing strange that the first really wide-ranging modern sociological survey, the otherwise admirable *Australian Society* (ed. A. F. Davies and S. Encel, Cheshire, Melbourne, 1965), barely mentions them. They have one index reference in the Commonwealth *Year Book*, which at least gives the basic statistics.

unions with a total of over 2,000,000 members, rather over 60 per
cent of the workforce. Many are very small, but about a hundred of
the larger are grouped in the Australian Council of Trade Unions,
again over 60 per cent of all unionists, though the largest single
union, the Australian Workers' Union, did not affiliate until 1967.
The AWU caters largely for rural and especially pastoral workers,
and its influence has been great – at times dominant – in State
politics, most consistently in Queensland but at times in Western
and South Australia.

One cannot generalise about union affairs. Some unions, like the
AWU and the Ironworkers', are definitely right-wing politically –
which need not exclude a fair degree of militancy; others, such as
the Seamen's and until very recently the Waterside Workers'
Federation, are virtually Communist pocket boroughs; one national
Union, the Federated Clerks, and several small Victorian ones still
support the Democratic Labor Party. Their leaders are normally
intensely practical and opportunist, adepts in the intricacies of
arbitration (which gives them a very powerful leverage into all
sectors of economic life), and very keen on the scent of anything,
however slight, which might be or be made to seem a derogation of
the rights of labour – or more correctly of their own members. In
this of course they are only exercising the Australian talent for
empirical bureaucracy, and exemplifying that curious anomaly
whereby the Australians, who are as individuals the most generous
of people and susceptible to the soft sell, yet become, once three or
four are banded together as an economic group, extraordinarily
grasping and parochial. This applies whether they are graziers,
dairymen, doctors, builders, returned servicemen, wharfies, or even
perhaps professors.

Since the unions are the financial mainstay of the ALP, they
naturally dominate the conferences which elect State Executives.
Conference or Executive nominates six members from each State
to the Federal Conference, which is formally the ruling body of the
party; it meets biennially and delegates normal operating to a
Federal Executive of two from each State meeting several times a
year. The State Executives meet much more frequently than the
Federal and are more highly organised – indeed, until 1963, the
Federal Secretary was always a State official, and even now there is
only a rudimentary Federal secretariat. Financially, the Federal
Executive is a poor relation dependent on doles of capitation fees

from the State machines. The State parties have thus large licence to go their own sweet ways, at least between Federal Conferences; and when the Federal Executive does exercise itself to discipline a State party, that means that a traumatic crisis has come to a head and the consequences may be devastating, as in the Lang and Democratic Labor breakaways.

In the circumstances, it is not surprising that intra-State factional struggles for power and patronage often obscure larger issues of national party effectiveness. The parliamentary caucus has autonomy in the election of its leader and the selection of those who are to be ministers, their particular assignments remaining with the leader; but even he is only rarely on the Federal Executive, and then only as a State nominee. The responsibility of the parliamentary party to the Federal Conference or Council is an obvious necessity in any party; but the extremely open, not to say crude, way in which the ALP Federal Executive has at times exercised its authority can be very damaging to the party image. The spectacle of the parliamentary leader, Arthur Calwell, in the middle of the 1963 general election, waiting in the lobby of a Canberra hotel, while behind closed doors 'thirty-six faceless men' deliberated on his instructions, lost nothing in the telling from Liberal and Country platforms. Hence, doubtless, his decision a couple of years later to accept a Victorian nomination to the Executive, to be in turn criticised for becoming a prisoner of the doctrinaire left-wingers of the Melbourne Trades Hall.

This union domination through the Executives is the more serious in that there is no reciprocity: the unions are very sensitive to suggestions of 'outside interference'. Yet, in Victoria at least, this does not always seem to apply to Communist interference, provided only that it is disguised by the device of a 'unity ticket'. Clearly Communists cannot in principle be debarred from Trade Union activity, in which they are not only militant but conscientious, for their own purposes, and skilled. In some unions the possibilities of rigged ballots are checked by supervision of voting by Commonwealth arbitration authorities, either optionally or by legal compulsion; but apart from malpractices, simply by working hard on dull day-to-day routine and on genuine or not-so-genuine union issues, Communists can secure influence out of all proportion to their negligible quantity electorally. A few unions, like the AWU, have barred Communists from office through their constitutions or rules.

Known members of the Communist Party[1] cannot, of course, be elected to ALP bodies, but they can and often do hold important union positions. On the principle – difficult to deny – that the best union activists deserve to be elected to the Trades Councils, they campaign for lists – 'unity tickets' – which include Communists, known or unknown as such, and ALP left-wingers whose tacit consent may or may not have been given. From such points of vantage they are able to exert indirect, but sometimes considerable, influence on ALP policy at grass-roots level.

The attempt to fight these tactics by similar ones on the part of anti-Communist Industrial Groups, largely inspired in turn by an outside body – the Catholic-oriented 'Movement' – in the early 'fifties produced a strong reaction from the Federal Executive, resulting in the breakaway of the Democratic Labor Party, which has remained an enemy so far irreconcilable and, owing to the electoral system, very powerful in a negative sense (below, p. 210). Many would-be friends of Labor wish that action against extremists on the Left had been no less vigorous. It is true that unity tickets have been denounced time after time (often when the damage was done) even in Victoria, and that even in Victoria this seems to be having an effect; but the apparently logical answer – an ALP ticket – is denounced by militants as tampering with union independence; this sometimes from open or crypto-Communists. 'This animal is very wicked: it defends itself when it is attacked.'

Obviously such anomalies, and the parliamentary difficulties arising from the rigidity of the machine, are as obvious to thoughtful Labor people as they are to candid friends and enemies; and the *débâcle* of the 1966 election, which reduced ALP Representatives to forty-two, is leading to a long-overdue setting of the house in order. It is to be hoped that the sense of shock will not be dulled too quickly; but for the hard-core professionals of the State machines, the internal power complex seems to obscure longer views. One factor that must be reckoned with – and the new parliamentary leader, Gough Whitlam, has stressed this – is the changing pattern of unionism itself, with the rise of professional associations of salaried workers.[2] It is clear that much more hard and rigorous thinking will be necessary if Labor is to have a coherent and

___

[1] Strictly there are two parties, following the Moscow-Peking split.
[2] It is perhaps significant that the Federal Clerks is the only large union adhering to the DLP.

generally acceptable programme; but there are ominous signs that some of the old guard subconsciously think of the ALP as a sort of national reserve which will be called upon when crisis comes, and which must guard its purity till then. Such an extremist view would not be clearly enunciated even if consciously held; and it must be conceded that such 'Left' leaders as Dr Cairns have a point when they ask whether the ALP must become merely a slightly more radical Liberal Party, and whether this would not deprive the electors of any real choice between policies.

Unfortunately, this reasonable and serious consideration tends to become confused with a doctrinaire adherence to old slogans, and to obscure the extent to which there is legitimate common ground between parties in a democratic state. The official nationalisation plank of 1921, for instance, is in itself innocuous enough; but its iteration is now economically irrelevant and confirms the impression of an old tired party living on its capital. There is in fact a good deal of nationalisation in Australia already, even if, for constitutional reasons, it is State rather than Federal; and not all of it has come from Labor governments. We have seen that the tendency of the Menzies régime was rather to make the clock tick more slowly than to turn its hands backwards. There is no reason to suppose that a firm policy of positive national development, in accord with Labor ethos and traditions, cannot be devised; and there is a good deal of reason to suppose that if it were devised, there is a large residual feeling for Labor which could once more be activated. Certainly many not in the ALP wish ardently, and anxiously, for the re-emergence of a party which could provide an alternative to the régime which has prevailed since 1949 and which, partisan considerations apart, has been in power too long for the good of a democratic political system. These people are not in the ALP because, on past form, they are reasonably doubtful of their welcome and of the extent to which they would have influence comparable to their contributions; and indeed their adhesion would, if allowed to be effective, modify the general cast of Labor thinking.

The remedy to the apathy of an affluent electorate is not in more apathy. But if Labor is to rehabilitate itself, not only must such scandals as unity tickets be done away with once for all, not only must machinery be overhauled and some more reasonable compromise between union-dominated base staffs and the parliamentary front line be found, but there must be real forward thinking. In its internal affairs the ALP is highly professionalised – too much so for new ideas to have much chance; but when it comes to dealing with wide national issues and establishing programmes to deal with them, it seems all too often hopelessly amateur. The other parties are little better, but then they are in possession.

Even on the line of waiting for a crisis which would show up Liberal-Country Party bankruptcy, not less but more, and more imaginative, forward thinking is needed. To secure it would involve a retreat from anti-intellectualism, which can still find surprisingly vehement, not to say bitter, expression from people high in ALP counsels. It would need less loyalty not to the party, but to the maxim that the party is always right and hence that outsiders are not worth listening to. Unless some such change happens – and it is a drastic one – then Labor will remain indefinitely in the wilderness, or come to power only in a context of unmanageable crisis. Either case would be to the national peril. Fortunately, the post-Calwell leadership seems well aware of this.

The Liberals

To some extent the Liberals can be considered a residual party when the more sectional labour and rural interests have been taken out and looked after by the ALP and the Country Party. This is apparent in its origins, for when, at the ALP's high tide of 1945, Menzies sought to establish a national union of non-Labor forces he had to weld together no fewer than eighteen parties and leagues, while the Country Party held itself strictly aloof. Much more than any other, the Liberal Party has been associated with one leader, Menzies himself; its structures are simpler than those of the ALP, if not so loose as those of the Country Party; and it makes much play with its claim to 'independence', both of extra-parliamentary pressures on it as a party, and as regards the parliamentary discipline of its members.

As we have seen (p. 176), the parliamentary system makes the latter aspect of its independence more nominal than real; and the former is also subject to qualification, especially on the State level and more especially when things are not going well.[1] In fact, it would not be very extreme to balance the ALP's 'thirty-six faceless men' with an unknown number of men nameless to the general

[1] This is brought out in detail in K. West, *Power in the Liberal Party*, Cheshire, Melbourne, 1965.

public, in say Collins House at Melbourne, the Adelaide Club, and various Chambers of Commerce and Manufacturers. Basically, then, the Liberal Party is the representative of non-labour and non-rural vested interests; but if it is thus a residual party, the residuum is a large one. There is also, of course, no one monolithic business interest, so that the party's role is quite as much that of a co-ordinator as an initiator, and indeed on larger economic issues it might well be argued that the real initiators are to be found in the higher reaches of the Public Service, particularly Treasury and Trade. On the whole, particularly at Federal level, the party takes its responsibilities seriously and has supplied competent if uninspired government.

Although it might be said that the Liberal Party is the nearest analogue to a British party (and specifically the Conservatives), the analogy is deficient in several aspects. Conservative as the party is, it is hardly Tory since there is really no strong central traditionalist element in Australian political and social life, no real Establishment – at least on the national scale, though there are of course pockets of such tradition in the armed services, in some grazing families, in a few 'public' (really private) schools, and perhaps incipiently in the Commonwealth Public Service, while South Australia is as Establishment as can be. But the general ethos is opportunist, and the compartmentalisation of the parties between the States serves to erode what little ideological consistency there is.

If challenged to state their positive contribution, Liberals would fall back on the virtues of free enterprise and competition, and they do the best they can to support these; but as we saw in Chapter 8, it is not always much of a best. In South Australia, for instance, where there is a single joint Liberal and Country League holding power from 1938 to 1965, its leader Sir Thomas Playford pushed through State nationalisation of electricity against the Upper House; in Queensland the Liberals are actually the most sectional of the three parties, being practically confined to metropolitan and large town electorates, and there they find their account in supporting compulsory Trade Unionism, which is anathema to the general Liberal stance and indeed to the formal Federal platform. All the eloquent Liberal (and liberal) generalities of Sir Robert Menzies were of little account beside the practical demands of the alliance between highly protectionist Chambers of Manufacturers, the great monopolies, and a Country Party which is anything but *laissez faire* when it comes to bolstering rural industries.

Post-war demographic changes strongly favour the Liberals. The increasing metropolitan and urban concentration will inevitably weaken the Country Party base, even with rurally biased electoral redistributions; but within the great crities, increasing suburbanisation weakens the ALP, whose major reliance was on the tight-knit loyalties of the inner-city industrial areas, now in relative decline. The Liberal image of getting on in the world has a marked appeal to the ever-growing white collar strata of suburbia; and the lack of a sectional ideology is a distinct advantage in the pragmatic climate of affluence. A non-ideological residual party is almost inevitably opportunist; gestures cost it little heart-searching, and less than either of its rivals is the Liberal Party burdened by a pedantic adherence to party shibboleths and traditions: in this sense it is hardly conservative at all. The Liberals were the first to drop from their platform support in set terms for 'White Australia', in 1960; after the 1961 credit squeeze had brought them to the brink of electoral disaster, they simply appropriated the opposition's clothes;[1] in 1963 Menzies adroitly introduced a small and apparently innocuous measure of 'State Aid' to non-State (dominantly Catholic) schools – merely grants for science laboratories – and thereby threw the ALP, with its twin tradition of Catholic support and egalitarian public education, into complete disarray.

One weakness at least – Sir Robert's sentimental over-emphasis on the 'British to the boot-heels' tradition – has vanished with him; doubtless his successor, Harold Holt, overdid the turn to America with his 'All the way with LBJ', but the turn itself conforms well to the widely diffused popular image of the United States as something Australia could and should grow up to, a genially helpful elder brother rather than a fussy Mother Country. So long as things are nice as they are, a party devoted to minor improvements in things as they are is in clover, and of all the parties the Liberals seem most assured of a comfortable future given 'normalcy'. Whether the times are or will remain 'normal' is another question, perhaps not admitting of the complacent answers which seem to come naturally to Liberal spokesmen.

---

[1] '... in one of the most dramatic somersaults of this highly gymnastic Government, Mr Menzies tossed out the entire philosophy of hard money ... in favour of almost the complete policy of the Labour Party', *Australian Financial Review*, 8 Feb. 1962, cited K. West, *op. cit.*, p. 256.

The Country Party

The Country Party has come some way from its rather crude agrarian beginnings – intolerant, xenophobic, and grossly anti-intellectual or even anti-intelligence – or even its adolescence, when its leaders could be succinctly described as 'men like the farmers whose interests they were sponsoring, one-eyed and single-minded horse-traders'.[1] Its maturity and sophistication, on the Federal level, are largely due to John McEwen, since 1956 very able Minister for Trade, who in 1962 seemed quite likely to succeed Menzies as Prime Minister, despite the handicap of belonging to the minority party.

Even more than the others, the CP is less a single party than a federation of State parties, and these carry out a remarkably independent line.[2] In Western Australia local electoral *rapprochements* with the ALP at Liberal expense are not unknown, and in Victoria – where the old radicalism of the mallee wheat farmers is not entirely forgotten – there was until 1950 a real three-party system, with, as well as Country-Liberal coalitions, CP and ALP on occasion supporting an ALP or CP administration. Since 1955 a Liberal government has held power, and the CP has been in opposition, an opposition at times almost as hostile as that of the ALP. In Queensland also local Country-Liberal relations give rise to friction. The Federal Council of the party has not much disciplinary power, and the Federal parliamentary party is in a much more autonomous position, both formally and effectively, than are the rival parties.

The CP is sectional not only in its opponents' propaganda, but in its own formulations, and probably still more in its intra-party ethos and its image of itself. For external consumption, however, this is neatly turned, by translating 'sectional' into 'specialist'; the party claims, and not without reason, to be the policy expert in all that concerns rural industries, and then points to the dominant share of primary products in export values, saying in effect 'Neglect us, and our special claims, at Australia's peril.' So far, fair enough: setting aside the irrational agrarian mystique and phobias which persist at the local level (and no party should be judged by its hard core of dumb loyalty), this is a rational and, given the export

[1] K. West, *op. cit.*, p. 220.

[2] In South Australia, there is no State Country Party; the strong rural gerrymander enables a Liberal-and-Country League to work effectively. Nor has there been a CP in Tasmania since 1925, though attempts are made from time to time to reconstruct one, mainly by Victorian influence in the north of the island.

figures, a reasonably valid claim. But where do we go from here? The interventionist principles, the 'Socialism without doctrines' going back to the selectors' problems of last century (pp. 47–48), marketing boards and export subsidies and price support, these have all been built into the Australian policy, and this is the party's achievement. In a sense, it has been too successful:

> ... it has forced the other parties to recognise that country people have problems which can be solved by political action, and both the Labor and Liberal parties now ... produce rural policies. It has gained many of its objectives, and the preservation of these gains is settled policy for all parties. As a result ... the Country Party finds it ever more difficult to explain why a purely country party is still needed.[1]

And all the while the great cities become greater, the countryside loses numbers (in many areas absolutely), and the Liberals in their hearts would like nothing better than to get rid of this nuisance and demanding ally and have the straight fight that Labor also desires. As Aitkin remarks, 'If present trends continue ... only tampering with the electoral system can save the Country Party from one day discovering that the Liberals no longer need its support to govern.' The figures of the 1966 election – 61 Liberals and 21 Country against 52 and 20 in 1963, may be the writing on the wall.

Faced with this prospect, the party in 1966 adopted a much less sectional platform. The old Jeffersonian innuendoes that cities and merchants and industrialism were little more than necessary evils, parasitic on the productive countryside, vanished. Cherished traditions such as the British connection, universal non-selective military service, 'White Australia', New States, even the banning of the Communist Party, were played down. In at least two respects – the future of New Guinea and a demand for more Australian equity in overseas investments – the platform is more 'advanced' than the Liberals', and these are matters in which, in the past, nobody would have looked for a lead to the CP. The old Adam appeared, naturally enough, in a demand for a 20 per cent numerical weighting in favour of country electorates. Apart from formal platform utterances, the stance of the party – at any rate of the rank-and-file –

---

[1] Don Aitkin, in H. Mayer (ed.), *Australian Politics* (Cheshire, Melbourne, 1966), p. 303.

probably remains reactionary, especially on such social issues as capital and corporal punishment and censorship; and it still hankers after a depressing conformity of manners and opinion. Nor has it ever yielded an iota on its special sectional interests, such as the protection of (often marginal) producers like the dairy or tobacco farmers.

All this change bears the stamp of McEwen, and would provide an admirable programme for a progressive party of the centre. For external consumption, it is very good; would it really be swallowed easily by the faithful? Is it not more likely that its constructive elements – like the old sectional ones – will be caught up by the Liberals and the ALP, leaving the CP to nurse its old-style bush agrarianism and its present relative electoral position, which is precarious in the long run? The programme is national; the name, the symbol, the myth are sectional, and sectional in an outmoded way: 'Change the name Country Party to Development Party, and who knows what allegiances it might eventually attract?'[1] But to become a truly national party of development, the CP would have to leave the bush and descend from the Tablelands to fight metropolitan electorates on a national scale, not as an occasional manoeuvre in one State. Quite apart from the risks of wrecking the alliance with the already restive Liberals, the activist core of CP support is still, in the last resort, self-regarding, backward-looking, based on an agrarianism distrustful of metropolitan contamination –

> A certain manner of knowing how to live,
> The pastoral rebellion of the earth
> Against machines . . .

So it is unlikely that the Country Party, an expression of values widely diffused and yet parochial, indeed in nothing so national as in its acceptance of a tough hard-headed down-to-earth economic sectionalism, can provide the new leadership which Australia badly needs. At best, the new programme warrants the continued independence of the party as a leaven within the coalition; even so, McEwen and one or two younger men apart, its leaders seem to have much more earthiness than yeast in their composition.

The Democratic Labor Party

No less sectional, but utterly different in origins and ethos, is the newest and in many ways the most interesting of the parties. The

[1] *Canberra Times*, 25 Oct. 1966.

Democratic Labor Party is a new and disturbing element in the political spectrum, not to be written off as just a breakaway Catholic faction of Labor, though it is undeniably Catholic-oriented and has to some extent reopened the old sectarian cleavage between Rome and the rest.

British observers, forgetting for instance the linkage between radicalism and Dissent, seem to find any correlation between religious and political loyalties so novel and aberrant, perhaps even a little indecent, that they have overplayed the importance of this cleavage. At bottom it was perhaps as much nationalist – the Irish underdog versus the 'Saxon' overlord – as credal; in some areas the squatter-selector struggle carried more than a hint of this. In two phases only – the debates of last century on denominational or secular education, and the 1917 conscription crisis – have religious considerations or influences had much direct effect on great political issues, as distinct from minor political patronage. In 1917, clearly Irish nationalism was more to the point than religion as such, and as we have seen (p. 75) the role of Archbishop Mannix has been exaggerated. And that the ALP has never been a Roman Catholic party or pressure group *tout court* is shown by the fact that it not only accepted but still defends a State system of secular education alongside voluntary denominational schools. About 82 per cent of these schools and their pupils are Roman Catholic, yet the ALP is the only party still reluctant to support State Aid, a singular position only explicable by the persistence of old radical tradition, and probably also by a doctrinaire refusal by the left wing to come to terms with anything sponsored by other parties, especially the DLP.

The 1955 crisis over the Industrial Groups was most catastrophic in Victoria, where after an unusually grimy factional struggle the ALP lost by defection or expulsion two-thirds of the State Executive, two-thirds of the branches, several affiliated unions, two dozen State or Federal parliamentarians, and £17,000 of party funds. These members had lost their seats by 1958, but the dissidents were confirmed by the State Supreme Court as legal successors to the old Victorian ALP and its physical assets. Elsewhere losses were contained, except in Queensland where in 1957 the State ALP split itself on basically similar issues, and in so doing ended a Labor régime which had lasted, with one interval of three years in the 'thirties, since 1915. The new Queensland Labor Party, now merged in the DLP, took with it the Premier, nine of his ten ministers, and twenty-four parliamentarians, all but one of whom had lost their seats by 1963. But while the ALP was thus able to deal with the defectors as individuals, it has been quite unable to liquidate them as the collective DLP.

In all this, but especially in Victoria, a main role was played by B. A. Santamaria, leader of the National Civic Council, a 'Catholic Action' type group; not formally a member of the DLP, his place in its councils might be compared to that of Mahatma Gandhi in those of the Indian National congress: influence amounting to power, but no formal responsibility. It may be added that in either case this agreeable position is owed to superior powers of thinking and leadership. Victoria is still the chief DLP stronghold, and here, until the death at ninety-nine of Archbishop Mannix in 1963, the Roman Catholic hierarchy strongly supported the DLP, and is still at least benevolent; elsewhere ecclesiastical favour is less warm, and in some dioceses it is replaced by disapprobation. The DLP is definitely not just a clerical party, any more than the old ALP was; amongst its leaders it has some Protestants (now and then they seem uneasy), its support by the hierarchy is far from complete, and its policies, while in accord with a general Catholic philosophy, are by no means specifically Catholic demands, except for State Aid which it shares with Liberals and Country Party.[1] Nevertheless, the party membership is dominantly Catholic, and its ideology is clearly inspired by the Santamaria interpretation of church teaching.

Apart from this, there is some evidence that the DLP has a certain appeal to young people weary of the platitudes and dreary bickering of the older parties. Its propaganda, especially on TV, has been adroit, full-blooded, and not too much hampered by scruple: consciously or not, it has played hard on atavistic fears of the Yellow Peril. It has cultivated the naturalised migrant vote, claiming marked success with eastern Europeans, less with Italians, little with Greeks – for fairly obvious reasons in each case. It has the dynamism which comes from the possession of an ideology in the midst of a chaos of expediencies, the sense of being a 'movement' of people set apart by their mission, a feeling which the ALP lost long ago. (In the long run, of course, with realisation of the sterility of being merely a veto party, this sense may go sour.) Whatever one

[1] Indeed, in its whole-hearted ardour for the Vietnam war, the DLP seems distinctly out of step with Catholic opinion elsewhere, including the Vatican.

may think of its premises, it might claim that it provides – or Santamaria provides for it – hard argument on fundamentals, with little or no hedging.

The policy itself is not very impressive. The DLP's basic *raison d'être* is simply and solely anti-Communism, but it realises that a simple negative is not enough. Hence it has developed, with some success, specific lines of approach on a variety of peripheral issues, the choice of which reflects its relict Labor radicalism: social services, needed reform of hire purchase legislation, Northern Development, decentralisation, more attention to migrants and their problems. These are laudable enough, but were the DLP to arrive at a position of some governmental responsibility it would find them extremely difficult to square with the added financial burden implied by the party's demand for major strengthening of defence. On the home front, 'Democratic Labor has dropped the Marxist objective of socialisation, and has adopted decentralisation or spreading of ownership widely by co-operatives, home ownership, breaking up of big estates, and so on. Democratic Labor opposes both State monopoly and private monopoly.'[1] This is even vaguer than Guild Socialism; there is a hint too of peasant agrarianism, and the National Civic Council, if not the DLP itself, has toyed with the idea of co-operative agricultural settlements of immigrants with a peasant background, thus fostering at once decentralisation, closer settlement, immigration, and perhaps irrigation. This is not very realistic, and critics were not slow to pounce on the suggestion of pocket boroughs, since the correlation of peasant Europe with Catholic Europe is obvious enough to friend and foe.

Nothing so vague, however, when it comes to foreign policy. Here the line is stern: everything must be subordinated to the containment of China, and secondarily the defeat of Communism everywhere. It is fair to add that this attitude would apply also to a nationalist Indonesia, a militarist Japan, or a non-Communist nationalist China were they actively expansionist, but defence against such threats would be matter of military and foreign policy; as against to-day's China, with its Fifth Column in Australia itself, 'self-defence involves internal political action as well'.[2] The DLP

---

[1] DLP Speakers' Notes for 1961 Victorian election, cited J. Jupp, *Australian Party Politics* (Melbourne Univ. Press, 1964), p. 105.

[2] B. A. Santamaria, 'We are Determined to Survive', in H. Mayer, *op. cit.*, pp. 475–96.

is fiercely critical of wheat sales to China, and demands much more aid to India; there is no more ardent advocate of the American alliance in its most hawkish aspects, and it also favours the development of an independent nuclear capacity. Although all this would mean a degree of austerity that one cannot see the Australian electorate accepting in advance of crisis, the party can act as a ginger group and may already have had some indirect effect on attitudes in the Liberal-Country coalition.

Structurally the DLP is organised on standard democratic lines; State divisions have more autonomy than in the ALP, but unlike the other parties, it has abandoned State parity in the Federal organisation in favour of a broadly proportional representation – which naturally favours the Victorian core. Its parliamentary representation is minimal, though four Federal Senators out of sixty-six (largely by the accident of proportional representation) provide a *point d'appui* when divisions are close. But, like the only other ideological party in Australia, its prime enemy the Communist Party,[1] the DLP does not worry too much about parliamentary numbers. Its power rests on a disciplined use of its voting preferences.

There is here a paradox. In a sense, the DLP is the most principled of Australian parties, and it would disclaim any totalitarian intent. Santamaria himself, calling for stringent internal security measures which would debar unions with Communist officials from representing workers in war production or transport, and individual Communists from such employment, states specifically that this would not 'interfere with the legal existence of either of the Communist parties . . . or with the right of trade unions generally to elect Communist officials'.[2] The DLP is then not Fascist; though one may recall Huey Long's dictum that if Fascism came to America, it would call itself Democracy. Yet it is impossible to avoid the apprehension that the DLP's tactics will be found in their working to be fundamentally anti-democratic.

Alone of Labor breakaways, the DLP has not withered away or come to terms within a few years. It has retained a first preference vote of 6 to 10 per cent in most States; in Victoria 15 per cent or

---

[1] There is believed to be also an Australian Republican Party; at least letters in the Press are signed on its behalf. But its politics seem emotional rather than ideological.

[2] In H. Mayer, *op. cit.*, at p. 493.

more. This is not enough to ensure parliamentary representation; but for the first time a continuing Australia-wide party has seized upon the possibility, inherent in the system of compulsory preferential voting, of exercising a permanent veto; and its ideological cast has ensured that its preferences have been distributed in accordance with the party line, with little leakage except in New South Wales. Should DLP discipline hold, and failing a most unlikely *rapprochement* with the ALP, this would mean that a body of voters, never less than 40 and often over 50 per cent of the electors, was disfranchised in the sense that its party, the ALP, was debarred from the chance of forming a government.

Party futures

The DLP's lesson in undemocracy has not gone unnoticed. In the 1966 Federal elections the Liberal Reform Group, an *ad hoc* organisation financially backed by a few businessmen opposed to participation in the Vietnam war, put up twenty-two candidates. Four weeks before the elections the Group did not exist, but in New South Wales it actually outpolled the DLP.

This could lead to a polarisation of politics, with extremist groups on either wing of the central parties forcing them into more radical attitudes or manoeuvres under threat of withholding preferences. As against this risk of rigidity in attitudes leading to the permanent exclusion of one major party, a recent tactic of the DLP in Victoria – the presentation of adroitly differentiated demands to all three major parties – might lead to an intolerable degree of bargaining and instability. Either way, the strain on parliamentary institutions, at least on the essentially two-party system, might prove excessive in a crisis.

The present position is paradoxical. On the one hand, there is really not a fundamental cleavage on domestic issues between the three major parties, though in effect the DLP is trying to make one. Emphases differ to a healthy degree, but major policy differences can be readily accommodated within the normal working of a democratic two-party system. As regards foreign affairs, where apparently minor changes in implementation may have incalculable effects, recent developments in the ALP have considerably reduced the likelihood of that party, if in power, operating any major reversal. On the other hand, the success of the DLP in freezing Labor into permanent opposition is far from a healthy sign, though it might conceivably contribute to a loosening-up of the present unduly static electoral situation by giving play to restiveness in the Liberal-Country alliance. In this regard, the viability of the DLP and the 'new look' of the Country Party suggest the possibility, remote as it may seem, of an intriguing realignment. After all, the two parties have at bottom a good deal in common, not least an essential xenophobia and some degree of antipathy to 'advanced' trends in modern social and cultural life. If China stopped buying wheat...

The central problem is still, however, what will happen to the ALP. Sooner or later, presumably, there will have to be a change of government at the centre; it will be hazardous if the present electoral complex lumbers along, like an ill-lubricated machine building up internal stresses, until a change must take place in an atmosphere of crisis and radical polarisation. There is some insurance in the inherent pluralism of a federal system.

Chapter 12

The Problem of New Guinea

NEW GUINEA is the world's second largest island, after Greenland; the eastern portion is controlled by Australia and (with adjacent islands such as New Britain and Bougainville) covers 184,000 square miles and has over two million people. The Indonesian portion, West Irian, is nearly as large in area but has less than half the population. The only larger areas still under colonial rule are Portuguese Angola and Moçambique. Such British, French, and Dutch overseas holdings as remain are much fragmented, and it is thus paradoxically true that Australia, Indonesia, and Portugal might well be ranked as the last major colonial powers.

That twelve million people should hold a continent of three million square miles, next to crowded monsoon Asia, may seem anomalous but is by no means without its justification, basically on historical grounds. But in this age the extension of Australian control over a region so manifestly un-Australian (though also un-Asian) can only be justified by the development of its resources and the advancement of its peoples.

Here any parallel with Indonesia in the west of the island breaks down. West Irian is not Indonesian ethnically, linguistically, or culturally, despite a long history of contact at spots around the coasts, and Indonesia's possession carries with it a responsibility for peoples still in a state of tutelage: so far this possession could be regarded as old-style colonialism. But if the advancement of the peoples and their self-determination might mean that they could enter as an equal and integral unit into the 'metropolitan' power, that is obviously very much easier of attainment for Indonesia, which already comprises much ethnical and cultural diversity, than for the basically European society of Australia. Such a merger is indeed Indonesia's avowed objective for West Irian; her methods may be questioned, her resources for meeting the most elementary responsibilities (such as the maintenance of order) demanded by the most old-fashioned colonialism may be doubted, but there is nothing inherently wrong with this aim.

No such clarity is possible on the Australian side. In the eyes of the great numerical majority of the nations, the bracketing with Portugal is far more real and significant than that with Indonesia, and Australia is far more likely to be called to account than Indonesia.[1] This is no doubt unjust – the principle is simply that imperialism is a crime which can be committed by white people only – but then we sought the responsibility for New Guinea just as eagerly as Indonesia did, and in the long view of history with just about the same kind and degree of justification. Australia's prime motivation was 'security', and Indonesians also have 'security' to think about, as well as their historical and legal claims. The position of both Australia and Indonesia in New Guinea seems essentially, though in neither case frankly, imperialistic, and it is stupid to blame history for the imperialist phase. Given the imperialist origins, however, everything depends on the working out of the responsibility so accepted; or should so depend, though one can have little conviction of a fair judgement in the world of the Committee of Twenty-four. There is also the judgement of our own consciences.

How this responsibility is met is – or again should be – of very material concern to Australians. The record so far is spotty, marked by some serious failings but, taken as a whole and in relation to Australian resources, by no means discreditable. But to put it bluntly, in the nature of the case, by misfortune rather than by any particular default, it will be very difficult indeed to launch into the world a reasonably well-found and decently-run state in Papua and New Guinea; but it would be easy – and this might be as much by our default as it would certainly be to our misfortune – to beget a second Congo on Australia's very threshold.

Origins of the problem

The formal written history of New Guinea, 'the last unknown', is centuries of blankness followed by decades of complications.

[1] Thus in April 1967 the efforts of some West Irianese exiles to secure a United Nations hearing on the grounds that Indonesian rule 'constituted Asian colonisation of a negroid race' were baulked by a ruling that the Committee of Twenty-four on non-self-governing territories had no jurisdiction. Such a self-denying ordinance is not characteristic when European countries are involved.

The first Europeans to sight its shores, in the first half of the sixteenth century, were Portuguese and Spaniards, who gave it its name on account of the physical resemblance of the coastal people to those of African Guinea.[1] In the west there were tenuous links with the Sultanate of Tidore in the Moluccas, the original basis of Dutch and hence Indonesian claims. In the Indies the Dutch policy was concentration on the more favoured areas, especially Java, staking a claim to the outer margins but not devoting much effort to them. There were some half-hearted attempts at control along the coast in the nineteenth century, but it was not until the end of Achinese and Balinese resistance was in sight, around the turn of the century, that the Dutch initiated solid establishments in New Guinea; they were perhaps motivated, in part, by rather brash Australian suggestions that the British government should secure an option should the Dutch wish to sell. Almost the only serious economic development was that on Vogelkopf oilfield in the extreme west, but this was not until after the second World War. Between the wars some settlements were used as penal stations for political offenders, including Sukarno, and this became a factor in the postwar Indonesian fixation on West Irian.

The real political history begins after 1870, with missionary activity and a minor gold and copper rush around Port Moresby. In the 'eighties, some Australian circles became apprehensive of European expansion in the Pacific, and in a small way expansionist on their own account. There was anxiety about French designs on the New Hebrides, overlooking the fact that French naval power, morals, and convicts were already settled in New Caledonia, 600 miles nearer the sacred shores of Queensland. Hence Australian commercial and missionary interests pressed a reluctant British government to intervene, which eventually led to almost comic-opera Anglo-French condominium in the New Hebrides. But meanwhile the expansionist Germany of Kaiser Wilhelm I became even more alarming, and in 1883 Queensland proclaimed the annexation, under the form of a protectorate, of the south-east of the island, Papua, the western half being tacitly admitted Dutch. This was done without any consultation with the British government, and was promptly repudiated by Lord Salisbury: Mother Country knew better than her excitable children, this was not the way colonials

---

[1] Since Guinea = Ghana, this has been adroitly used by one or two Ghanaian visitors to suggest if not affinity, then at least fellow-feeling.

should behave, and agreement with Germany in Africa was far more important. It is to be hoped that the home government felt remarkably silly when in the very next year the German New Guinea Company 'protected' the Bismarck Archipelago and Kaiser Wilhelmsland, that is all the north-east, and much the better portion, of the island. There is no record that it did so feel, but it picked up the leavings – Papua – later in 1884. All this came to a head in Deakin's outburst at the Imperial Colonial Conference of 1887, and played its part in fostering federationist sentiment.

Papua was the end of the line for the British Empire, a dead end; it was policed along the edges, and that was about all. In 1906 it was transferred to the Commonwealth, and became the end of the line for Australia. It did attract one remarkable man, Sir Hubert Murray,[1] Lieutenant-Governor from 1908 to 1940, who pursued a cautiously paternalist policy, perhaps not quite so high-minded as it was often made out to be, but most certainly not so high-handed as the arbitrary and at times brutal German policies on land alienation and labour recruitment for plantations. At least there was no flogging ethos, while in the north 'coon-bashing' was firmly in the German tradition and, to say the least, was not very sternly discouraged under the later Australian administration between the wars.

The shade of Lord Salisbury may have smiled at the threat actually presented by German New Guinea in 1914: the Australian Official War History is a fat volume of 412 pages, the actual fighting accounts for twenty pages, and the Australian casualties were six dead and four wounded. Von Spee's Pacific squadron was at large somewhere in the waters to the north, and this prevented the Australians from going on to German Micronesia – the Marianas and Carolines – and by the time this obstacle was removed, the Japanese were moving in. The Germans left behind them their missions (now mostly American-run), a few words in Pidgin, a few place names, reckoning in hectares, and a system of appointed village officials that persists even to-day.

After the war, 'security' took on a new and more realistic aspect: the Japanese in Truk and the Carolines were now only 2,000 to 3,000 miles from Australia, and their metropolitan base was about as far again: a different proposition from that presented by the Germans based on the other side of the globe and shut in by the

---

[1] Brother of Gilbert Murray, the translator of Euripides.

British Navy. As we have seen (p. 77), W. M. Hughes at Versailles left much to be desired in courtesy and argument, but outright annexation would have avoided the current inconvenience of a joint, but formally divided, administration for Papua and the Trust Territory (once the League Mandate) of New Guinea.[1] Under the new régime the most important inter-war development was the discovery in the 'thirties of the open grassy vales of the Highlands and of gold; the sectional airlift of heavy gold dredges across the mountains was a notable step in aviation history.

The Japanese war was a traumatic shock to people who, in the Highlands, had met their first Europeans ten or even five years before; and scarcely less traumatic, along the coasts, was the spectacle of undreamed of stores of wealth in the American bases, the raw material of many a cargo cult. The war also shook Australia into some recognition of the challenge. A Labor Minister of Territories, Eddie Ward, earned much disfavour by an almost demagogic assault on the right divine of planters and traders to rule the roost. This brief but exciting incursion was succeeded by the long régime (1951–63) of Paul Hasluck, a man with a strong if somewhat doctrinaire sense of mission, under whom new vigour and a new administrative sophistication came to New Guinea. As Dutch prospects dimmed in the west, Australia faced the disturbing prospect of a land frontier with an Asian nation; gestures of support to the Dutch were made, but nothing more was possible. By 1960 the stage was set for a classic example of the difficulty either of colonisation or decolonisation in a country where, far from it being necessary or even possible to divide to rule, it was essential to unify in order to administer.

The country

When empires were still empires, there was a useful distinction between colonies of settlement and colonies of sojourn or exploitation.[2] From its geographical nature, as a very difficult tropical land,

---

[1] A joint name for the two Territories, acceptable to both Papuans and New Guineans, is obviously desirable, but has eluded the collective wisdom of the political scientists of Australian universities. 'Paradisia' has been locally proposed, but has understandably met with little response externally. The initials of the new Papua and New Guinea Union Party – Pangu – would seem a neat solution.

[2] 'Exploitation' with no moral overtone; the exploitation of resources, not of people, is meant. In practice of course the two exploitations were very far from mutually exclusive.

New Guinea could really be only a colony of sojourn; unfortunately, owing to its proximity to the metropolis – unique in the annals of colonialism, if we exclude Ireland and Algeria – it was easy to mistake it for a colony of settlement. When, in the 'thirties, the Highland valleys, so exhilaratingly broad and open after the savagely dissected jungly mountains which surround them, were first penetrated by white men, the slogan was 'a second Kenya'. This has understandably been dropped, but as late as the 'fifties there were plenty of people who wanted 'economic soldier settlement', which on any significant scale would have created either an intolerably uneconomic financial burden or a poor white class; probably indeed both together.

Luckily in the long run, the country was much too difficult for a really serious attempt to create a White Melanesia before White Australia had been fully settled; but had the distinction been realised, and the moral drawn that most Australians in New Guinea would have to be (as they have been) sojourners rather than settlers, we might by now have trained more indigenous people for the minor, and some of the major, jobs now done expensively by expatriates. Some settlement by Europeans is inevitable and useful, and so far the export economy has depended mainly on European plantations and mining, though with an increasing indigenous contribution on the agricultural side; European capital and know-how will long be essential in mining and really large lumbering projects. But on the whole and in the long term, the country does not lend itself to economic development directly by European producers, and certainly not to large-scale white settlement. This is apart from the tradition that alienation of native land should be carefully controlled and in general narrowly restricted. This did not apply to any great extent in New Guinea under the Germans, and paradoxically Hubert Murray himself sometimes advocated white plantation-type settlement in Papua; but on the whole the tradition has been honourably upheld by all Australian régimes. There can be little doubt that the way of advance, in the main and except for large-scale mining and some forestry, can only be by the fostering of indigenous productive energies, though this is by no means an easy way. This seems to have been generally accepted by the Commonwealth government since the second World War, if not always whole-heartedly.

This limitation stems from the topography of the island, which is for the most part either swampy or extremely rugged, and in both cases usually covered with dense rainforest or secondary growth. The axis of New Guinea is a great cordillera, rising to 16,000 feet but including the broad grassy vales and plateaus of 'the Highlands'. The cordillera is flanked on south by foothills which are largely very wild country and everywhere densely forested, in places a tangle of limestone sink-holes and knife-edge ridges; in western Papua these fall to the swampy delta of the Fly River and the dry scrubby Oriomo Plateau, little more inviting than the savage foothill country. North of the Highlands is the long trough of the Markham, Ramu, and Sepik valleys: it has large grassy areas, probably the result of long-continued burning for shifting cultivation and hunting, but the great floodplains are swampy mosquito reserves.[1] North again are complex mountains, flanked by the recent and active volcanoes of the offshore islands and New Britain. These can be disastrous, as in the terrible eruption of Mount Lamington (on the Papuan mainland) in 1951, but they have contributed greatly to soil fertility, especially in the Gazelle Peninsula behind Rabaul in New Britain – the area of longest European contact, German and Australian, of greatest plantation development, and, so far, of the most marked diffusion of indigenous economic enterprise and the most advanced indigenous local government.

Climatically, New Guinea is not as bad as its Australian image, based on the unfair test of war experience, would suggest. The Highlands are superb, the lowlands, except in swampy deltas, at least no worse than most tropical lowlands. Soils are patchy: not a few tracts are reasonably or highly fertile, but comparisons with the great areas of very fertile recent volcanic soils in Java, though popular, are grossly misleading.

The people

The two million dominantly Melanesian inhabitants of Australian New Guinea are naturally distributed very unevenly: both population and economic development are very patchy. This is strikingly obvious from the air; pockets of settlement stand out from the jungle background, but they are few, and far between. There are a few roads, notably one from the port of Lae into the Highlands, but no integrated system; it is indicative of the difficult terrain that

---

[1] The Sepik mosquitoes are said not to attack aircraft in flight.

most of the interior can only be reached on foot or in a plane. The first wheels that many inland tribes ever saw were on aircraft, and in the primary school syllabus the Safety First lesson begins grandly 'Do not play on the airstrip.'

There are thus very few tribal groups with high population density over a reasonably large and accessible area, so that in all sectors, administrative and economic, activity is much fragmented. Some such groups there are: the Tolai around Rabaul are perhaps already in the stage of self-generating entrepreneurial activity, and they may be joined in the not too distant future by the tough and shrewd Chimbu of the Highlands. But there is only a handful of little towns – perhaps only Port Moresby and Rabaul really qualify – which have any truly urbanised indigenous groups; and the urban natives are often transients from other parts, so that a United Nations Mission was deeply shocked to hear the term 'foreign natives' – and yet what other term could apply in a country which is still more a congeries of tribes than a nation? All this means that any sort of 'advancement' must meet high overheads, since the effort must be thinly spread over many scattered nuclei with very poor intercommunication. It is perhaps a pity that for many years an insistence on as much 'uniform development' as possible hampered the attainment of a really high level anywhere. Doubtless regional disparities are bad, and élites open the way to internal injustices and exploitation; historically, no people has ever got very far without them.

Everywhere the life of the people was based on subsistence gardening, supplemented by hunting and coastal fishing. This means that the staples were fruits and roots such as yams, taro, and sweet potatoes; these are difficult to store and transport (consider the waste space in a bag of rice and a bag of potatoes) and with rare exceptions such as some types of yams, are quickly perishable: this inhibits both exchange over a distance (except for valuables such as gold-lip shell) and the building-up of a marketable surplus, though this Neolithic agriculture was often technically highly ingenious and very locally supported surprisingly high densities. However, there were no political structures beyond clans or tribes covering at most a few villages and up to 4,000 to 5,000 people.

Internally, the most serious division is the confusion of tongues: there are not scores but hundreds of languages, and a 'large' language is one spoken by a few thousands. Only in the Highlands are there groups of up to 250,000 people speaking languages sufficiently close to each other for intercommunication to be easy: once more the keynote is fragmentation. 'Police Motu' is a *lingua franca* in Papua, Pidgin in New Guinea: the latter is the most widely-used medium and is gaining ground in Papua itself. It poses a serious and very controversial educational problem. While it is certainly not just a bastard English patois, but a real language, Melanesian in structure, but mainly English-derived in vocabulary, it is probably fair to say that it is circumlocutory and not well adapted to abstract discussion: it is fine for saying 'Take out the spark-plug and clean it', not so good for explaining the function of the spark-plug as an electrical component of an internal combustion engine. However, this would be disputed: some authorities think it should be the basic medium of education to a fairly advanced level. Some serious students think of Pidgin as doomed and damned for being 'tokboi' ('boy-talk'), with all the servile connotations of 'boy' applied by their masters to grown men; others hold that it may become a badge of nationalism.

Just over half the people are at least nominally Christian, and all but a handful of leading Papuans and New Guineans received their formative education in mission schools. So far as a coherent world-view has superseded a congeries of tribal myths and cosmogonies, it is a Christian view. This has not always been a factor of unity, owing to sectarian conflict; and some missions – especially newer Fundamentalist sects – have been guilty of outrageously terrorist propaganda[1] and reckless assaults on indigenous culture. The older missions, Catholic and Protestant, have for the most part learnt something, including Christian humility, in 150 years of endeavour in the Pacific. While many indigenous Christians are still at heart quasi-animist or at any rate firm believers in sorcery, there are others with a reasonably high standard of faith, conduct, and understanding: it is not for the average Australian to throw the first stone in this respect. And although half the people are still heathen, in some ways New Guinea is a more Christian country than Australia: incipient co-operatives and Trade Unions often begin their proceedings with prayer.

Yet, while Christianity of varying quality has provided the only

[1] For instance, by showing films of the Lamington eruption with the gloss that this is what will happen to *you* if you do not heed the Word – in areas with no record of volcanism for millions of years.

really large-scale reintegration of values, it has been 'such as to fit [the New Guinean] for participation in the world of Christian society *as it was a century ago*'.[1] The contrast between this proffered ideal and the practical conduct of many white men must be, to say the least, deeply unsettling. Christianity, then, may be no abiding comfort; and on the whole it has failed to open the way to the material welfare which was a main, and very practical, objective of the old tribal and fertility cults.

It need hardly be said that the impact of the 'modern world' has often been totally bewildering. It came not gradually over generations, but of a sudden: the *oldest* contacts with missionary, trading, and administrative activity along the coasts took place under a century ago; in the interior, where lives the majority of the population, it is a matter of the last thirty years – thirty years interrupted by a large-scale and savage modern war. Small wonder then that the reaction, against both government and missionary interference, was often that of the 'cargo cults'. These are millenarian movements drawing inspiration from the Old Testament or the Apocalypse and from memories of the purposive discipline of the war, the mighty 'cargoes' piled up in the war-time bases. These cargoes represent treasures that were once known or owned by the Ancestors, but the white man has filched, hidden, intercepted them. If the Ancestors knew, they would surely help; so to invoke them villages are replanned, primitive docks and airstrips made to receive the cargo, old rituals revived, new disciplines imposed, against the day when the Ancestors will return with the cargo, and the white man and his hangers-on be plunged into the fiery pit. . . .[2] There is a core of rationality in these desperate attempts to adjust to an incomprehensible situation; and on occasion, with imaginative guidance, the sense of purpose and striving can be led into productive channels and really add some elements of a better life. Such guidance, however, is a difficult and delicate matter, and has not often been vouchsafed.

[1] C. D. Rowley, *The New Guinea Villager* (Cheshire, Melbourne, 1965), p. 129; my italics.

[2] Cargo cults have been wide-spread in the Pacific and have analogues in other 'primitive' regions such as the backlands of Latin America (and in medieval Europe). One of the most recent involved the purchase, for $4000, of President Johnson, whose reputation was such that he was thought to show promise of being a most useful and adroit local representative in the New Guinea House of Assembly.

The economy

Apart from gold mining, which reached its peak before the war and now seems declining, and lumbering, the economy is almost entirely agrarian. Geological structures strongly suggest the presence of oil, and for some years in the 'fifties oil search was a main economic activity. It is surprising that no serious strikes were made, but the search has now tailed off, though not completely. There are definite reserves of natural gas, but what can be done with them at this stage of backwardness? A beginning is being made on the extensive copper deposits on Bougainville Island, but the reluctance of the local people to risk their land, and their demand for a large share of royalties (which in the official view should go to general development) presented the Administration and Conzinc Rio Tinto with an acute, if local, social and political problem – a pointer to the difficulty of exploiting resources without exploiting people, or appearing to do so.

So far the market economy, as distinct from subsistence agriculture, has rested on a very narrow base: apart from gold, only on copra (50 to 75 per cent of exports), rubber, cocoa, coffee, and timber; tea, tobacco, groundnuts, pyrethrum, and passion-fruit are grown on a small scale. This enforced reliance on a few products, vulnerable in world markets or to world output restrictions, is a very serious weakness. Coffee, for example, was ardently propagated by the Department of Agriculture and became very popular with indigenous farmers in the Highlands; but it is very difficult to explain falls in prices, or why, after the official propaganda effort, expansion must be restricted by the International Coffee Agreement. As it is, however, indigenous producers are responsible for about one-third of the main export crops.

In 1965 an important survey was made by a team from the International Bank for Reconstruction and Development.[1] In summary, the team recommended quadrupling rubber area, more than doubling cocoa, adding 70 per cent to coco-nut acreage, and introducing 16,000 acres of tea. Livestock should be increased ten-fold, to 300,000 head, while forestry output should be quadrupled. If the ten-year programme were carried out, export values, $27,000,000 in 1962–63, could rise to nearly $68,000,000 in 1973–74 and $100,000,000 by 1982–83. But annual budgets would have to be

[1] Published as *The Economic Development of Papua and New Guinea* (Johns Hopkins, Baltimore, 1965).

increased to about $100,000,000; this is about a third greater than the 1963–64 level, and the amount raised internally would have to rise by about 10 per cent per annum (largely through increased excise), though the proportion contributed to Territory revenues by the Commonwealth would rise from nearly two-thirds to nearly three-quarters.

On the technical side, this report is an impressive document, if somewhat deflationary on social services. It marks a trend away from 'uniform development', favouring concentration on areas where returns are likely to be surest and quickest. Its projected increases in output include a considerable indigenous component – two-thirds of the copra, half the cocoa, half to two-thirds of the meat, and half of the tea and rubber; at present practically no part of the last three items is native-produced. Nevertheless, the team's apparent reliance on increased expatriate investment in plantations seems both backward-looking and doubtfully realistic.

There is probably more un- or under-used land (some in European hands) than is needed to meet these recommendations, though whether it is where it is needed is a very different matter, and indigenous opinion looks very askance on alienation. Demographic data for the Territory are confused, but the really remarkable spread of medical services is responsible for a high rate of population increase – among the Tolai, so far the most pushful entrepreneurs, it is very high indeed, probably over 3 per cent per annum. Labour therefore should be ample; but again, is it ample where it is needed? Considerable shifts of population might well be needed, and the history of directed resettlement (for instance, in Indonesia) is not encouraging. On the money side, better judges than the present writer hold that underwriting the programme would not be an intolerable strain on Australian finances. The worst bottleneck is likely to be in the supply of the large numbers of trained staff needed, especially agricultural research and extension officers, who are in short supply in Australia itself.

While the World Bank survey thus contains a mass of careful argument and clearly stated recommendations, which in themselves could lead to notable advance, it pays too little attention to the social factors which underlie and ramify through the life of peoples such as those of New Guinea. In such traditional societies, traditional Western economic thinking, however excellent in its own terms, is much less than half the story. New Guineans cannot be expected suddenly to behave like New Zealanders, literate capitalist farmers who have lived for generations by producing for the market. Both in this matter, and in the matter of finding trained leadership in administration (and politics) for the great productive effort demanded, education is of paramount importance. Unfortunately, it is probably in education that the Australian record in New Guinea has so far been weakest.

The educational problem

Before the second World War, education was to all intents left to mission schools, of which some were good, most mediocre, too many frankly bad. There was no lack of devotion, but they were starved for money, and (naturally enough) as a rule evangelist rather than primarily educational in approach and aim. Apart from limited subsidies to such schools, the direct contribution of the Administration was ludicrous: in the Trust Territory, £A18,000 in 1923, only 5,000 in 1937; in Papua, one school in Port Moresby – for European children!

Since the war, government action has been much more positive. More efficiency, and teaching in English, were demanded of the missions, and the Administration itself made a much greater direct effort. In 1963 some 40,000 out of 220,000 primary pupils were in Administration schools, and in secondary education Administration outranked missions, although at this level the start was very late (about 1957) and there are still only 12,000 secondary enrolments. The Department of Education in recent years has attracted able and forward-looking men at the top, and indeed this is true of other sectors of the Administration, though there is sometimes a distinct and uncomfortable gap in quality between the directing and the subordinate cadres. The imbalance as between primary and second-ary education stemmed largely from the policy of 'uniform development', which distrusted the formation of an élite and aimed at levelling or reducing regional disparities; but it has produced a terribly narrow base for training the people needed to run the country in a time of rapid political advance.

Education in the Territory itself was supplemented by scholar-ships, mission or Administration, to Australian schools; nobody seems to have reflected that this might produce an élite even more alienated than a home-trained one. So far there is only a tiny handful, half a dozen or so, of indigenous university graduates. A crash educational programme is perhaps New Guinea's greatest need, and one devoted not to planting a bush school in every hamlet, but to producing a system balanced and integrated at all levels, geared to Territory needs and not (as in the very recent past) to Australian syllabuses.

Such was the view of the Commission on Higher Education which reported in 1964, recommending the establishment of an Institute of Higher Technical Education and a completely autonomous university. The case for the latter is simply that, whatever happens politically, increasing numbers of Papuans and New Guineans must be trained for the task of running a modern government and its agencies, however modest their scale; and that this training can best be given in an independent university, so that its methods and approach can be adapted to meet the real needs of the country instead of being subordinated (as in a University College) to institutions designed for the very different society, culture, and economy of Australia.

Although the Interim Council of the university was not formed until October 1965, by a remarkable effort of improvisation it enrolled sixty students for a pre-university year in 1966, and commenced proper first year degree work in March 1967. The 'preliminary year' was designed to offset as much as possible the lack of background of the local secondary school leaver; its classes were held in adapted buildings, almost literally 'tin sheds', on the Port Moresby showground. Despite this less than modest beginning, it is fair to say that both the quality of staff attracted and the showing of the first student intake surpassed the anxious hopes of those who had advanced the bold project of a full university in an environment academically so unpromising. The pity is that the construction of a solid secondary foundation was left so late.

Political advance

Here there is a different story, one of striking progress, but progress made to some extent (despite disclaimers) under pressure from United Nations missions to the Trust Territory, and uncoordinated with the general development of New Guinea.

The lack of any indigenous system either of hierarchical chiefs or elected leaders led the Germans, and later the Australians, to appoint village officials, *tultuls* and *luluais* in New Guinea, constables in Papua, who were supposed to be important local figures capable of transmitting the Administration's directives. In reality, they were often local nobodies put up as 'front men', while in the background the old 'big men' kept a watching brief and saw to it that as little as possible was changed, and indeed developed considerable, if unobtrusive, political skill in manipulating the situation. In 1950, however, a first step towards indigenous participation in affairs was taken by setting up the first Local Government Councils in the Gazelle Peninsula and at Hanuabada close to Port Moresby, 'uniform development' being subordinated to the sensible selection of areas favourable for the experiment. By 1966, rather ahead of target, these Councils covered over half the population, and the first experiments in multi-racial local government were being made. Councils raise revenue, mainly through a poll tax set by themselves, and have a wide range of minor functions. Their efficiency of course varies widely, and few can as yet stand firmly on their own feet; some may do little more than rubber-stamp the District Officer's advice, but they provide, at the very least, valuable training in running affairs, however parochial.

On the Territory scale, it is sufficient to say that the House of Assembly has a majority of elected indigenous members; its autonomy is limited, but it is by no means a subservient tool of the Administration, and is beginning to reach out towards the budget. There is already the beginning of indigenous executive participation, at 'under-secretary' level, and a quasi-ministerial system may not be long delayed. The quality of understanding about representative democracy is of course only rudimentary in many areas, as the President Johnson cargo cult indicates, and is perhaps not very advanced even in the capital, Port Moresby. It is difficult to see how it could be otherwise, given not only educational backwardness but also the paternalism, not to say authoritarianism, inherent in colonial rule. Nevertheless, the numerous surprises in the 1964 election (held by compulsory preferential voting) demonstrate that the electoral officers, who had to fill in the ballots for the illiterate majority, did their duty, and that this was no rigged plebiscite. It was in fact a remarkable experiment, and achievement, in political education, an example which might be taken to heart by many anti-colonialist régimes more prodigal of advice to others than of democratic measures at home.

This political advance may fairly be claimed as a bold experiment, to be justified on the belief that people only do their best when set a task rather above their estimated current capacity, but not so far above that the challenge becomes a paralysing nightmare. But given the as yet very small diffusion of post-primary education, and the dependence of the Territory on the Commonwealth for two-thirds of its budget, it could well be argued that the political sector is out of phase with the economic and educational; not that politics have gone too fast (for instance, they lag badly in the essential matter of party formation, which is as yet only incipient), but that the others have gone too slowly.

The future

The bills for education and for economics will be heavy, and most of them will be addressed to the Australian taxpayer. But the easy antithesis of economic versus educational development as first priority is a shade too facile. Any solid economic advance will demand much larger and better trained indigenous cadres than are now available – unless continued reliance is placed on expensive expatriates; but here recruitment is already discouraged by political uncertainty, and there is a risk of exacerbating race feeling. Solid educational advance will need as well as help economic development. Political stability obviously depends upon and affects both.

Many are the unresolved problems and perils: the danger of forming an élite alienated from mass opinion in the villages; the danger of over-raising expectations – and even in the conservative Highlands, impatience is already sometimes voiced; the great difficulty of staffing the economic programme. Most dangerous of all, perhaps, is the inherent sectionalism of rival regions, languages, and tribes, which is often deep and has potentialities of violence. The armed force – the Pacific Islands Regiment, in which there are already a few indigenous subalterns – seems to be developing a supra-tribal solidarity and to that extent may become a unifying factor; yet the recent history of Africa shows that such a development is itself not without hazard.

One thing may be said with confidence: on any view of the future of New Guinea, and of its relations with the Commonwealth of Australia, things can only worsen if the necessary quantum of trained indigenous intelligence is not secured by an economic and educational programme at once comprehensive, co-ordinated, and not run on the cheap. Refusal to take up this challenge can only lead to greater difficulties for Australia as the social, economic, and political developments become more lop-sided: the three legs of a stool must be of approximately equal length and strength if it is to be stable.

The balance of advantage, then, lies in meeting the educational and economic bills; if they are not met, the country will become increasingly susceptible to what are delicately styled 'outside influences', which will have a fine culture medium if expectations already aroused are disappointed. So far the Australian government has shown much greater readiness to meet the concrete economic challenge than the educational one. Its attitude to university financing contrasts with its spontaneous addition of $20,000,000 a year to the $100,000,000 recommended by the World Bank Mission. In itself a fine gesture, made in the hope of doubling export values, this action yet suggests a rather simple materialist approach to the priorities of what is much more than a simple problem of material economics.

The fact remains that at best the Territory will long remain a poor relation, a dominantly agrarian country with poor prospects unless it continues to receive a good deal of outside aid. Since Australia justifiably regards New Guinea as highly important to her security, and since she is already exclusively involved, this means in effect Australian aid. It should not be overlooked, as it often is in official hand-outs and popular articles, that the Australian contribution to New Guinea, honourable as it is in relation to Australian resources, is not just altruism. Apart from the primary motive of security, private interests derive a good deal of gain from New Guinea; and nothing is more striking than the way in which, for instance, the great trading firms of Burns, Philp and W. R. Carpenter – mighty economic powers in the land – are usually left out of the reckoning.

The present condition of New Guinea is a source of embarrassment to Australia; it costs a good deal of money and yet, inevitably if unjustly, it is the failings rather than the achievements that are publicised at the United Nations and determine the Australian image in the eyes of the Afro-Asian majority of nations. New Guinea's future is of high importance to Australia; will it be a modest but well-run friendly country or a second Congo?

There have been rather vague suggestions of a Melanesian federation including New Guinea; when originally aired, before 1963, such notions seem to have reflected last-minute desires to provide some framework by which West Irian could have been kept out of Indonesian clutches. This is now a lost cause, and a more limited Melanesia is not practical politics, if only because of the presence of the Indians in Fiji and the French in New Caledonia, the other significant components of the projected structure. There is talk also of the Territory becoming a seventh State of the Commonwealth, and indeed this is called for by one of the embryo parties. But one cannot have a second-class State, and the costs of ensuring parity of administrative standards might well amount to much more than those of aid to an autonomous New Guinea. The prospects of unlimited 'Panguan' immigration, or (if this were avoided by some convention) of the digestion into the Australian political and social system of some 2,000,000 people of such vastly alien culture, are sufficiently daunting.

The official attitude in Canberra is that when the (unspecified) time comes, the people of Papua and New Guinea must decide for themselves, and meantime nothing must be done to prejudice their freedom of action. But of course every decision made in the Department of Territories affects the conditions in which the choice must be made, and therefore affects that choice. A good example was given in the decision to divide the Territory Public Service into two grades, essentially indigenous and expatriate, with a very large salary differential. It is very true that a self-governing Territory could not possibly afford to carry a Public Service on Australian rates of pay; but the manner in which the operation was performed was tactless and untimely to a degree, and the derisory increases awarded by an appeal to arbitration (decided on narrow legalist and fiscal grounds) gave rise to bitter allegations, from educated and responsible Panguans, of racial discrimination. It is astonishing that the well-tried alternative of similar basic rates plus generous expatriate allowances was not thought of until the damage was done.

The racial situation in itself gives cause for disquiet. On the whole, relations are not so bad as they might be; evidence of recent trends is conflicting and probably mirrors the preconceptions of the witnesses. There is adequate legislation against discrimination on grounds of colour; but the enforcement of such legislation in the social sphere is notoriously difficult. It is encouraging, for instance, to look through the sporting columns of the local Press and note the high standing of many indigenous players; but good relations on the oval are not always carried over into the club or pub. As usual, sexual fears, sometimes imaginary but sometimes not without some foundation, add to tension, and there is a mutual incomprehension of *mores* which can lead to nasty incidents. Yet on the whole, and with limitations, there is much more interplay between the races than there was even ten years ago.

Meanwhile, great play is made in official hand-outs of the reluctance of the people to see the Australians depart. A good deal of this reluctance is genuine enough, motivated partly by a recognition of the existing need for guidance in modern ways, partly by fear stemming from bad news on the bush telegraph from West Irian. But probably rather more of it is 'induced' than the official spokesmen realise; and increasingly it is concentrated in the Highlands and the Sepik people, apprehensive of domination by the Tolai of Rabaul or the Port Moresby folk who have had a longer start in education and economic development. The continued official distrust of élites, the myopic reliance on the presumed unwavering conservatism of the backblocks, may not reflect any conscious feeling of 'divide and rule' (in which respect Australia has had a good record of avoidance) but is very reminiscent of die-hard miscalculations in India and Africa.

In Rowley's informed and thoughtful *The New Guinea Villager* there is no passage more moving, nor more to the point, than that in which he reports the words of an old man of Manus Island. Until he was quite sure of his interrogator – and that 'native apathy' and 'suspicion' so often designedly mask a considerable astuteness – the old man was loud in his assurances that all 'loved the government'. But this was while he still suspected that the talk was a government trap; afterwards: 'If only you would not hide your real thinking from us, we could be brothers. . . . If only the white man would open his hand, we would be brothers. But he keeps it tightly shut. He has locked all his knowledge in a box, and where are we to find the key?'

It has been traditionally found – and lost again – through the apocalyptic cargo cults. Perhaps the mission of the new university will be to unlock the box; perhaps, as has happened elsewhere, the white man's knowledge will prove but a Pandora's box, 'the greatest of the cargo cults'. At least, some of the cargo cults, failures as they must seem whether measured by their own millenarian dreams or by more prosaic Western standards, have left a residuum of better living. One of their leaders, Paliau who founded the New Way on Manus, became President of a Local Government Council and a Member of the House of Assembly. Perhaps all that New Guinea needs is that scarcest of resources in the modern world, the world of the Committee of Twenty-four – time.

Part Four

SOCIETY

Chapter 13

The Dark People

T HE FORMAL – that is, European – history of New Zealand is
shorter than that of Australia; yet in New Zealand the
traveller with a perceptive feeling for the past may well sense
a greater historic depth, for there the indigenous Maori was strong
enough to clash in real and not altogether unsuccessful conflict with
the white invader. One could write a good history of Australia
without mentioning any aborigine by name; this would be unthinkable in New Zealand. For a century and a half, the Australian
aborigines were simply swept under the carpet of history, an
irrelevance to the story of 'progress'. The constitution of the
Commonwealth refers to them twice: in providing that they shall
not be counted in reckoning the population of States or Territories
(Section 127),[1] and that the Commonwealth should have powers to
make special laws for the people of any race for whom this was
thought desirable, 'other than the aboriginal race in any State'
(Section 51 (xxvi)). Ironically enough, the purpose of the latter
clause was to reserve to the Commonwealth the power of discrimination against Asians, which impinged too much on external
affairs to be left to the States, while it reserved to the 'men on the
spot' full powers to handle their own natives their own way; at this
time there was in fact no Commonwealth Territory at all. With the
changes of sixty years, the exception came to be seen as a discriminatory restriction on powers to make laws *for* aborigines rather
than *against* Asians.

On 27 May 1967 (the day on which the preceding paragraph
was written) the people of Australia voted, by exception, 'Yes' in a
referendum, and by the overwhelming majority of nine to one
endorsed the repeal of these sections of the constitution. Only in

---

[1] There is some popular confusion about this section: it did not preclude a
census enumeration of aborigines, which was first attempted in 1961, but
simply taking any account of them in any reckonings based on population,
e.g. electoral or fiscal arrangements.

Western Australia did the total of negative and informal votes reach a bare 21 per cent; surprisingly enough, not a single outback electorate in Western Australia or Queensland (the Northern Territory has no referendum vote) recorded a 'No' vote. The immediate practical effects may not be striking; there will be no swift millennium for the aborigines, and indeed the huge majority might even induce a comfortable complacent feeling that Australia had wiped her face clean of an obvious stain, and that was all that was needed. But psychologically, as a symbol, the vote is of immense significance: it may be simply a salving of conscience and a purgation of guilt, but still the nation has gone on record as admitting a vast injustice, and that is an essential step to righting it. Fundamental to this of course, was the climate of world opinion; it simply would not do, in this age, for an avowedly democratic nation to maintain in its very constitution provisions which on the face of them appeared blatant racial discrimination. But there has also been in reality a change of heart, muddled no doubt but genuine. Perhaps the most significant feature, in the long run, is that while all political parties, all churches, and all important newspapers save one supported the amendment, most of them seemed to take success very much for granted and hardly anybody made much of a campaign, the few and weak aboriginal organisations themselves, for the first time, raised an aboriginal voice throughout the nation.

Estimates of the aboriginal population in 1788 range from 200,000 to 300,000. There are now about 46,000 full-bloods, of whom 4,000 or so are still intermittently following the traditional life, but now at best as semi-nomads. This decline is 'equivalent to the death every year since 1788 of two large tribes totalling 1,700 souls'.[1] There may be something over 75,000 'half-castes', though many other Australians must have some forgotten aboriginal strain. These figures exclude the 8,000 Torres Straits islanders, Melanesians attached to Queensland by historical accident. Of the full-bloods, all but a handful were in the north and west; New South Wales has 2,750 and Victoria 300. However, in the real outback full-bloods are by no means a small proportion of the total population: in the Northern Territory, they number 20,000 against 37,000 others, of whom 20,000 were in Darwin. The race which even in 1938 seemed dying is living and multiplying.

[1] W. E. H. Stanner, 'The Aborigines', in J. C. G. Kevin (ed.), *Some Australians Take Stock* (Longmans, London, 1939), pp. 3–38.

The century of wrong

From the beginning, official policy was well-meaning; but the gulf of incomprehension was too wide to be bridged. Some of the officers of the First Fleet were liberal and intellectually curious, Phillip himself was anxious to do well by those he was dispossessing; but within a few years the aborigines around Sydney became what their fellows throughout the continent became as contact spread – despised hangers-on, subsisting on handouts on the dustier fringes of society.

As the sheep and cattle stations covered the land, the aborigine lost his waterholes, but gained – briefly – a new type of game, far easier to hunt than the kangaroo. This was theft, and must be punished; too often the most convenient mode of punishment was murder. Officialdom frowned on this, and issued plaintive proclamations; but officialdom was a long way off from the frontier. After the 1838 massacre of twenty-eight aborigines, including children, at Myall Creek in New England, the government – in face of furious protest – re-charged seven men acquitted by their peers, and eventually hanged them. Methods were usually more discreet thereafter, even if the most ghastly charge of all – the hand-outs of poisoned flour – are in the nature of the case unproven. There was retaliation, of course; but very rarely were the aborigines sufficiently well organised for more than raids on isolated homesteads or the spearing of lonely shepherds. It is more than difficult to accept the distinction made in an Australian schoolbook that in America the Indians were 'driven out or exterminated', while in Australia the blackfellows 'withdrew before the advance of settlement'; perhaps no recorded people is so thoroughly extinct as the original Tasmanians. In fact it was often not so much retreat from European contact as a movement towards it, once the fabric of traditional life began to break. At the best, aboriginal material life was a struggle for existence in a generally harsh environment; often, especially in drought, a desperate struggle. Such things as axes and knives became almost essential to survival, tobacco and tea became cravings.

The black record is of course only one side of the story: protest and sympathy were never entirely lacking, there were official Protectors of Aborigines. But in a pre-anthropological age, the protectors themselves were unable to appreciate the problem in meaningful terms. At the worst, they were frauds; for the most part, paternalists working in a spirit of contemptuous compassion, avowedly 'smoothing the pillow of a dying race'. Many, or most, of those who devoted themselves to aboriginal welfare were Christian missionaries, and they included men of devotion and even heroic constancy, such as the Spanish Benedictine Dom Salvado who in 1846 founded New Norcia, north of Perth, which still exists as a great boarding school and training centre for aborigines, a massive and incongruous piece of Iberian Baroque in the bush. Colonial and State governments, even in this century, have found it convenient to shuffle off a large share of responsibility to missions, as agents or principals, and a large proportion of aborigines still live on mission stations. Some of these display a sympathetic attitude to old aboriginal values, or attempt a creative training in new ways; but one cannot but suspect that many were (and some still are) run in the spirit of an old-fashioned reformatory, bound down with a net of regulations and petty (but humiliating) penalties designed to crush any impropriety, which means any hankering after the old ways, any attempt to live a life of one's own, with such consolations as the dispossessed may find. The missions offer material security but psychological tension and frustration; it is not surprising that many prefer the material squalor of camp life, which has at least some psychological comforts and readier access to that most universal solace of the despised and rejected, drink.

If this harsh monitorship was (and sometimes still is) the stance adopted by the servants of a religion which proclaims the brotherhood of all men, the attitude of the average man in the bush, in the full flush of White Australianism, may be imagined. Incomprehension was often total and brutal, accompanied by vilification and physical brutality; aborigines were barely human nuisances, tolerated because easily exploitable – in some remoter pastoral areas, 'station natives' provided a good deal of essential labour, but as late as the 1930's received food and clothing (of what standard?) but no wages at all.[1] And in an otherwise all but womanless land, the aborigines could provide women; once more, the consideration was usually tobacco. Such attitudes were common, but not universal: station owner-occupiers (not so often managers) not infrequently developed a patriarchal attitude to their pastoral charges, and it must be remembered that widely-extended families were

[1] For a general survey, see Stanner, *op. cit.*

supported as well as actual workers. In the last century, when the itinerant bush worker often enough lived at a material level not greatly above that of some aborigines, there was at times a rough and ready mateship which did not pay too much attention to colour, except that the white man 'naturally' took the lead and the black 'naturally' accepted this.

Signs of change

As the 1967 referendum demonstrated, the awakening of social consciousness and conscience since the second World War has been striking. While it has been in no small part induced by external factors in the age of Afro-Asian decolonisation, the groundwork was laid in the 'thirties. In this, the writings and personalities of some old hands, whether pastoral respectables like Daisy Bates, Mrs Aeneas Gunn, or the Durack family, or picturesque 'bush identities' like Bill Harney, played a part; even if they were on the whole paternalist (though Harney and Daisy Bates were fraternal enough), these were people who believed, and acted on the belief, that 'one touch of nature makes the whole world kin'.

But at least as important were the churchmen and the anthropologists, including one man who was both – A. P. Elkin, the Anglican clergyman who for twenty-three years held the Sydney Chair of Anthropology. Aboriginal life had been a rich quarry for such classical anthropologists as Tylor and Frazer, but they were remote, though of course they drew their data from observers in the field. But at this stage, while the aborigines were a 'dying race', it seemed more urgent to rescue their record than themselves, and the approach was external and strictly academic. The later generation of anthropologists have been no less academic – indeed, more sophisticated in technical discussion of such delightfully and endlessly debatable matters as kinship systems and what (if anything) 'totemism' really means. But more and more attention has been paid to the contemporary problems of aboriginal change and survival. Again, the aesthetic richness and the true spirituality of the aboriginal tradition were displayed: the deep devotion to the land; the mystical bond between man and his environment; the complexity and beauty of the myths of origin, of the 'Dream Time'; the fundamentally religious view of life summed up by W. E. H. Stanner in one lapidary phrase: 'man is of value in himself and for others, and *there are spirits who care*'.[1] This was a far cry from the mid-nineteenth century, when even religious men denied to the aborigines religious beliefs or even moral sentiments; and after this the old write-off was no longer possible.

However important the post-war external pressures on Australia to put her house in order, the real turn in policy dates back to 1937–40, when Commonwealth and States agreed to further the 'assimilation' of the aborigines into the general society. There were several factors: revulsion against atrocities, some at the hands of the police, as recently as the early 'thirties; Donald Thomson's journeys in Arnhem Land, which exploded the myth of 'wild and treacherous natives'; the discovery of the aborigines by writers in search of new and exciting local colour, artists and poets anxious for new myths and symbols; and a formal remonstrance to the Commonwealth from the Royal Anthropological Institute in London.

'Assimilation' sounds well, and appeals to that vast majority of Australians who believe in a 'fair go' and neither have nor are likely to have any contact with aborigines. But the difficulties are immense; there is not one aboriginal problem, but several, springing from the widely differing internal structures and external socio-economic environments of these depressed and fragmented people. It is a gross over-simplification to speak of aborigines *en bloc*: those lumped together under this omnibus term range from full-blood nomads to urban quadroons and octoroons; beyond this last point assimilation has probably come about through natural processes.

Attitudes to 'assimilation'

Aboriginal attitudes to assimilation are very mixed. At one end of the scale is a small educated élite of part aborigines who wish nothing more than to take their place as 'ordinary members of society'; at the other, outright rejection. And this rejection is by no means confined to those groups in the north-west who retain a good deal of their customary *mores* and rites, but is strong among the completely detribalised fringe-dwellers of the south-east, not to mention the 500 Bandjalang of New South Wales who have established their own almost savagely independent Pentecostal Church.

---

[1] In R. and C. Berndt (eds), *Aboriginal Man in Australia* (Angus and Robertson, Sydney, 1965), p. 216. This book and Marie Reay (ed.), *Aborigines Now* (Angus and Robertson, 1964) are the most useful contemporary general discussions available.

Moreover, insistence on maintaining traditional organisation, or at least a considerable internal togetherness and external separatism, does not rule out acceptance of European material goods: indeed, in one area candidates for initiatory circumcision rites may travel by air to a European hospital for the actual operation.[1] In the long run, however, this is obviously an unstable adjustment; the cross-currents are too confusing. For example, whose law shall prevail? Tribal justice would accord a husband or father, or a set of kin collectively, the right to inflict corporal or even capital punishment for sexual and religious offences; but this is a crime to white man's law, which offers no redress whatever for what in aboriginal eyes is serious outrage. It would be callously imperceptive to ignore the existence of such tragic dilemmas, which might be multiplied many times and in other contexts, but there is little consideration for them in assimilation policy – unless indeed we count as this the fact that murders at custom, as it were, are not punished by hanging; but then hanging is now rarely if ever inflicted on white men who have not the sanction of custom. Something of the tragedy may be sensed from Stanner's life-history of Durmugam, who 'came to good terms with Europeanism' – with its axes and its guns – 'but found it saltless all his days and, at the end, bitter too'.[2]

However, relatively few aborigines now live in anything approaching the old way of life, though kinship ties and elements of the tribal ethos, such as sharing of goods amongst kin, are still strong, even in the relatively sophisticated part-aboriginal community of Melbourne. This group could perhaps be equated with the less well-off immigrant groups from southern or eastern Europe, and to that extent is assimilated. So also are a few industrial or casual workers in the larger towns of New South Wales, who are accepted on the unskilled or semi-skilled level; they are not very different in standard of living or manners from their white fellow workers at that level.[3] But most aborigines, full- or part-blood, live on pastoral or mission stations, or government settlements in the north and west, or on the fringes of small country towns. Apart from the

[1] Catharine Berndt, in R. and C. Berndt, *op. cit.*, p. 240.
[2] W. E. H. Stanner, 'Durmugam, A Nangiomeri', in J. B. Casagrande (ed.), *In the Company of Man* (Harper, New York, 1960), pp. 63–100; a deeply moving essay which covers a much wider range than the point made above.
[3] For the former group, see Diane Barwick in Reay, pp. 20–31; for the latter, J. H. Bell in Berndt, pp. 414–17.

romantic tourist image of the traditional aborigine, it is these 'degraded' groups who provide the stereotype, and the obvious problems.

Facts of aboriginal life

Whether the station was pastoral, government, or mission, the tradition has been strongly paternalist. The pastoralist opposition to granting award rates of pay to aboriginal stockmen was based on the argument that with few exceptions they were slow, poor, and lazy workers, and that as well as the minimal wages, the hand-outs in kind supported many non-workers; it was not stressed that these hand-outs themselves were often subsidised by government. There is something in these arguments, but certainly one factor is a re-action to the long tradition of contempt: often enough the aborigine of set purpose lived down to his bad name, and met exploitation by the very natural device of dodging the column to the maximum extent possible. It is not only in Australia that the poor savage's untutored mind is shrewd enough to use 'stupidity' as a shield.

Changes are afoot in the cattle industry; in 1961 a Darwin news-paper warned the cattlemen that they 'will just have to do their part in the gigantic, heart-breaking task of bringing independence and dignity to a people stripped of these qualities by the white pioneers who, in their struggle for survival, could do little else at the time'.[1] The response has been on the whole grudging; as we have seen (p. 163), the reluctant acceptance by the cattlemen of a compromise was accompanied by threats of replacement of native by white labour, which would certainly lead to strain on govern-ment and mission resources. But it also led on three stations to withdrawal of aborigines to strike camps; this move, like the attempted formation of a mining co-operative at Pindan in Western Australia, owed something to outside white helpers, some of whom probably deserved the 'Red' tag they promptly received. But Wave Hill and Pindan do also represent a stirring of self-help and a striving for a new aborigine-oriented form of organisation.

Government and mission stations offer very little of a lead in this direction; they are in a sense the institutional form of what Elkin called 'intelligent parasitism'. A less formal mode is that of the

[1] Quoted in L. R. Hiatt, 'Aborigines in the Australian Community', in A. Davies and S. Encel (eds.), *Australian Society* (Cheshire, Melbourne, 1965), pp. 274–95.

'professional aborigines' who 'donning tattered garments, and borrowing babies if they have none of their own' prey on the ignorant curiosity or sympathy of tourists by begging, thinly disguised as selling a few crude 'genuine native artefacts'. This scarcely enhances the dignity of the aboriginal image, but it does after all conform to the expected stereotype. And the black may not unreasonably feel that the white, who has stolen his old hunting grounds, should be himself fair game.

The aborigine has been helpless before the infinitely superior strength of white society; he has had no option but to accept this helplessness, to find his account in it, and to live by it. To many aborigines, the rations and hand-outs for clothes and blankets are no more than a return – and a pitifully poor one – for the land which has been taken. There is a vicious circle – dispossession, contempt and degradation depressing men into a helpless apathy, then rescue work in a paternalist spirit, leading to more helpless dependence. The attitude seems often to be that these are wayward intractable children, who must be helped by protecting them against themselves – and consequently kept helpless. Very rarely is there even a pretence of consultation; everything must be done from above and from outside.

For the efficient conduct of this 'rescue work', the managers of such stations are still often vested with powers which are supposedly necessary to maintain discipline, especially in matters of drink and sexual behaviour. Perhaps they are; but at least in Queensland, where managers can refuse permission to leave the reserves, there is evidence of serious abuse and the complete denial of personal liberty in the most trivial matters: as late as 1962, 'Conduct prejudicial to the good order and discipline of the Settlement, viz., Evading Work, being Found Asleep' received ten days' imprisonment.[1] This is often bitterly, if silently, resented: there is surely a moral as well as grim humour in the true tale of the settlement which was reported 'wiped out' by a bushfire; later reports showed that the aborigines, with typical Aussie initiative and self-help in a crisis, had made fire-breaks around their own houses, but had unaccountably overlooked the manager's bungalow. . . .

It is forgotten that over-strict parental control means retarded development, and perhaps irrational rebellion, and that the wayward child longs for that which is forbidden. It is all very well to

[1] Hiatt, *op. cit.*, p. 285.

instil sobriety and morality, with the carrot that sometime or other, if you are good, you will be allowed to go out into the world, while that world itself is very often not conspicuously sober or moral. The aborigine can hardly be blamed for taking the line of least resistance: outward conformity, dodging the column, tasting the illicit delights of drink, sex, or gambling, of sorcery or tribal feud, as and when he can. He is not fooled; he recognises, and duly exploits, the guilt element in all this care for him; and he is aware of the divergence between the picture of a virtuous and sober Christian society, and the reality which lies around him.

Drink and kin

So far the discussion has been mainly concerned with the real outback station or mission natives of the north and west. But in the more developed and settled south-east, where hardly a trace of tribal organisation remains and where the economic obstacles to assimilation are if not absent at least much attenuated, there are still pressing and difficult problems. Here it is not unduly cynical to say that the test of assimilation is the ability to hold one's drink and ignore one's kin. This is also, probably, the measure of the desire for assimilation.

Until recently, this was officially explicit; in Western Australia legislation made the acquisition of citizenship rights conditional, amongst other things, on abstention from association with natives other than first-degree relations; in all States aborigines were legally prohibited from drinking until the mid-'sixties. There was exemption for 'those whose behaviour had been exemplary' – in practice, those who did not drink.[1] Such citizens were equal, but not so equal as others; and for their unexempted kinsfolk – well, nobody could be so completely de-assimilated from Australian society, more conspicuously marked out as inferior, as the man who cannot legally enter a country pub.

As Beckett and Bell show, the drink-and-kin nexus or syndrome is very clearly displayed in the part-aboriginal group of New South Wales. The same small town may have a little group of 'black' citizens, of no great standing but holding jobs and living in decent houses, perfectly respectable and on the whole accepted – they have 'passed'; and a disreputable group, usually larger, supporting them-

[1] J. Beckett, 'Aborigines, Alcohol, and Assimilation', in Reay, *op. cit.*, pp. 32–47, on which much of this section is based.

selves by casual and often seasonal labour, living in squalid tin
shacks and humpies on scrubby reserves or in camps on the out-
skirts. The two groups hold themselves very much apart, are in fact
castes; the citizens look down on the fringe-dwellers, though some of
them may be kinsfolk, as dirty debased reprobates; the reprobation
is mutual, the fringe-dwellers scorning the 'flash' climbers who
have sold out to the whites and their way of life. In the camps, life
is warm, casual, free-and-easy; everybody knows everybody else
intimately, goods are freely shared when one has them, in the
certainty of reciprocation. Above all, amongst many (not all) of
the men drinking is almost formalised as a social bond and a social
protest. It must be remembered that the formative contacts were
with the bush society of last century, when the only recreation very
generally available was liquor, and the bushworker, with nowhere
but the pub to cash his pay-check, not infrequently drank it out in
one glorious debauch; and even to-day no discredit, but often a
certain prestige, attaches to the hard drinker.

It was illegal; but the law was not very stringently enforced
against the white supplier, and there is a whole folklore of songs
about drinking exploits and resultant brushes with the police;
penalties were limited and predictable. Beer is bulky, difficult to
carry or conceal; spirits, usually cheap rum, and cheap fortified
wine – 'plonk' – were preferred: they produce results more quickly.
Not only was the drinking bout the only opportunity for an uninhibited projection of personality; it was also a defiance of white
man's law, an assertion, paradoxical as it may seem, of identity and
independence. It is most doubtful that these cheerful anarchists are
greatly disposed to accept the cramping limitations which go with
assimilation.

Their 'unco' guid' fellows inside the towns have accepted these
limitations, including that of contemning and avoiding their own
kin; that is part of the human price of assimilation. The penalty for
failure may be bitter: Albert Namatjira, at that time in all probability the most popular painter in Australia, lost his citizenship
rights and was jailed for supplying liquor to his kin, and the most
famous and 'successful' aborigine ended his days in misery and
disillusion. Much the same fate befell Robert Tudawali, the star of
the film *Jedda*. They failed as assimilated aboriginal citizens, one
may say as 'black white men'; they lost dignity and respect. Yet
this was in response to an age-old moral imperative, the strength of

which can hardly be truly assessed by a modern European: that the last crime is to desert one's kin. Is it better, or worse, to fail as a white citizen or as a black human being?

Education and economics

One of the most over-worked clichés of modern times is 'Education is the key'. In a sense, it happens to be true in a great range of problems; but its mere enunciation does not help much. Much has been done since 1950, when there were *no* trained teachers in Western Australian native schools; but what economic opportunities are open to the educated aborigine? Where in the outback are the urban centres which could provide settled jobs or markets for small truck farmers? What is the use of agricultural training, such as has been carried out for a century in South Australia, when even the 'reserves' are not legally native landed property, and in some cases, as late as 1960, have been partly leased out to native share farmers while aboriginal residents on them were unemployed?[1] Even if he is trained and has access to land, where is the aborigine to find the capital for even a modest farm? In such circumstances, can 'education for assimilation' mean anything more than education for a pool of seasonal rural labour, pea-picking and the like? Perhaps the answer lies in education for some form of community development, but the lessons from its multifarious and often chequered history seem very little known.

Such questions apart – and they are obviously very serious ones – there are definite special problems in aboriginal education. While special aboriginal schools, and more particularly specially trained teachers will be necessary, the objective will be defeated if aborigines are confined to a separate education system of their own; yet there are obvious practical difficulties in adjusting curricula to aboriginal needs in a mixed school and in running two streams without emphasising separateness. Very naturally, aboriginal children are easily discouraged by scholastic difficulties; often they have little incentive and can see little point in scholastic training. Next to European children, they feel the disparity in background and in home conditions and can be demoralised by relative failure. On the other hand, among some groups there is a strong conformity to old anti-individualist and non-competitive traditions; it does not do to excel one's fellows too obviously, that is 'flash' and will be met by the derision

[1] Fay Gale, in Reay, *op. cit.*, p. 104.

of the group. It is clear that an effort at once intensive and imaginative will be needed, and there are pointers on the way; for example,
there is evidence that in the earlier stages an approach through art
does much to level the disparity with European children and to give
a much-needed sense of achievement. Yet a Western Australian
experiment, which showed much more promise than the commercial art developed in the missions of the centre, was abandoned
for lack of financial backing by the State.

'Assimilation' versus 'Integration'

The long history of dispossession and rejection has shattered
aboriginal morale, and on any showing, Christian or pagan, morals
also have suffered. It is clear that for an indefinite time some
special provision for aboriginal welfare and advancement will be
necessary. The status of aborigines has varied greatly over the last
few decades and from State to State; assimilation has been adopted
as a general policy, but on the one hand it does not seem to have
any settled body of principles, apart from the general objective;
and on the other it is increasingly recognised that the problem is
multiplex, and that the methods appropriate to one area or group
are not likely to be of universal validity. Assimilation has not been,
and cannot be, unquestioned.

In the last resort, the demand is for absorption into a way of life
in which the material advantages are more conspicuous than the
moral superiority or the psychological comfort. For the aborigine it
amounts to a hard decision in a context of no other choice being
possible; it is not a matter of being able to make some sort of terms.
All the spiritual surrender must come from one side; a people
which has been robbed of all else is asked to yield its one remaining
possession, the sense of immemorial identity, and to transmute its
deepest and most cherished modes of thought and feeling into
almost their opposite. Proponents of assimilation do not of course
see it like that, in terms of surrender; rather in terms of the righting
of a wrong, of opening the way to a better life. The ideal is the full
mingling in the community, at any level open to talents and training, of people who will be indistinguishable from their fellows
except by their colour and their name, and retaining a pride in their
ancestry.

This has been the achievement or the fate of many peoples, those
subsumed into the Roman or the Chinese Empires for example, or,

say, the once-tribal Celts of Britain. But rarely, perhaps never, has the gap between the assimilating and the assimilated been so great, the habits of thought so antithetical, the shattering of the old society so catastrophic, the demand so total and so abrupt. Usually, also, there has been some tangible homeland, however remote in time and space, retaining some autonomy and nourishing a continuing sense of identity, even though the individual may be totally absorbed in an entirely different society from that of his ancestors. The aborigine's road is much harsher than that of any other such people, and he is given a shorter time to traverse it.

Faced with this stark prospect, some advocate as the ideal what is called 'integration'. This is very vaguely defined, but seems to imply the acceptance of a plural society, in which people of differing *mores* and social structures would live side by side, subject to common restraints of law but otherwise with, as it were, internal social autonomy. This has its appeal, but how would it work? The main positive contribution of this current of thought, as distinct from its critical underlining of awkward questions, is in the demand that aborigines should have a voice in running aboriginal affairs. Undoubtedly this is a necessity; but again, how shall it be applied? As we have seen, in practice the camp-dwellers do to a considerable extent run their own affairs with 'internal social autonomy', but this is hardly what is meant; the general level is not acceptable to a modern welfare state community.

Another way of life which in practice is a form of 'integration' is that of some of the missions, and undoubtedly some of the more conservative mission areas would like to keep it so, with little self-sufficient and aloof communities like the old Jesuit missions in Paraguay, the State forgetting, by the State forgot. But it must be admitted that by and large the aborigines have not found in Christianity the 'reintegration', in the sense of the replacement of the old congeries of beliefs by a new and fairly coherent philosophy, that has been achieved by some of the coastal peoples of New Guinea (and even here the prevalence of cargo cults shows how fragile the new philosophy so often is). For one thing, the white missionaries inevitably appear as the agents, or sometimes even the principals, of the invasion which has subverted a society materially poor but at least extremely well adjusted to its environment and skilled in the use of it; for another, the contrast between the official Christian doctrine and the realities of outback European life is often sufficiently striking to discredit the message: it was a monk of New Norcia who wondered whether the missionary effort might not be better applied to white society than to black. But if Christianity has on the whole failed – not of course without exceptions – to provide a reintegration of life, the old religion has been destroyed. Though some missionaries have made a fundamentalist assault on aboriginal belief, perhaps in isolated cases being as convinced of the existence of 'spirits who care' as the aborigines, but regarding them as devils, this destruction is not so much the result of direct Christian teaching as of the destruction of the bases of aboriginal society. Few systems of thought can have been so much entwined with the 'genius of the place' as that of the aborigines; but the sacred places are lost beyond recall and the aborigine is left wandering between two worlds, spiritually as well as materially. Little wonder that he turns to grog and gambling.

Aboriginal societies are small and fragmented, often highly ethnocentric between themselves. The time has gone by, if it ever existed, when an aboriginal quasi-autonomous territory, on a large enough scale to be economically viable, could have been reserved; and the attempt to construct one now would be immediately labelled discrimination, 'keeping them in an anthropologist's museum', *apartheid*.

There seems, then, no real alternative to assimilation, applied, it is to be hoped, with discretion and local adaptation in timing and method. But it must be admitted that the price will be high, not only in cash but in human terms. How high, no European can truly know.

The picture so far is and must be sombre; but there is light on the horizon, and it is not only the artificial light of official brochures and documentary films. Especially in small country towns, prejudice is still often bitter, but it is certainly easing, if gradually. Despite many petty tyrannies, those responsible for missions, stations, and reserves are increasingly recognising the need for trained and sympathetic approaches; the long and patient work of the anthropologists is beginning to bear fruit. And there is a changing image of the aborigine, and the emergence of an élite not forgetful of their still submerged fellows.

There are many cross-currents in this: some of those who voted 'Yes' in the 1967 referendum probably did so with the idea that the Commonwealth would now pay, a few with the hope that the

Commonwealth would take a tougher line with the aborigines than the States, and in the north the aboriginal vote itself must have counted for a good deal in some electorates.[1] But the general motivation, apart from considerations of Australia's reputation abroad, was probably simply the desire to 'give a fair go'.

Many factors have gone to the surprisingly wide-spread change in attitude shown by the referendum. A good deal, of course, is simply rather woolly do-good liberalism on the part of those who have no direct contact with the problem; as Paul Hasluck, who as Minister for Territories had a strong sense of mission towards his charges, once suggested, there may have been a shortage of good causes. There is a certain fashionable *réclame* in taking aborigines seriously, expressed for example by exploiting the fictional possibilities offered by studies of local race prejudice and miscegenation: it is an easy way of establishing one's reputation as a man of strong social conscience. However, unthinking do-gooders are better than unthinking do-badders: they give the thinking do-gooders some leverage.

The referendum opens the way – and aborigines themselves have been quick to demand that the way shall be taken – for positive action. The initial response of the Commonwealth was cool; a bright symbol is all very well, and may easily become a substitute for effort. There is no lack of immediate problems: health, and especially the very high infant mortality; a fresh approach to education, housing – in some cases the euphoria of assimilation has led to gross neglect of housing in aboriginal settlements, since it was optimistically assumed that the need would dwindle; the provision of economic opportunity. One problem which demands attention is the levity with which aboriginal reserves have been disregarded when minerals are found on them: the aborigines have no legal claims except to more or less *ex gratia* compensation, and while some companies have striven to provide education, employment, and amenities, the general record is deplorable. And one cannot but suspect some window-dressing in the more readily accessible government settlements.

But the most significant factor is surely the emergence of articu-

---

[1] Since 1962, all aborigines may vote in Commonwealth elections, including referenda, though the Northern Territory, like the Australian Capital Territory, has no referendum vote; and they may enrol as State voters. Enrolment is not compulsory, but once enrolled voting is.

late aboriginal spokesmen; people like the poet Kathy Walker, the Sydney graduate Charles Perkins, to mention but two, who have made the grade themselves and are not prepared to sit back and do nothing for the less fortunate.

The earliest pathway to recognition of individual merit in aborigines was in sport: it is safe to say that before the war such as were in any degree known to the man in the street were boxers or footballers, whose renown was in the nature of the case ephemeral. Perhaps the first real break-through in other fields, even if a rather equivocal one, was that by Albert Namatjira, whose landscapes, in a style too derivative from a European model and heavily loaded with those mauves and purples beloved of Australian suburbia, are to be found in hundreds or even thousands of homes. There is of couse a phony element in this: it was odd and exciting to be able to say 'Just think that it was really done by a blackfellow, my dear.' Nevertheless a break-through was made: one aborigine at least was known by name throughout the country in an honourable context. There are now others, increasingly engaged in the conscious promotion of aboriginal interests as such. The Negro struggle in the United States has not gone unnoticed; Sydney students, led by Charles Perkins, went on a Freedom Ride in northern New South Wales, and this was not without its effect. Until very recently, everything that was done was done by outsiders *for* aborigines; it is already necessary, and will be increasingly so, to work *with* them.

The tragedy of the aborigines is not unique: it is the tragedy of all weak peoples, living by kinship and custom, forced into the omnipotent world of the market, of contract and money. It is more poignant than most such tragedies because the odds were so hopelessly disparate and the devastation so complete. But at least it is a problem not insuperable, except at utterly unbearable cost, by reason of sheer scale, as the South African problem is, and perhaps also that of the American Negro. The individual suffering, in personal humiliation and in the agonising wrench of the breaking of kinship bonds, will often be intense; but given time and patience, one can see assimilation working in the long run. At any rate, since the referendum two things are sure: the old brutal rejection of the aborigines as a general Australian attitude is gone for ever; and aborigines themselves – even if as yet only through a small élite – have begun to share in the shaping of their destiny.

Chapter 14

Aspects of Australian Culture

A DISTURBING AMBIVALENCE runs throughout the Australian social and cultural scene. A 'developed' country of high technology and even affluence, and inordinately proud of the trappings of modernity, especially American modernity – an attitude aptly summed up in the coinage 'Austerican', which has only the flaw that it suggests a non-existent austerity. At the same time, an 'underdeveloped' country, incapable of exploiting its resources without massive overseas aid in money and know-how, uneasily aware that it must indefinitely remain if not a colony then at least a client. Superficially, egalitarian to a degree, and yet attached to status symbols, sometimes of the most inane kind.[1] Young and dynamic in its image of itself, and in truth with plenty of energy and not a little creative capacity, yet so often timid, conservative, traditionalist in its attachment to tired political and social institutions. Boastful and self-depreciatory, euphoric and anxiety-ridden; living for the day and yet on occasion gloomily introspective; given to simple pleasures and longing for sophistication; a hedonist society in a Puritan tradition.

The arts

In the arts this ambivalence is most clearly seen in the constant tension between the desire to be firmly Australian and the desire for universal, or at least cosmopolitan, values. Both desires are entirely natural, indeed inescapable, and by no means confined to Australia; but the dichotomy is particularly acute here by reason of a remoteness which does not amount to a protective insulation, within which a truly autonomous culture could grow, but only to an isolation which inhibits the full development of either the cosmopolitan or the local genius.

---

[1] Some 'economy' air services from small country towns have lapsed because nobody in the local society who could afford to fly could afford to be seen 'flying tourist'.

Since the decline of patronage in the eighteenth century, any considerable cultural development (excluding odd essentially parasitic coteries) has depended on a reasonably wide commercial market. Until recently, the Australian society was simply too small to support a high culture of its own; other small societies, such as those of Holland or Hungary, were able to do so because they had their own language (which provides as it were a protective cultural tariff against the dominance of English), were strengthened by long historic tradition, and yet were well placed for participation in the general stream of European culture. None of these factors applied in Australia; nevertheless, the attempt to build an indigenous culture was made, aided or compelled by isolation, and with a fair measure of success. But today the effort made to perpetuate this abortive culture in some circles, ever on the *qui vive* for 'the great Australian masterpiece', is merely pathetic.

It is unfair to the colonial poets, Kendall and Gordon, to dismiss their efforts (the quaint old word applies well) as mere reflections of Tennyson or Swinburne; but, however well they occasionally brought off the marriage of the contemporary English Muse to the Austral environment, the way to an Australian culture was not up this blind alley. But by the 'nineties there was a genuine local tradition: it is because Paterson and Lawson mirror a world as authentic, integrated, and complete as those of Jane Austen and Trollope (though much less complex) that their work, so artless as it appears, has yet some satisfactions for post-Eliot readers. Even now there are those admirable survivors one meets in outback pubs, rolling stones who have gathered no moss but an immense store of living anecdote and legend, boisterous always, often witty, sometimes wise, which gives to the short and simple annals of the rural township something at least of a tradition: salty, earthy, grotesque, but genuine.

This tradition stands in no need either of apology or of boosting, and it has its literary remains; it cannot be forgotten. But as a contemporary thing it is moribund, and there is no point in artificial resuscitation. It is suffering the horrible fate of commercialised parody, for all the world like the revival of Egyptian dynastic motifs in the squalor and garish décor of modern Cairo. Bush culture survives in *Waltzing Matilda*, which few people can sing beyond line four and chorus, and in the tourist propaganda in which the dinkum Aussie is cast as a rugged pioneer. Ten years ago one wondered how long it would be before the conducted tours would include a Reserve with real live bushmen really boiling the billy; with the exploitation of Ayers Rock, this seems coming about already. And when a township which had certainly not reached its century held sesquicentennial celebrations on the ground that 150 years ago Matthew Flinders must have sailed past its site, and might have seen it – well, why be in such an unconscionable hurry to grow old ungracefully?

This last example is of course the expression of an exhibitionism which provides some outlet from the narrowness of small town life; and this exists on a higher and more respectable level, with those who would still cling to the dream of O'Dowd's Utopia. On this plane we have the apotheosis of everything aboriginal, which the 'Jindyworobak' poets have taken to the point of seeking a mythos completely at one with the Australian environment, to be attained by jettisoning all European modalities in favour of a symbolism drawn from the aboriginal dream-land or dream-time of Alcheringa. Certainly it is to the advantage of poets to develop new myths and symbols, but this does not imply a deliberate and unnatural turning away from one's own times and culture. Longfellow after all tried the same thing, and nobody would say that *Hiawatha* is nearly so much of an indigenous American thing as *Spoon River Anthology* or *John Brown's Body*.

Fortunately this is an aberration only (and not without some agreeable lyrics as incidental side-effects); the central problem remains: how to find an expression which combines the local genius of Australia with some approach to universality? The old tradition has been swamped by the increasing sophistication of the great cities, stricken mortally as much by improved communications, internal and external, as by anything else. Yet the intellectual in Melbourne or Sydney is too much in touch with the outer world to be content with local material and well-tried techniques, too much out of touch to avoid a distressing time-lag. A good deal of modern writing looks too much like inter-war Bloomsbury; very little is really *avant-garde*, though in some circles this is not for want of trying. This applies also in the plastic and graphic arts and in architecture: there is very good modern work, but it is sometimes painful to see a competent artist presenting an eclectic *mélange* of half-a-dozen styles, some genuinely experimental but some too suggestive of the currently fashionable band-wagon.

For all that, the cultural achievement of Australia is not small, and it is no longer necessary to become an expatriate to secure fame and (more rarely) modest fortune. One must distinguish between what may be called the public and the private arts. On the whole, it seems to be fair to say that Australians at home have excelled mainly in the latter – lyric poetry, fiction, painting. For such public arts as theatre or film, expensive to create or display, the base is too small to support a really solid development as yet, though it will surely come. There are good Australian plays but so far hardly an Australian theatre – there might have been but for the intrusion of the picture-house and of television. The latter is far too dependent on material imported (especially from America) which is cheap and fitted to the lowest common denominator of taste; the public which would be glad of something better does exist, but is not large enough to call the tune. In music the Australian record is much stronger on the executant than on the creative side.

In such arts, and in ballet, the real rewards are still overseas, and the Australian emigration has contributed substantially, both in quantity and quality, to theatre, ballet, film, television, and even opera, in Britain and America. So much indeed is this so that the 'Earls Court expatriates'[1] are something of figures of fun in Australian intellectual and artistic circles. A good deal of the fun derives from their patronising commiserations with their fellows left at home, accompanied by laboured attempts to prove that they are as good Aussies as any, but compelled reluctantly to leave their ungrateful and unrewarding native soil. To Australia, their loss is perhaps offset by those *émigré* intellectuals from Europe who, like the present writer, are reasonably happy with their antipodean lot.

Overseas market factors operate less strongly in painting and in non-dramatic writing, and in these fields the Australian harvest is fully mature. 'Henry Handel Richardson', whose *The Fortunes of Richard Mahoney* (1917–30) is highly accomplished in the manner of the classical English novel, was an expatriate; but she could be matched at home by Furphy's *Such is Life*, a work of more original cast, and by Eleanor Dark's historical trilogy of the first

[1] To Australians, 'Earls Court' is synonymous with a more or less Bohemian colony or enclave of *émigrés*, just as Sydney's 'King's Cross' is synonymous with a wildly exotic enclave of continental Bohemia in Australia. Both views ignore the workaday penumbra of ordinary people, English or Australian, who surround these islands of rather sordid romanticism.

settlement. To-day Patrick White is recognised as a novelist of world stature, in whose work the local and the universal meet: the explorations of *Voss* are of Australia and of the human heart. The English language has no more gifted Symbolist poet than Christopher Brennan, unless Yeats be counted as such; and few 'older contemporaries' in England or America surpass the trio Judith Wright, James McAuley, and Alec Hope. They do not form a school, but the work of McAuley and Hope is rooted in a reflective intellectualism which is far from excluding human emotion: indeed, it would be difficult to find a purer or more beautiful expression of physical love than McAuley's *Aubade*. Hope's best verse, often sharply satiric as in *Advice to Young Ladies*, maintains a tough classic stance before 'the regimen of the disorder'd world' which is akin to the stoicism of de Vigny or Robinson Jeffers.[1]

Painting, if not Royal Academic or purely abstract, must needs have a local colour, and the difficulty of judging, buying, and importing pictures from the other side of the world (not to mention a 15 per cent sales tax on the works of foreign artists) gives an automatic protection.[2] Affluence, status-seeking, and modern tendencies in interior decoration have led to a market boom, accompanied by remarkable incongruities of taste; when it is said that more Australians are interested in art than ever before, what is usually meant is that more people are talking about the prices of paintings. The older generation – Russell Drysdale, Sidney Nolan, William Dobell – is every sense native to the soil, blending successfully the traditional and the local with the contemporary experimentation of their day. The younger men, as everywhere except in countries of Socialist Realism, go a-whoring after the latest strange gods: abstract, action, and pop art flourish. The general competence, in both quasi-traditional and *avant-garde* modes, is high, and the versatility of contemporary graphic artists is full of promise.

As for sculpture, it has suffered from lack of intelligent patronage: allowing for their scanty resources, the Australian colonies shared to the full the nineteenth-century passion for the memorial perpetuation of the illustrious obscure and the degradation of sculpture

---

[1] It would be pointless to enumerate the ever-changing minor constellations which surround these stars of magnitude. For an admirable survey, see Geoffrey Dutton (ed.), *The Literature of Australia* (Pelicans, 1964).

[2] Until recently, this was fortified by actual tariff duties. The recent expansion of patronage is analysed by J. M. Main in A. F. Davies and S. Encel (eds), *Australian Society* (Cheshire, Melbourne, 1965), pp. 176–89.

from an integral part of architecture to an *appliqué* adjunct. The results were bathetic. To-day the idea that sculpture is not just monument, funerary or patriotic, is taking ground. There is now a market for non-representational sculpture in various modes, and experimentation is lively, if at times too conscientiously derivative from the latest overseas fashion.

Architecture: heritage and trends

Before the gold rushes, most public building was Georgian in style and temper; the time-lag was dependent not only on isolation but on the survival of a society simpler and more authoritarian than that of England after 1800. Except on a limited scale in Tasmania, however, there was nothing really comparable to the flowering of American Colonial; there was no large leisured class of the plantation type. Rural Tasmania, where there really was something like a landed gentry, has a treasury of excellent Georgian building, including whole villages like Bothwell; but elsewhere little survives, although around Sydney some is hidden behind the barbarous re-modelling of several generations. Only recently – and that is much too late – has the preservation of this heritage (admittedly difficult for economic reasons) been seriously taken in hand on National Trust lines. On the domestic level an indigenous style, with hipped roofs and verandas, was developed, unassuming but not unpleasing even when the roofs were of corrugated iron.

It is indeed difficult to think of Australian development without the 'tin roof', which has been neglected by social historians – above their heads, often enough, but beneath their notice. It was introduced as early as 1830 and almost universally supplanted shingles and expensive imported slate, until in this century red tiles have taken over in the vast spreading suburbias. The advantages of corrugated iron were many: it was easy to install, relatively easy to transport, fireproof, and above all it provided a reliable catchment for rainwater; on the other hand it is of course very hot in summer and cold in winter. Along with corrugated iron goes the decorative cast iron of innumerable balconies, which gives to many older city areas something of the charm of the Vieux Carré in New Orleans. In both cases there was an economic factor – cast iron came cheaply from Britain as ballast for ships which would return with bulky cargoes of wool or cotton.

The inflation of the gold rush decade was accompanied by a

dilution not only in taste but in craftsmanship; the falling-off can actually be traced and dated in single buildings of the 'fifties. The progressive shortening of the cultural time-lag produced some curious results. Thus in secular or municipal architecture the reign of Gothic was relatively short, and the more spectacular and sometimes horrific buildings of the later nineteenth century are more likely to be in eclectic but vaguely Renaissance styles, which cry out for an Osbert Lancaster to record them. Ballarat, Bendigo, fashionable Toorak in Melbourne are veritable museums of architecture as grandiose as that of the Third Republic in France, though less cluttered with gigantic nymphage. But where money was less plentiful, building was often remarkably successful, as in the banks and post offices built in New South Wales country towns between 1870 and 1890, in a distinctly Italianate style in cream stucco, sometimes a little heavy but always solid and dignified. This phase was succeeded by the vogue of Art Nouveau exteriors, relatively much more common than in Britain and sometimes bizarre. But the inter-war suburban spread produced leagues of monotony, relieved by a safe and easy 'modernism' here and there.

The modern 'international style' is not the first of its kind: one has only to look at the commercial offices of the 'nineties around the ports of the colonial world. The new concrete-and-glass mode is now firmly rooted, but while on the one hand insufficient regard is shown for the unsuitability of acres of glass in the Australian climate, on the other there is still evident a desire to play for safety by being 'modernist' rather than truly modern. The public buildings of Canberra, for example, are with some exceptions distinguished – or better undistinguished – by an unadventurous anxiety to avoid the possible ridicule of posterity. However, though 'Pseudish' in all its many branches is still dominant, architecture at least in the public and commercial sectors is sharing in the general and quite startling increase of urban sophistication since 1950. The cores of the capitals are becoming clusters of skyscrapers, some university building is very good indeed, and even in remote country towns ecclesiastical clients are no longer content with Tutor's Tudor and seedy Gothic. By and large, the urban landscapes of Australia, in the countryside as well as in the capitals, are becoming brighter, more colourful, and more impressive.

Education and its ills

Australia has produced good scholars, scientists, poets, painters, soldiers, politicians, and a few who at least verge on greatness. Often enough Australians have made their names overseas and are not generally recognised as Australian-born; one may instance Gilbert Murray, Grafton Eliot Smith, Jack Lindsay, Errol Flynn, Lord Florey.... But perhaps the really great names in Australia's history – not all country-born, but Australian by virtue of their work – are the men of the land and the laboratory: Macarthur; Ridley and Mackay with the strippers and harvesters, the Smiths with the multiple-furrow stump-jump plough; Lowrie with his work on superphosphates and rotations; the Chaffeys who brought irrigation from California to the Murray; Farrer the wheat-breeder; Watt who destroyed the prickly pear and saved the bananas; Mort who pioneered refrigeration; and a long line of keen and intelligent pastoralists, forever experimenting with new strains whether of stock or pastures. To-day the tradition is maintained more vigorously than ever, by the universities, by the Commonwealth Scientific and Industrial Research Organisation (CSIRO), and by a host of State agencies.

In 1945 there were six universities, one in each State capital; there are now fourteen. The Australian National University, initially devoted to research only, was founded in 1946 and began effective work at Canberra in 1951; two were added in both Melbourne and Sydney, one in Adelaide, and University Colleges at Newcastle and at Armidale in New England attained full status. Next in line are the Colleges at Townsville and Wollongong and a second university for Brisbane. This numerical expansion has been accompanied by intensification in the traditional disciplines – long past are the days when the Sydney Department of History consisted, for thirty years, of the foundation Professor – and by an immense diversification, though some disciplines (most notably perhaps anthropology and sociology) are quantitatively still below the level they need to give their full contribution.

Academic standards in general are high. Initially, the older universities – Sydney 1850, Melbourne 1853, Adelaide 1874 – began with a very narrow range of arts subjects and were staffed almost exclusively from Britain, and while in a strictly academic sense their staffs were good and sometimes brilliant teachers and scholars, the criticism that they were aloof ivory towers was not wholly unfair. They were essentially élitist, and their main contribution to national life was in supplying lawyer politicians and doctors. By the turn of the century the obvious importance of engineering and of the applied and field sciences – especially geology and botany – enforced an uneasy compromise between Oxbridge and Redbrick; and the next wave – Tasmania 1890, Queensland 1909, Western Australia 1912 – were Redbrick from the start; the shift from city to State names may have been unconsciously significant. Criticism then changed in emphasis: the universities were and are condemned as being much too utilitarian-biased degree factories (and often enough as being of little practical use!). There is something in this, but despite the cant of Academe, it is very questionable whether, in most ages and places, more than a small (but crucial) minority of students went to the university for spiritual and intellectual enrichment for its own sake, rather than social and vocational advantage.[1]

It is of the utmost importance that universities should indeed foster free intellectual enquiry and development; and to the best of their ability those of Australia endeavour to do so. But this is an increasingly difficult task in an age of mass education, of the 'two cultures', of academic specialisation and technological sophistication, and of the increasing bureaucratisation of learning rendered inevitable by the sheer size and complexity of a modern university, which must be amongst other things a large business organisation accounting for a great deal of money. University finance is governed, at least notionally, by the recommendations of the (Commonwealth) Australian Universities Commission, the equivalent of the British UGC, the Commonwealth contributing to State universities on a fixed ratio. This system runs into difficulties when State governments do not feel able to meet their proportion.

The task of the universities is rendered more difficult by the failings of the educational infrastructure; though it must be admitted that academics themselves, by and large, do not greatly trouble themselves in the improvement of the schools.

Education is a State subject, and the Commonwealth Office of Education has been concerned mainly with research and overseas contacts; not until 1967 was a definite, and mainly co-ordinating,

[1] Were ever universities more vocationally-oriented (and in effect to the single vocation of the church) than unreformed Oxford and Cambridge? Or more socially biased than the same universities between the nineteenth-century reforms and the first World War?

Commonwealth Department of Education and Science set up. The State systems vary in efficiency, but all of them are strongly centralised, and one cannot but suspect that a good deal of Australian 'education' is rather 'schooling', marked by mechanical criteria of efficiency and a slavish adherence to sometimes outmoded syllabuses.[1] With exceptions, such as the central schools of rural Tasmania, they are all cut to a pattern, or rather six patterns between which there is little communication. This means, amongst other things, that the textbook market, small enough to begin with, is cut up into six, and that in the more specialised fields there are hardly enough qualified teachers to maintain active and truly professional organisations, as distinct from general teachers' unions. Only ten years ago many textbooks were quite simply disgraceful to their authors, their publishers, and the authorities which permitted their use. There has been a good deal of improvement, but in general the standard is not as high as it should be; and the current talk of uniform Commonwealth-sponsored collective texts for what are assumed to be 'factual' subjects seems a desperate remedy, perhaps worse than the disease.

The State centralisation of education undoubtedly results in undue rigidity; but were the schools to be devolved to local boards, as in the United States, one may very reasonably wonder how many of them would have the intellectual resources to maintain really good standards, let alone adequate finance, which would in most non-metropolitan areas still have to come largely by State subsidy.

Although education is a major item in State budgets, and total expenditure on it rose from 2.2 to nearly 4 per cent of gross national product between 1954 and 1967, it is still definitely low compared with that of most countries with a similar general level of development. Although few, if any, would like to see education further centralised federally, it can scarcely be doubted that the Commonwealth could and should do much more – though not by way of uniform textbooks! Library appropriations for instance are often scandalously low, and this would seem a fit and easy field for central aid. The Federal government did not accept the recommendation of the very responsible Martin Committee on Tertiary Education (1964)

---

[1] There are some amusing, but also saddening, examples in R. F. Butts, *Basic Assumptions underlying Australian Education* (Australian Council for Educational Research, Melbourne, 1955). There has been some improvement since Butt wrote, but how substantial may be a matter of doubt.

that it should directly engage in or specifically subsidise teacher training. Yet the shortage of teachers, as well as the shortage of class-rooms in many places, seems to be approaching crisis proportions.

In 1959, no fewer than 10 per cent of the children in large Victorian primary schools were in classes of over fifty; over half of them in classes of over forty. In such conditions it is clear that the word 'education' hardly applies; 'schooling', in the chronologically Victorian sense, may. In 1963, the Australian average for State schools was one teacher to 27.5 pupils; to reach a desirable ratio of 1:20 would need over 23,000 extra teachers, against an annual out-turn from training colleges of rather over 6,000; the wretchedly low allowance to trainees, in a context of affluence and nearly full employment, is a main factor. This of course neglects non-State schools: about one-fifth of over 2,500,000 pupils are in Roman Catholic schools, and in many of these conditions are worse than in the State schools.

Serious as this quantitative inadequacy of the teaching body is, its lack of specialist training, especially in science, is quite as alarm-ing. In 1960, 59 per cent of all science teachers had no science degree, 31 per cent had not even passed in any science subjects.[1] In a technological age, these figures for a country which boasts of its affluence and its high development are quite simply appalling. University enrolments, partly as a result of the post-war 'baby boom', are swelling, from 30,360 in 1950 to 76,188 in 1964, and the universities are adjured to put more and more effort into science and technology, though already quotas must more and more be applied. Selective quotas should improve the average student level, and a greater outturn of trained teachers should theoretically be-come possible; but this must surely depend on a more realistic – which means a more liberal – attitude to the training colleges and their trainees. And this, with other demands on government for money, might well lead into inflation. . . .

Beside the State systems are the denominational, which range from poverty-stricken Catholic parish schools to Anglican founda-tions which are close copies of Public Schools in the peculiar English sense, and a very tiny handful of progressive schools. It is an inter-esting comment on 'Australian egalitarianism' that about half of Liberal Federal parliamentarians were educated at private schools, and that of the 15 per cent of Melbourne University arts students

[1] J. R. Lawry, 'Education', in Davies and Encel, *op. cit.*, p. 87.

taking honours courses in 1959 over a quarter had been to one of the 'Great Public Schools', which represent a very much smaller fraction of secondary enrolments.

Of course, whatever the system, good teachers and good students there will always be, and when they meet they produce good well-rounded, well-equipped citizens. But this is leaving much too much to chance, and implies a dreadful wastage. The malaise of Australian education has struck deep, and it is not only a matter of money, though that is important. Except – perhaps – in New South Wales, there seems to have been little attempt in recent years, on the official level, to think out a coherent philosophy of education for our times, though there has been much detailed pedagogical research. Part of the trouble may well stem from the fact that in higher education Australia has taken a middle way, at first sight sensible and attractive, between the old British élitist model and the American emphasis on college education for the mass.

In itself, the Australian pattern of university courses appears to hit the happy medium between the undue specialisation of the British honours course and the diffuse and amorphous mass of 'credits' which make up many American first degrees. But with increasing professionalisation, almost all non-manual and some quasi-manual occupations demand some tertiary qualifications. The universities are in part inhibited by the residuum of the British tradition from going whole-heartedly on the mass vocational line, and in any case are just not equipped, even with the post-war expansion, to cope with the numbers that would be involved. Their public image is ambivalent: on the one hand, professors rate high in sociological rankings, and must expect to receive more personal publicity, sometimes of a rather lurid kind, than their fellows in Britain; on the other, they are condemned at one and the same time for giving their students routine utilitarian drill instruction and not creative ideas, and for failing to keep students with ideas under control. Any student expression of social or political radicalism, or even of high spirits, is likely to be visited with grotesquely disproportionate moral indication by the 'unco' guid' (especially in Melbourne), and the sins, if they are such, of a minority are transferred to the whole organism of the university.

The question of technical education for those not academically inclined or qualified also looms large. There is a reasonably good range of technical colleges, although the provision of a really modern system of technical education is hampered by the addiction of the Trade Unions, and some employers, to apprenticeship systems which were appropriate enough to nineteenth-century Britain but are irrelevant in an age of universal education. A start has been made, especially in Victoria, with the establishment of what would be in effect 'Junior Colleges' on the American model. In principle, this would seem a good solution of the problem; in Australian conditions, one may well apprehend that they may become an untidy compromise, perhaps withdrawing needed finance from the universities and producing a dilute mixture of semi-academic and technical skills.

Nowhere in Australia is there less room for complacency than in education. It would not be fair to say that the governments have been entirely complacent, but there are so many calls, and education is dull – not least in the prose of professional educationists. While all parties pay lip-service to the problem, it is far from clear that official agencies are really seized of the urgency of the case. The teachers do what they can to emphasise its gravity, but they are hampered by the fact that their claim to professional status is sometimes difficult to square with the facts of their training and outlook and hence they are too easily written off as just another interested pressure group. The universities, on the whole and with bright exceptions, pay too little attention to the schools. Meanwhile, it can hardly be said that overcrowding, staff shortages, and inadequate teaching qualifications are being liquidated: rather it is a case of running hard to stay in the same place.

In this, as in other social matters, Australia has a tendency to live on the capital of past achievement. The State educational systems in their origins look crude to the hindsight of a psychologised age; but considering their scant resources, they were great things in their day. Our times are infinitely more complex and demanding than the Australia of say 1900; and a country with Australia's population, in an environment at once very difficult and potentially rewarding to trained and intelligent effort, cannot afford to neglect the most intensive fostering of its considerable resources in brainpower.

The mass media

The efforts of the educationists are not, on the whole, well served by the mass media; though it may be questioned whether, all things considered, Australia is really much worse off than the rest of the world in this respect. Lenin's dictum, that freedom of the Press means the freedom of the man who can afford to own a paper to debauch the mind of the man who can only afford to buy one, has a good deal of point everywhere; but at least if there are several owners (as there are not in Lenin's state) one has a choice of poisons and can compare one with the next. It is true that in Australia this choice is limited by the high degree of Press oligopoly.[1]

Once again this is largely a function of the small size of the market and its combined concentration and fragmentation into six metropolitan nuclei – or seven if we include Canberra, whose role as the national capital to some extent offsets its small population. The percentage of people who would be interested in a 'quality' newspaper is perhaps not much below that in Britain; but the British minority is a fraction of a total five times as great, and is well enough concentrated geographically to be served from the one centre of Fleet Street. Conversely, the absence of anything like America's multiplicity of second-order metropolitan centres makes impossible the existence of solidly-based provincial papers with more than parish-pump coverage. There are many local papers, mostly weeklies, in Australia, but they are in every sense small-town, and it is hardly too strong to apply this term to the dailies in the minor State capitals. Only Sydney and Melbourne are big enough to support really mass circulations, and there is as yet no really 'national' paper. It is significant that the youngest big paper, *The Australian*, which was founded in 1964 and has made a gallant attempt at being a national organ, had by 1967 to shift much of its organisation from Canberra to Sydney.

But if the demographic geography enforces fragmentation in the distribution, and hence in the physical production, of newspapers, it imposes no such restraint on ownership. Two chains produce three out of every four copies sold. The most serious aspect of this con-centration is perhaps in its depressant effect on journalism as a profession; even in Sydney, where there is most competition, it may be difficult for a man of any independence of mind to carve his way once he has fallen foul of an editor or proprietor, and there is a brain drain either overseas or into public relations and so on;

[1] See the chapter on mass media by Davies and Encel in *Australian Society*, pp. 205–09, to which this section owes a great deal, and H. Mayer, *The Australian Press* (Landsdowne, Sydney, 1964).

radio and TV are not altogether adequate alternatives as many of their outlets are themselves controlled by newspaper interests. This of course conduces to mediocrity. Overseas news is syndicated, and even in the best papers scarcely adequate to real understanding; inter-State news is usually provided not by an independent staff in other capitals but from a linked paper. There is thus a good deal of sameness in the news stories; and – perhaps a reflection of egalitarianism? – not much differentiated reader appeal. The main distinction is between the staider dailies and the abysmal tabloids, which – to cite the summary of one of them by its rival – 'always get worried and confused when confronted by any issues more serious than bosoms and bottoms'.

All things considered, it is perhaps surprising that the few 'big' papers maintain a reasonable standard – not that of *The Guardian*, but recognisably of the same family as the old *News Chronicle*, though more conservative; the tabloids rank with the British *Mirror*, minus its verve and its radical line. Perhaps the most interesting are *The Canberra Times*, a fascinating blend of the national and the small-town, and *The Australian*, which is schizophrenic in a different way: it has elements of a 'quality' paper in an unusual provision of special articles of some length and weight, but is often unduly sensational in news treatment and coyly descends to an astrological column. Once a week, on Saturdays, the 'big' papers go all cultural, and the standard of features and book reviews is remarkably high.

It is doubtful how far the dailies could really qualify as 'organs of opinion' (though their own editorials entertain no such doubts), and even the continuing *Bulletin* has lost a great deal of its one-time impact. There is no Australian *New Statesman* or *New Republic*, though persistent efforts are made to supply one to offset the conservatism of the *Bulletin*; but they are generally short-lived and the most successful, *Nation*, while lively enough is not impressive in format and has not a large circulation; once more, the market is too small and fragmented for anything more solid. There is of course a wealth of technical journals, as well as radical (and one or two reactionary) dissents, comments, outlooks, voices, and so on preaching to the converted, and half-a-dozen literary quarterlies, of which *Meanjin* and *Quadrant*, radical and conservative respectively, are the best-found; but most of these literary journals depend to some extent on subsidies from the Commonwealth Literary Fund.

The giants of periodical publishing are such things as *The Australian Women's Weekly*, which it is claimed goes into every other home, *People*, and *Pix*, whose effect would seem to stifle rather than to foster opinion of any sort.

Nor do radio and television do very much to redress the balance. There is a dual system: the 'national' Australian Broadcasting Commission, and privately-owned commercial networks. The ABC is not a very close equivalent of the BBC: it is controlled by nine commissioners appointed by the Federal government and they are formally independent of government interference; but it is difficult to envisage the ABC playing the really autonomous role of the BBC, though it does try. But in a monocultural democracy, really fundamental questioning is difficult to carry through, and there are just too many little incidents of shifting or demotion of staff after programmes which have aroused criticism from churches, the Returned Servicemen's League, or government parties. In isolation, most or perhaps all of these could be written off as not exactly 'interference' but merely response to presumptive pressure from the right-thinking; but cumulatively they are rather disquieting. The internal organisation of the ABC seems too heavy and to subordinate creativity to administration, while the personalities of most of the Commissioners themselves seem to be a guarantee of impeccable caution. How immoderately moderate the ABC can be is shown by the replacement, in a script for broadcast to Asia, of a reference to 'negro slavery' in nineteenth-century Brazil by the words 'involuntary coloured servitude'.

Nevertheless, there is some reflection in the ABC of the Reith ethos in the BBC, and a definite desire to maintain standards. The ABC's news services are on the whole good; its support of symphony orchestras and of visits by overseas artists has certainly provided good music to many who would otherwise have been denied it; and its special services for outback schools, 'kindergarten of the air' and so on, are excellent, though the TV 'University of the Air' is perhaps rather too conventional in approach. With all its weaknesses, life in Australia would be a good deal poorer without the ABC.

It is the commercial stations which 'give the people what they want', and which hold the greater audiences. Press interests are very strong in local radio and TV, but churches, the Ansett industrial group, and even the ALP take a hand. 'Drama', which covers a multitude of sins, and pop music are the staple fare, naturally enough; and despite legislation to maintain some locally-produced content, there is a great deal too much reliance on the imported second-hand and third-rate. Although TV has taken a very firm hold, it is doubtful whether its overt social effects – replacement of reading as a habit, fostering of violence, and so on – have been very deleterious; it may in fact have served to integrate family life. In small country towns, the chatty atmosphere of the commercial programme, in which any group can buy a few minutes to say a word for its own concern (which may be spiritual as well as commercial), contributes to an easy-going local togetherness. This should not be despised, and yet here perhaps is the real snare of TV for a people already given to complacency and with a limited vision of the outside world: 'The bland beam on a mirror they take for a window.'[1]

The religion of sport

In no ironic sense, sport in Australia must be treated with serious respect. In 1960–61, it was ascertained that of 770 Australian army recruits, two-thirds were unaware of who Pontius Pilate was, while what events were celebrated on Good Friday, Easter Day, and Whitsunday were known respectively to two-thirds, one-half, and 0.9 per cent. It is a safe bet that were say Dawn Fraser or Lew Hoad substituted for Pilate, and Melbourne Cup Day for the Holy days, the successful score would be nearly 100 per cent.[2] For in truth sport is the secular religion of a large proportion of Australians.

Like that of the Trade Unions, the role of sport in Australian society has been sadly neglected by academic enquirers; yet it is replete with fascinating sociological problems which one would think far more amenable to the questionnaire approach than more intimate matters such as religious beliefs and marital habits. There is for example the changing spectrum of sports rankings: the old domination of cricket as a summer sport seems yielding, if it has

---

[1] Davies and Encel, *op. cit.*, p. 229.

[2] One-sixth did not know who Christ was. The phenomenon is not altogether new: half a century ago the Very Reverend Monsignor Patrick Hartigan, better known as 'John O'Brien', published an unexpected reply to a bishop's query, at Confirmation time, about what Christmas stood for:

> The ready answer bared a fact no Bishop ever knew –
> 'It's the day before the races out at Tangmalangaloo.'

not already yielded, to tennis; since Bradman no cricketer has had quite the universal fame now accorded to the stars of tennis, swimming, and golf, in which the index of individual participation is high. There are, for example, over 200,000 tennis players who take the game seriously enough to belong to one of 5,000 registered clubs. Judging by the courts one sees lost in the bush, at dirt-road junctions or by isolated homesteads, tennis is a social factor of great importance in the countryside: one forms the impression that they are kept in repair just so long as the marriageable daughters are not placed. . . .

The historical geography of the football codes alone would be more seriously worthy of a Ph.D. thesis than many a favoured subject. The 'National Code' – Victorian or (officially) Australian Rules – dominates over Rugby, League or Union, everywhere except in New South Wales, and Queensland: why? In Melbourne, indeed, the attachment to Rules teams reaches a fanaticism reminiscent of the feud of the Blues and Greens in Byzantium; it is said that one can obtain even gas stoves in one's team colours.[1] Most fascinating of all is the rise of soccer, which now rivals Rules and surpasses Rugby in attendances. Before the last war it was hardly played outside the coalfields of the Hunter valley, where such place-names as Aberdare, Gretna, Morpeth tell their own story; in 1952 there were 25,000 registered players, there are now about 200,000. It is very easy to form a soccer club; the British pools are always ready to extend a helping hand to preserve their continuity through the northern summer. Apart from the Hunter, soccer came to Australia very indirectly; the British managed to sell it to all the world except Anglo-America and Australia, and it is the 'New Australians' from the continent of Europe who have been its spearhead. This is not without its inconveniences: when say Beograd plays Croatia United, or Budapest meets Prague, there is apt to be a certain edge to the proceedings, and in the interests of peace and progress the official Association discourages unduly segregated national teams.

If cricket has not quite its former hold, the same cannot be said of racing, although Melbourne Cup Day is perhaps a little less sacred than it was. But Phar Lap, whose heart is solemnly preserved

[1] What happens if a Collingwood supporter falls in love with a St Kilda girl is not known: it would be quite as scandalous as a Montagu-Capulet union. Perhaps endogamy is the rule.

at Canberra, is still as strong a legend as Ned Kelly, and leading jockeys share the limelight with the stars of swimming and Rules. Racing is indeed the biggest sporting industry, with over 4,000 meetings a year at all levels from the Cup to bush events, and betting must be one of the largest items of consumer expenditure, though its true extent is never likely to get into the statistics: a recent estimate suggests three-quarters of a gambling bill of $2,000,000,000.[1]

In all this, climate and affluence play a big part. The average Australian is not a bushman but a city-dweller, but even so he is likely to be more of an outdoor man than his fellow in Britain. The camping holiday, for instance, is a standard part of the way of life of families of all classes. In the nature of the case, individual sporting participation cannot be measured, but it is certainly high, and it reaches down a long way. This is very clear in such sports or recreations as fishing – a summer religion to many – and yachting, or at least sailing. The beach itself is a highly developed social phenomenon: it has even been said that Australia should cease to follow tamely after European culture, since she has already advanced beyond Europe or even perhaps America – the evidence being, forsooth, that they have nothing like our wonderful life-savers on the beaches. More seriously, the life-saving clubs, apart from their undeniable primary value in saving lives and their training in tough team-work, provide an element of ritual and pageantry which on occasion gives a centre when the *dolce far niente* in the sun begins to pall. More individualistic is the popularity of surf-riding, which with some young people amounts to an obsession.

The general level of culture

Visitors to Australia may be divided into two broad classes: those who give interviews to the local Press, in which they tell us what a wonderful youthful country we are, dynamic and expanding and offering such splendid opportunities for development and (overseas) investment; and those who go home and write books. The latter usually give us full marks for hospitality and mateship, but often tend to be pained at our low cultural level, our emphasis on business and sport. They do remark on the excellence of some cultural manifestations – poetry and painting, perhaps – but rather in the spirit of Dr Johnson's comparison of a woman preaching to a dog standing on its hind legs: the wonder is that it is done at all.

[1] *The Australian*, 7 Oct. 1967.

However, it seems fair to say that the main daily preoccupations of most people anywhere and at any time have been with getting a living and with family relationships; and as for the emphasis on sport, it is surely imperceptive and insensitive to rule out of 'culture' an element which for so many thousands of people is the very salt of life. Culture is not confined to Hampstead Garden Suburb or Oxbridge common rooms, nor is the possession of the *New Statesman and Nation* its last word; and even in England, how much of the culture of the industrial north has been built around the local football team as well as the choir and the Literary and Philosophical Society? It is true that Australia's 'cultural organs' are few, small, and struggling, and that despite an early lead – *teste* James Anthony Froude – in the provision of the great truly public library, open to all, Australia has faltered sadly, in this century, in library provision. Yet there are statistics, which certainly cannot be taken quite at face value and which yet cannot be easily or completely discounted, which indicate that Australians are amongst the world's largest book-buyers and have relative to population more bookshops than the British and very many more than the Americans.

Once more, it is not very likely that the percentage of Australians who really care for things of the mind and spirit differs greatly from that in any large society; but it is a fraction too small in absolute numbers and too dispersed in six widely separated nuclei to support a large integrated superstructure. Comparisons are odious, and perforce leave out too many variables; but it may be worth mentioning that when the United States had 12,000,000 people, around 1830, they could show a magnificent galaxy of political talent, trained in the school of revolutionary war and nation-building, but the strictly 'cultural' contribution was slight: some fine architects, a few respectable painters, some scientists, but hardly any creative artists in prose or verse. Australia's contribution, in 150 years, stands up well in comparison. Nor, in evaluating 'culture', should the scientific life of the community be forgotten; 'applied' as Australian science so often is (and must be), it has struck very deep roots.

Australia was a late starter in the cultural stakes, and hence it is very difficult, for instance, to build up a really first-class and comprehensive art gallery, for the simple reason that such prizes as remain outside the great collections of Europe and America find higher bidders on the spot. Booksellers' catalogues arrive weeks late, and the bargain is often lost before Australia knows of it; yet the National Library is alert to the market, and not only for Australiana, as is shown, for example, by its acquisition of such collections as David Nichol Smith's library of Augustan literature.

One reason for the prominence of sport can be stated very simply: what else is there to do? There are buildings well worth looking at as buildings, but in the nature of the case there cannot be anything like the great cathedrals and palaces of Europe, still less a town like Carcassonne or Cracow, enshrining centuries of tradition. Canberra itself is increasingly a tourist centre, but its sights can be done in a day with no strain whatsoever. The bush appeals to many, but on the whole the places of spectacular scenic attraction are few and very far apart; there is nothing like the concentrated variety of New Zealand. So: with what can the average man fill his leisure, except sport? And to this the climate is a standing invitation.

Nevertheless, all allowances made, the lowest common denominator is a very powerful factor in Australia: the whole historical tradition tends towards 'the middling standards'. Can a high tradition of intellectual culture be other than to some extent aristocratic or exclusivist? There have been limited exceptions – the Elizabethan drama, perhaps – but on the whole the answer must be 'probably not'; and although Australians are by no means so egalitarian as they are reputed to be, still there is the persistent distrust of élites. The relative popularity of the ABC and the commercials suggests an answer to the awkward question: is the provision of programmes intellectually worthwhile (to intellectuals!) really compatible with 'a nice evening's entertainment' for Mr and Mrs Norm Everage of Humoresq Street, Suburbia?[1] Who pays the piper calls the tune. And something must be allowed for the aesthetic values of sport, and the opportunities it gives for the emergence of individual excellence, even if this is limited and ephemeral – like that of the actor or the singer.

The intellectual shrugs his shoulders: it is all he can do. Yet there are the pleasures of being in a minority: it is so easy to be *avant-garde* and to shock the bourgeois, and even the censorship adds something to the gaiety of life. There is a very spirited, if somewhat coterie, intellectualism, assisted by a lack of inhibition in public comment which paradoxically owes much to the rough plebeian

[1] The illustration is borrowed from Barrie Humphries' recordings, *Wild Life in Suburbia*.

tradition of calling a spade a bloody shovel. Anyone reading the Press correspondence about the 'betrayal' of Joern Utzon, the Danish architect of the Sydney Opera House, would think that the country was rocked to its depths by a cultural problem: the fate of a magnificent conception faced by costs exceeding the estimates some seven or eight times. It was not so; the storm agitated only the surface layers. The outraged intellectuals might have reflected that it was *l'homme moyen sensuel*, who could not care less for opera, who flocked in his thousands to buy the lottery tickets without which the project could not even have been conceived. Yet it must be said on the other side that the *persistence* of passionate dispute about the Opera House is significant of a very deep and abiding concern with cultural life among some circles, even though they are minority circles.

Recent local commentators show a certain penchant for the portentous, a mode in which most Australians do not live and move and have their being. Perhaps, in view of the perils which environ them, they should do so; but spiritual anguish is at least one privilege which they are prepared to leave to an élite. Yet the garden and the oval, the beach and the pub, are not enough; the art of living runs a poor second to the standard of living. In the last resort the Australian dilemma is probably not so much intellectual as spiritual. Alongside the extrovert dynamism there is an *ennui*, underneath the complacency a malaise.

Chapter 15

Mores and Morale

FUNDAMENTALLY, the current malaise of Australia is not in its nature different from that which affects the western world in general, and seeps through the Iron Curtain, most notably in Poland and Romania but even, at least in the thoughts of Chairman Mao, in China. In Australia the cultural variables are simpler than in continents which have experienced millennia of struggle between richly diverse cultures and creeds, and the roots of malaise, though still complex, are more clearly seen. Among them are the factors standard everywhere – the atomisation of life in the vast suburbias, the frustrations of modern urbanism, the problems of increasing affluence and leisure, the sexual revolution; and there is the special problem of guilt and fear springing from the contrast between empty comfortable Australia and the crowded misery of Asia. Essentially the problem is one of adjustment by a society which since the first World War has increasingly lost its isolation and its innocence.

This older society, though most of its members lived in a few cities, still had something of a rural stamp in its ethos; its preferred image was that of the bush, and the cities themselves were citadels if not of the rural then of the bourgeois virtues. This was offset by a certain raffishness, but this was simply uncomplicated reaction to undue respectability, and expressed itself mainly through drink. There was commercial and political corruption, but again of a straightforward kind. Amongst advanced intellectual circles in Sydney and Melbourne there was some self-conscious and rather old-fashioned Bohemianism, as there still is, though of course the cultural time-lag is now much shorter in sin as in other human activities: psychedelic ripples have reached at least Sydney's Kings Cross, the Greenwich Village of Australia. But by and large the pattern of society in the early Commonwealth was unsophisticated, and the rebels and aberrants were unsophisticated too.

The place of religion

The society is still largely Puritan in official theory, but increasingly hedonist in unofficial practice. By the Census statistics, Australia is overwhelmingly a Christian nation: 88.2 per cent in 1961. The Census question is optional, and this figure was 99 per cent of those who gave their religion: only 0.4 per cent were avowedly 'of no religion'. This tiny fraction is gradually increasing; but when we come to examine the quality rather than the quantity of Christian adherence, we may well feel that, far from indicating moral collapse, the change reflects a mild improvement in truthfulness.[1]

By the Census, the largest denomination is still Anglican, with something under a third of the total population; Roman Catholics are next, and gaining rapidly. Methodists and Presbyterians each number about one-tenth of the population, and other substantial denominations are Lutheran, Greek Orthodox, and Baptist. Half, or perhaps a little more, of Catholic, Greek, and Lutheran increases since the second World War have been directly due to the arrival of new settlers rather than to natural increase.

Answering a Census question is one thing; practising a religion seems to be quite another. From a Gallup poll of 1961, it would seem that the Census answer, for a very high proportion of respondents, is little more than a stock response stemming from family habit. 'C. of E.' in particular may be evidence not so much of a religious conviction as an absence of anything so definite as unbelief. In the same year 1961 that nearly nine out of ten adult Australians told the Census that they belonged to a Christian church, a quarter of the respondents to the poll claimed that they attended service weekly, but another quarter disclaimed attending at all.[2] Over half of the Catholics did attend weekly, but for Presbyterians (the 'residual' church for those of Scots descent) and Anglicans the figures were respectively 14 and 13 per cent. And the survey cited on p. 268 above is not alone in suggesting an ignorance of the most elementary facts concerning the faith to which the mass of Australians nominally subscribe; an ignorance so thorough that

---

[1] The increase in infidelity, or of veracity, in the Australian Capital Territory between 1961 and 1966 was striking: 0.91 to 3.19 per cent, 536 to 3,066 persons.

[2] This, and many other factual statements in this section, are drawn from the brilliant essay by K. S. Inglis in A. F. Davies and S. Encel, *Australian Society* (Cheshire, Melbourne, 1965), pp. 43–75.

it may well shock even the unbeliever who has any regard for cultural tradition.

This does not mean that religion, whether as a belief or as social convention, is a negligible factor in Australian life; though it may be that the social rather than the spiritual aspect is often in the ascendant. This is particularly marked in the rites of passage. If christening, except among Catholics and Orthodox, has hardly the place which it holds in the English tradition, the percentage of marriages celebrated in church is actually a few points higher than the Census percentage of Christians, and the proportion of civil marriages, after a sharp rise in the 'twenties, increases very slowly, while the great variation between the States rules out any easy correlation between those not stating a religion and those not marrying in church. Addiction to ecclesiastical nuptials is proportionately over twice as high as in England and the United States; yet curiously enough cremation, which as late as 1964 was barred to Roman Catholics, is as frequent as in Britain (about one funeral in three) and five times as popular as in the United States. However, in other respects the American mortuary style is encroaching: minor editions of Forest Lawn, with the same appeals, have been introduced, and two-thirds of funerals are conducted from funeral parlours where the rites of religion tend to be heavily overlaid by the arts of the mortician. No less pagan, as Inglis points out, is the gushingly sentimental and mildly erotic music without which few Australian brides – or their mothers – would think they had been properly married.

The Australian family, then, is Christian as to the shell; but often enough its kernel may be eaten into by paganism. Even the quality of obedience of professed Roman Catholics may be found wanting: at least, half of those polled in 1957 approved of desertion, as well as adultery, as grounds for divorce; whatever their personal ethos, they were too democratic to extend the prohibitions of their own church to those beyond its pale. Incidentally, the Federal divorce legislation of 1959, denounced by Roman and some Anglican leaders as yet another nail in the coffin of the Christian family, must have been rather disappointing in its effects: although if current trends are maintained about one in ten marriages will be dissolved, the percentage rise for divorces lags well behind those for population and for new marriages.[1]

[1] The average number of divorces for the five years 1948 to 1952 was 7,142; for 1960 to 1964, 7,246.

It seems also that in practice numbers of married Catholics must evade the official teaching of their church on the use of contraceptives. Although both in rural and in metropolitan areas Catholic families produce more children than non-Catholic ones, the essential differential is not so much between the creeds as between the enviroments, and the higher rural rates for both groups run parallel. In the generation before the 1954 Census, the median size of families was halved, and this 'massive decline' affected both the religious and the environmental groups.[1] It seems improbable that this decline, so far as it affects Roman Catholics, is entirely due to the use of the safe period, or that they are entirely unrepresented in the demand which makes Australia probably the largest per capita consumer of 'the pill' in the world. By what soul-searching individuals reconcile the dictates of humanity, or expedience, and of doctrine cannot, of course, be known.

One must indeed sympathise with those priests and pastors who ardently desire to make of the Christian ministry a living force in the national life, and who find themselves reduced to tolerating the religious marriage of patently irreligious couples in the faint hope that some slight odour of sanctity may linger on. Yet it is a little too facile to say that the ministry is exercised in a society to which it is not so much wrong as irrelevant. There is as it were a residual desire that Christianity *should* be relevant; but it is exceedingly difficult for the churches to translate this into a practical policy, by reason of divisions both within their own body and in the body politic. Some assert that the only cure for the ills of the world is individual conversion; but, though all are present in Australia, neither the revivalism of Billy Graham, nor the Moral Rearmament Crusaders, who might be described as the Jehovah's Witnesses of the upper middle classes, nor Jehovah's Witnesses themselves, have anything but a fleeting or a narrowly confined impact. Attempts by the collective body of the churches to enunciate a forward-looking policy are faced with the dilemma that any programme with really concrete objectives is likely to repel as many as it attracts: they can support the government's warlike policy in Vietnam and be denounced as conformists serving Mammon, or oppose it and be denounced as dupes of the Reds. There is of course a wide range of good causes in which the churches play an active and honourable part; but it would be difficult (and ungracious) to

[1] L. H. Day, in Davies and Encel, *op. cit.*, pp. 156–57.

assess the relative contributions of humanitarianism directly inspired by Christian belief, and by simple decent human feeling.
Australia is certainly a far less Christian country than it appears in
the official statistics; but probably a less heathen one than the
impressionism of the Press would suggest.

Matters of morals

There is one sphere in which the churches are still able to mobilise
the residual feeling that they should stand, and speak out, for pre-
scriptive social values. Opposition to divorce, pagan funerals, and
even contraception may be virtually a lost cause; but the residual
Puritanism of many Australians can still be rallied in support of
moral restrictions on the exercise of other people's tastes.

However, there are ambivalences. There can be scarcely a shadow
of doubt that gambling and drinking on the Australian scale are
seriously anti-social, but there is here a marked divergence between
Catholic and non-Catholic attitudes. Great was the shock and loud
was the outcry of 'depth of moral cynicism, travesty of every
Christian principle' when the Christian Brothers raised funds for
their schools by a lottery in which the first prize was a Tasmanian
pub. But as well as strange divorces, such issues make strange bed-
fellows. During the first World War, temperance pressure groups
were able to translate their normal appeals into a patriotic demand,
and – with many of the soldiers conveniently overseas or under
voting age – referenda in New South Wales and South Australia
enforced the closing of hotel bars at 6 p.m.; Victoria did not bother
about voting. This introduced the '5 o'clock swill', when cheerless
bars were packed tight with men drinking quickly, on their feet,
and on empty stomachs. The results were predictably revolting, and
few things did more than this so moral measure to establish
Australia's ill-fame as a nation of boozers: no visitor to Sydney or
Melbourne could escape the nasty spectacle.

The shock once over, however, brewers and publicans found their
account in restriction: everything, including the legal requirement
to provide overnight accommodation, was subordinated to larger
bars for the one hour in which about nine-tenths of the beer intake
was consumed; and another Australian reputation, for dreadful
hotels, was created or at least enhanced. Early closing was supposed
to be a temporary war-time measure, but it was not repealed until
1954 in New South Wales, 1965 and 1966 in South Australia and

Victoria. Despite the coyness of both parties, it is clear that the only opposition came from the brewers and publicans, fearful of the higher labour costs and overheads of late closing, and a hard core of Nonconformist 'temperance' men. Alcoholism remains a very serious problem; but since late hours were reintroduced, public drunkenness has become much less obvious, reasonable drinking in comfortable surroundings much more easy to secure. Another factor in the general advance of decency in drinking was the rise, in the 'fifties, of the licensed club, though in New South Wales (but only there) the installation of poker machines, the 'one-armed bandits', offsets this improvement; the licence tax is too useful to State revenues for the machines to be prohibited.

If the Catholics are reasonably permissive on liquor and lotteries, they are at one with their fellow churchmen (or rather ahead or behind, according to taste) in the field of sexual regulation. This is expressed mainly through censorship, in which, amongst Western countries, Australia shares a bad eminence with Eire and Portugal. If the British public periodically made itself ridiculous by a wave of excessive morality, a good deal of the Australian public is chronically in this state. The results can be diverting, as when a demand was made for the withdrawal of John Wyndham's *The Day of the Triffids* from school libraries on account of its sexual content, or when an Inspector of Schools (in English!) denounced A. D. Hope's poems, blissfully ignorant that they had been prescribed as a set book in the State's Leaving Examination. But they can also be serious.

Censorship of books and journals produced in Australia is a State matter, though it is likely to become more uniform and in so doing to conform more closely to the standards of the more restrictive States, Queensland and Victoria. Imported material is subject to Customs control, and one cannot discern that the officers in charge have any particular qualifications for their indelicate task. Moreover, a book passed by the Commonwealth Customs may fall under police displeasure in a particular State – whence lively publicity and (naturally) a lively inter-State parcel post traffic. This has applied to so serious a work as David Holbrook's *The Quest for Love*, which is banned in Victoria although it is largely devoted to a forthright attack on the immorality of *Lady Chatterley's Lover*, which itself was banned as a matter of course.

Customs control is exercised largely by examination of invoices, and a good deal depends on title – both *The Rape of the Earth* and *The Rape of the Lock* have been temporarily held up, and students of oriental linguistics must furnish translations of titles in Asian scripts, though there the possibilities of evasion are as obvious as those of corruption are slight. This indeed is the worst aspect of the system – not that the Australian public is debarred from reading such works as the *Kama Sutra* or *Fanny Hill*, but that legitimate workers, for example in medicine and psychology, are subject to humiliating demands for supervision at the hands of people who cannot understand the technical language of these subjects, to 'protect' people who could not read a page of it. Meanwhile, when one contemplates the locally produced sexy magazines and the sex-and-sadism paperbacks which crowd the airport bookstalls – well, one often wonders what the censors ban one half so grubby as the stuff they pass.

The Guardians: police and RSL

Amongst the Guardians are two potent forces, the police and the returned servicemen. The old Australian distrust of authority and of the agents who enforce it persists, and while there is no reason to doubt the devotion to duty of most of the police forces of Australia, there are enough doubtful interpretations of duty to foster this distrust. In country districts, where one constable may be in charge of a large area with a few people most of whom know each other, he may of course be compelled to wink at minor irregularities to be sure of co-operation on the big ones; in the early closing days, for example, the bars would be closed and emptied at 6 p.m., but by 8.30 would be full of '*bona fide* travellers' many of whom might have journeyed as far as one mile, few the statutory twenty. But in larger places, there is little doubt that strong-arm tactics and the reckless use of fire-arms are resorted to – only occasionally, but yet too often; some groups – homosexuals, demonstrating students, aborigines – do not get a fair deal; and some corruption is inevitable. Yet it should be added that many policemen give beyond the strict demands of duty in such activities as clubs for adolescents, and that in really hard-luck cases they often rally round in an admirably humane spirit.

The Returned Soldiers', Sailors', and Airmen's Imperial League of Australia, understandably better known as the RSL, is nearer the American than the British Legion. Like the latter, it has as its official *raison d'être* the protection of the legitimate interests of ex-servicemen in such matters as pensions, hospital treatment, and re-employment, and here its record is admirable. Indeed, alone of all bodies of organised opinion in Australia, it has a statutory right of direct access to the Cabinet, and it is perhaps not surprising that it is on occasion tempted to overplay its hand; there seems little reason to demand preferential employment for servicemen twenty years after they have ceased to serve, by which time, one would think, they would be either employed or unemployable. Many people would have liked to say what only Sir William Slim, with his prestige of Field-Marshal and of Governor-General, could say: that the RSL should hesitate to claim for its members special privileges for having done what all good citizens had done – their duty.

But beyond this constructive work the RSL, or its leadership, like the American Legion, considers itself a watchdog of the national interest, interpreted in narrowly chauvinist terms. It does not indeed intervene overtly in party politics, but its influence is very generally thrown on the illiberal side of any issue, and it rarely bothers to inform itself of the arguments, motives, or standing of those it chooses to regard as dangerous dissenters. So innocuous an activity as the formation of a mainly clerical committee not to advise conscientious objection, but to give legal and moral advice to lads who are already conscientious objectors – a matter of simple Christian charity – can be visited with vulgarly abusive attacks and strong suggestions that this is a matter for Security to investigate. To some RSL leaders it is unthinkable that people should be allowed to forget Japanese atrocities, while Hiroshima might never have happened. Whether this accurately reflects the views of the RSL membership is another matter. Probably it does, in a general way; the structure of the League is fairly oligarchical, and the rank and file are generally content to follow along, although it must be added that on occasion there is fairly strong internal criticism of the more illiberal leaders, and this seems growing in effectiveness.

A great part is played in RSL life by its clubs, which in the countryside are often the only general male meeting-places apart from the pubs. Their great occasion is of course Anzac Day, and there is no warrant to suspect or denigrate the sincerity and the often moving ritual of this 'one day of the year' given over to remembrance. For the rest, the main functions of the clubs are social, or perhaps more accurately convivial. People are entitled to drinking clubs, of course, and perhaps without an organisation and a crystallising point like the RSL the network of goodfellowship could not exist; but to some the association with patriotism jars.

A word for the women

The discussion so far has been concerned with respectable and often majority opinion; it is time to turn to the less privileged sections of the community. One of these is barely a minority and in a strict legal sense is but slightly underprivileged: women.

The popular impression is that Australia is still very much a man's country, and this is confirmed by Norman MacKenzie's detailed study *Women in Australia*.[1] Some sociologists have queried this view, but their evidence does not seem very convincing: it suggests that Australian fathers leave to their wives a good deal of household decision making and parental guidance, more than do Americans and Mexicans, and this becomes 'matriduxy'. But the quality of decisions is not analysed, merely their number, and this may be only the correlate to the outer world being a man's world: woman's place is in the home, but the home is the place reserved to her.

There is a good deal of prejudice against women in employment. This is sometimes limited to, and often rationalised by, an objection to working mothers on the ground that this means neglect of the family; but it goes beyond this. The most classic expression of prejudice is perhaps the Public Service denial of permanent posts to married women, only lifted by the Commonwealth in 1966 and still the rule in most States. The professions are theoretically open on equal terms; in practice the share of women in most of them is very small. It is safe to say that an Australian woman free of attachments finds advancement beyond a middle level much more difficult than her sisters of equivalent ability in the United Kingdom or the United States, even in such fields as university teaching where one might expect prejudice to be weakest. Nor has the principle of equal pay for equal work been widely accepted; Mr Justice Higgins' thinking on the basic wage was posited on the needs of the man as a breadwinner. It seems likely, however, that the 'rate for the job' concept will more and more prevail, however slowly and grudgingly it is adopted.

[1] Cheshire, Melbourne, 1962.

South Australia gave women the vote in 1894, only a year after New Zealand and not long after the pioneer western American States; Victoria, the last State to fall into line, did so in 1908; the Commonwealth suffrage was universal from 1902. Women had local government franchises much earlier, and their right to be elected to parliaments had been conceded in all States by the early 1920's. All this was attained with much less storm and strife than in Britain; and yet the role of women in political and public life has been strangely limited. There are obstacles to women undertaking jury service, and there are no women magistrates. Women are legislators at all levels, but there is nothing to compare with the quantitatively strong and qualitatively distinguished role of women in British local government. The proportion of women appointed to advisory boards and councils – even those dealing with health, hospitals, and cultural activities – is scandalously low.

This attitude of resignation would be in conformity with the degree of tacit sexual segregation in Australia; is it significant that the women who take part in voluntary associations are often grouped separately, sometimes under the quaint but revealing title of 'Ladies' Auxiliary'. In some spheres segregation is formal. Only recently, in face of competition from motels and clubs, have Australian hotels shown much tendency to become more than machines for drinking in, and it must be conceded that in early closing days the bar was no fit place for a woman (nor for a man of much sensitivity). In certain bars in the big cities certain women may be found; but almost universally women are shepherded into a room, usually bare and cheerless, known as the Ladies' Lounge, where males may penetrate only under escort. Even private parties tend to split up, by unspoken common consent, the men discussing the footie at one end, the women talking domestic shop at the other, with perhaps the secondary sexual differentiation of beer and sweet sherry.

To a point, such separatism is natural enough; so long as there is any sexual division of labour, interests will differ, and in all societies women like to gossip of house and home among themselves. But, while it may be exaggerated, it is difficult to resist the impression that the division of interests, in Western societies, is rarely so overt and almost formalised as in Australia. This is perhaps a factor in the generally admitted gaucherie of many Australian males, whose relaxed fellowship with their mates is often in marked contrast to an off-hand awkwardness in female company – even, to judge from literary impressionism, solitary female company. To a large extent this is probably another hangover from the nineteenth-century dominance of masculinity – as late as 1881 the male : female ratio was 116 : 100 – and the image of bush mateship. The psychologists are most portentous about it, but some think that the competition of New Australians with more gallant traditions is changing this. . . .

For all her laggardness as a political animal, there is plenty of liveliness about the Australian woman. In the countryside, she is often a tough confident bushwoman, fully capable of taking on a farm as well as a family. If her cultural standards sometimes seem pitched rather low, she *has* standards, which is often more than can be said for the males. Nowhere is this better displayed than in the activities of the Country Women's Association, one of the most admirable self-help organisations to be found anywhere. Country life for the woman is often rough, solitary, and harsh; the CWA brings companionship and amenity, mainly by its hundreds of rest rooms in country towns and townlets. Wandering around a little township, say in the Western Australian wheat belt, one may observe (wistfully, from without) at least one building, in the crude dusty waste of tin and fibro, which is neat and even a little gay: an oasis of civilisation.

'New Australians'

The old boast that the Australian population was over nine-tenths of British stock is no longer possible; the bi-partisan post-war immigration policy decisively broke with this tradition. In 1947 the Australian-born were 90 per cent of the population, and of the nearly three-quarters of a million born overseas, only 110,000 came from the continent of Europe. By 1961 the native-born were only 83 per cent, those born outside Australia were 1,779,000, and of these over 840,000 were continentals including, in addition to the Germans, Dutch, Poles, Italians, and Greeks mentioned earlier (p. 95), sizeable contingents of 'Displaced Persons' from the Baltic States, Hungary, and Yugoslavia. These newcomers were styled 'New Australians' in a well-meant official effort to divert prejudice from them, but the new term itself took on derogatory overtones, and is now replaced – formally – by the colourless 'migrants' or 'settlers'. Except for a relatively small number of

Yugoslavs who still enter, this Displaced Person immigration had practically ceased by 1951.[1]

Trends in immigration fluctuate with economic and social conditions in the countries of origin; on the whole the 'pull' of Australia is probably by no means the overwhelming attraction that the native-born like to think it – some southern Europeans actually dislike the climate, than which there could be no blacker token of ingratitude. And, except for Greece, southern Italy, and (after austerity winters) Britain, the 'push' of home conditions is by no means so strong as it was. The British and north-western Europeans are regarded as the most desirable immigrants, certainly in the popular mind and implicitly (as shown by policy) in official circles. But Australians are slow to realise, if they realise at all, that for north-western Europeans, and even some northern Italians, the vaunted social services and opportunities for advancement are not notably superior to those of the Europe of the Common Market; some social services are definitely not so good. Moreover, the problem is not only one of attracting migrants, but of keeping them when they get here.

The preference for the northerners is shown by the considerable expenditure on recruiting and the facilities for assisted passages. British migrants can get all but $20 of their passage money paid, and the majority of them are in fact assisted to this extent. Unfortunately, they show a greater tendency to return than do the less-assisted southerners. They are many factors in this.

Perhaps the worst retention problem is that of the British. For the professional or semi-professional, who may be coming to a firm which provides housing or who has sufficient savings for a house deposit (after paying the mere $20 for his fare), it is relatively easy to find a comfortable niche. However, many even in this group do return: fundamentally, perhaps, the reason is that they expected to find, but do not, simply another England with a sunnier climate. While the meteorological climate may be agreeable enough, the social climate with its casualness, its poorer health services, its often mediocre school standards, may be harder to take. Conversely, Australians often react with more or less open resentment to any

---

[1] Factual information in this section comes largely from J. Jupp's *Arrivals and Departures* (Cheshire-Landsdowne, Melbourne, 1966), though it is fair to say that this summary was valuable as confirming and supplementing impressions from a variety of sources, rather than creating new ones.

hint that things were not so bad in the old country, which is well-known (in Australian eyes) to consist of little but the drabbest slums, under almost perpetual rain and fog, and overlain by a rigidly snobbish ruling class.

Of all the northerners, the most disgruntled are likely to be the skilled and semi-skilled workers, who find the openings by no means so easy as they have been led to expect – partly by their own romanticism but often, it is to be feared, by somewhat disingenuous official information.[1] There is no question of conscious deception, but the public servants in Australian agencies overseas have rarely any real knowledge of working-class life either at home or abroad. It is their job to attract migrants, they naturally do not wish to sell their own country short, and it is difficult indeed to maintain the balance between gilding the lily of migrant hopes, and blasting it by a dose of realism.

Some three-quarters of Commonwealth assisted migrants usually begin their Australian life in hostels, and there is no doubt that hostel life is responsible for much reasonable discontent, and many premature returns. Most hostels are virtually barracks of Nissen huts; they may be neat and even colourful from outside, but drab and cramped inside, in some cases with inadequate sanitary facilities, and always with institutional food. To maintain a decent family life in them is a difficult and distasteful task. Many were expected to be only temporary, but in Australia there is nothing so permanent as the temporary and *ad hoc*; and some hostel managers seem to think that if they were made too comfortable, the migrants might want to stay in them for good and all instead of the maximum of two years. But if they are made too uncomfortable, the migrant's efforts will soon be directed to not staying in Australia at all, which is a waste of a good deal of his own and the Commonwealth's money.

The rates charged for hostel board and lodging are certainly far from excessive; but they may not leave much money over for home-building. One of the boasts of Australia is the very wide prevalence of home-ownership; but this is only obtained at a price. Building societies are little developed, and (except at very low standards in some inner-city areas) working-class *family* accommodation for

---

[1] The climax of unimaginative, if unintentional, misrepresentation is surely the use in an official pamphlet of photographs of children in a fee-paying private (= English Public) school (Jupp, *op. cit.*, p. 132).

rent is extremely scarce; yet this is what a high proportion of migrants are accustomed to. It is very much more difficult to become possessed of one of those nice little suburban homes, so popular in the illustrated brochures, than the migrant realises. This of course goes for the non-British migrant too: with little English, or none, he is much more readily victimised by the small print of the house-agent or the hire-purchase salesman. Once the initial testing period, which may be very gruelling, is over, however, the British or northern European migrant may readily pass into more or less full membership of the Australian community.

The southerner may have an assisted passage, on a less generous scale, but he has much less done for him officially; he may indeed be packed off from the hostel to some seasonable job in the country-side almost as soon as he arrives. But very many of the Italians and Greeks arrive through chain-migration; there are extraordinarily close links between some Calabrian villages or Aegean islands and small communities, both urban and rural, in Australia, despite the fact that until recently there were rather severe obstacles to bringing out relatives who would not contribute directly to the work-force. Many inner-city areas, especially in Melbourne, have very strong concentrations of Italians and Greeks; so long as he is content to mill along among his compatriots, life to the southerner may even be not quite so 'foreign' as it is to the English newcomer, though the combination of restrictive liquor laws with drunkenness is unnerving. But it is far more difficult for the southerner, or easterner, to break out. To begin with, especially for older women, Australian family *mores* are distressing, particularly the weakness of family solidarity and of parental authority. This is not altogether distasteful to the young, of course, and hence family tension may be the price of assimilation.

A grievance common to both British and continentals is the difficulty of gaining acceptance for technical qualifications. This is not confined to the Trade Unions, indeed perhaps the greatest obscurantism is shown by some professional associations, such as the medicoes of Victoria. There is a self-regarding habit of mind which simply ignores the obvious fact that professional and technical training is just as highly developed in Europe as in Australia, and in some fields is superior. Certainly conditions are easing, information services are improving, and there are now far fewer tragic stories of Europeans with the highest qualifications, and good

English, compelled to work for years in relatively menial occupations, when in theory Australia was crying out for their skills. Yet
much disability remains, and falls with greater incidence on the
continental than the British migrant, and this not only on account
of the language difficulty. There are of course official language
classes, but they are too often taught by mono-lingual Australians
using antiquated methods and quite innocent of the special problems of teaching English as a foreign language. There seems indeed
a general failure to use the services of already integrated migrants;
interpreting services are rather poor, and there have been instances
of strike meetings when union officialdom had to avail itself of
interpreters obligingly provided by the Communist Party. . . .

It is of course natural that the continental migrant should seek
out his own folk – often they have brought him out – and enjoy his
own language and such cultural satisfactions as may survive, in an
attenuated form, in this strange land. Even without prejudice on
either side, this would happen; but it is in part a reaction to
Australian prejudice, which it in turn fosters. On the whole, this
large body of non-English speakers has been incapsulated (rather
than assimilated) into Australian life with singularly little serious
friction, and there is no doubt at all that prejudice is much weaker
than it was in the earlier stages of the continental migration. Young
toughs may still beat up 'Ity' boys who 'could be saying anything
about you in their own lingo' (and indeed they do not confine
themselves to such recognisable minorities); but there are no longer
the ludicrously chauvinist letters to the papers demanding that
migrants should be legally prohibited from speaking anything but
English within earshot of an Australian. Nevertheless prejudice
persists: much more publicity was given, for example to allegations
of a Mafia in the Melbourne markets than to the subsequent police
retraction. More serious is the tendency of some migrant groups,
especially the Croats, to bring with them their old political hates;
national rivalries have brought soccer into some disrepute, and the
eastern Europeans now and then show their opposition to Communism in ways which may be a little too militant even for the
DLP.[1] It is popular fallacy that migrants are more addicted to
violent crime, or indeed just crime, than genuine Aussies; perhaps

---

[1] However, as Jupp remarks (*op. cit.*, p. 90), the three Australian branches
of the Society Devoted to the Sacred Memory of Tsar Nicholas II are
'perhaps the ultimate in harmless political nostalgia.'

because when they are violent, it is likely to be with knives rather than boots or broken bottles. But statistically this is proven non-sense; though when Joe Smith and Josef Zubrecovich are both in for a pub brawl, it is the latter name which catches the eye.

One reason for the relative smoothness of relations between old and New Australians is that the latter are not so much 'a large body' as a number of discrete smaller bodies. In some inner-city areas the naturalised migrant vote is in aggregate significant, but as a rule it is too fragmented to give rise to much political skulduggery. Indeed, to a large extent the migrant communities are out of public life, not part of the *pays légal*. This is obviously true of the non-naturalised, who even if ratepayers, as many are, do not have a municipal franchise; but even the naturalised have as yet not had much impact on affairs. The Trade Unions have not paid very much attention to them, other than collecting dues; nor have the political parties, with the partial exception of the DLP. As for religious bodies, the Catholic Church to some extent looks after its own; the Greeks and other easterners have their own Orthodox Church (not exempt from the usual separatism and factionalism of that faith); Protestant ministers are prominent in the officially sponsored Good Neighbour Councils. These are supposed to extend a friendly hand to the newcomer, but on the whole, by reason of language difficulties and class composition, they are most effective with those who least need help – the middle-class British. Neverthe-less, many non-British migrants have made breakthroughs, some-times quite spectacular ones, in business, sport, academic life, and the arts – including the much-needed art of cooking, which has shown much diversification since their advent.

In all this, Australians generally tend to adopt an over-simplified view of the problems of migrant life; it must be remembered that though they travel widely, they rarely settle permanently overseas, except in positions of relative privilege such as those afforded by the brain drain to Britain or America. They point with pride to the not infrequent success stories, and to the generally successful adaptation of migrant children in the schools, and their attitude is 'they come to our beautiful free country for their own advantage, they should take on the responsibilities'. This is seen in the strong pressure for naturalisation after five years; it is not realised what a wrench formal naturalisation implies, what a burning of boats it really is. Many migrants who would be willing enough to accept the responsibilities of Australian citizenship are repelled by the unnecessarily total and public repudiation of their old allegiance which is demanded. (This seems to apply with peculiar force to the otherwise admirable Dutch, some of whom have the bad taste to think that Queen Juliana is just as good as Queen Elizabeth.) No thought is given to the position of the Greek or Italian who may fall upon evil days and wish to return to his old family and friends – in a country where he is no longer a citizen.

The issue of conscription for Vietnam has made this dilemma acute; the more so as probably quite often an unstated motive for migration around the world is a desire for one's son to escape Europe's wars. Yet even the naturalised migrant seems too often to be regarded as not quite a first-class citizen, and the conscription of unnaturalised aliens, loudly demanded by the RSL, would raise serious problems of international law. Americans, for instance, would automatically lose their nationality, and on the other hand one can imagine the clamour if an Australian living in Greece were conscripted there. Granting that there is something in the 'sharing responsibility' argument, the effect of enforcing it might seriously jeopardise the continuance of immigration on the scale that Australia desires and needs.

The post-war migrants have served Australia well. Immediately after the war the expansion of basic industries relied very heavily on Displaced Persons, who in return for passage and admission were virtually drafted; in 1952 they formed 20 per cent of the workforce in the steelworks of Newcastle and Port Kembla. Migrants were very prominent on the Snowy, and are strong in the building and construction industries. There is still a tendency to regard the continentals as hewers of wood and drawers of water, necessary to do the rough menial jobs which do not attract enough Australians. Such an attitude is not very realistic in the age of the Common Market; yet it seems likely that for a fairly long time to come Australia will need a considerable migrant intake for full development – the Vernon Committee put it at 100,000 a year. In this context, undue pressure for naturalisation, and over-expenditure on importing northerners who will not stay, could lead to serious difficulties. It is a sign of the times that in 1961 Italy refused to renew the bilateral assisted migration scheme except on wholly unacceptable (and indeed unrealistic) terms, although agreement was reached on most matters at President Saragat's visit in 1967. It looks as if Australia will have to find some 'honorary Europeans': Turkey is considered as a source, even (less seriously) Egypt, and there are already 10,000 Lebanese. But efforts in this direction have to meet the pull of the Common Market countries, and would bring in elements less assimilable than the Italians and Greeks.

Wider anxieties

Finally, affluence notwithstanding, it is not true that there are no slums and no problems of poverty in Australia. It is true that there is nothing like the wide-spread slumdom of old Europe and some of the great American cities; but there are certainly areas of very poor conditions in the cities, and here and there in the bush enclaves reminiscent of the hill-billy country of the Appalachians. Australia's Skid Rows are faint replicas of those of America, but they do exist, and are occasionally brought to public notice, perhaps by a fatal fire in an Old Men's Home. Old age pensioners often have a very grim struggle for existence; and one factor in the strong tendency for the unskilled and semi-skilled to try to hold down two jobs is simply the difficulty of making both ends meet for a family at the lower end of the wage scales. This in turn is not conducive to efficiency. Some estimates suggest that poverty is much more widespread than the general picture of affluent Australia allows for, embracing at least half a million people. This is not 'the other half' of the old saying, but it is certainly true that many Australians begin and end their days in an abyss of loneliness and deprivation.[1]

More pressing than these internal anxieties are the external ones. Indeed, so long as primary export values hold up, the internal problems are by no means on an intractable scale. Our cities are not so much out of hand as those of America, though there is no room for complacency here; still, the aesthetic quality of Australian townscapes is on the whole improving. Given the will and the effort, it is still possible for conservation to do much to check the devastation of a continent too big and for the most part too empty to be completely clogged by the commercialised ugliness that the motor-car brings. Alcoholism is an endemic disease both chronic and acute, there is an incipient drug problem, and there is quite serious delinquency; but except for alcoholism, these and poverty are again, relative to

---

[1] John Stubbs, *The Hidden People: Poverty in Australia* (Cheshire-Landsdowne, Melbourne, 1966), presents a sombre picture, which does not however seem overdrawn.

America and perhaps Britain, tracts rather than large regions. Political life is uninspired, but on the whole not incompetent to meet the internal tasks facing the nation, and it is free from ideological violence or really serious corruption. Our economy is still too little diversified on the export side, still too dependent on rural and extractive industries; our business world still too much the client of overseas know-how; the balance between foreign and domestic investment, both in gross and in detail distribution between industries, presents problems we have hardly begun to face. And education, with striking advances at the higher levels, has serious weaknesses in the substructure.

Our vices and troubles, as well as our virtues and achievements, might be unkindly described as still approximating 'the middling standard.' Culturally, we are not really ruined by not being able to read the *Kama Sutra*; and even with the censorship and the banality of the mass media, artistic life flourishes in all its branches. The aborigines present a grave moral problem (and one that gravely stains our external image), but they are too few to foster a shattering fundamental crisis like that of the Negro insurgence in the United States; there are failings also in our dealings with the continental migrants, but no such problem as exists in Britain to-day.

With all these, and more, we could cope, if only we were left alone to be 'The Lucky Country' or the 'Lotus-land' of the publicists. But in this divided world, 'Betwixt the pass and fell incenséd points Of mighty opposites', no country, however small and however isolated, can be left alone.

Chapter 16

Australia and the World

THE PHRASE 'to be left alone' can be taken in two ways. It may mean being left free of outside interference, or it may mean being left without outside support. This was sharply and painfully brought home to Australia by two British initiatives of 1967: the renewed approach to join the European Economic Community, and the announcement of a definite policy of phasing out British military strength east of Suez, until by the mid-'seventies or even in three years it would seem hardly even a token presence. These moves were received with a flurry of excitement in the Australian Press, exhortations to get out of the 'Lotus-land' and stand on our feet, to recognise the necessity of living dangerously. Superficially, however, the flurry might seem as brief as it was intense, and succeeded by the old insouciance of 'business as usual'. This would be unfair: however little it may appear in the Press, and still less in the speeches of politicians, some hard thinking goes on in the higher reaches of the Public Service and in some academic circles.

The dilemmas are hard and basic. The essential ones are probably that, as we have said, Australia is at once too big to discount herself and adopt an attitude of helplessness mitigated by *ad hoc* tactical shifts, and too small to count as much of a 'Power' in her own right; and that there is a probably unresolvable tension between considering Australia 'a part of Asia' and maintaining a distinctive European-derived culture with its concomitant of an immigration policy somewhat tempered to new times but still basically anti-Asian.

Asia and 'White Australia'

When we are told by the Prime Minister of the Commonwealth that 'Australia is geographically a part of Asia' it is surely pertinent (though it may be deemed impertinent) to remark that the only glimmer of geographical validity in this claim is that once upon a time part of Australia was linked with part of India in the ancient continent of Gondwanaland; but since this part-identity was shared by South Africa and Brazil, and in any case broke up some 60,000,000 years ago, it has little relevance to current affairs. The phrase substitutes a single, though important, geographical factor – location – for the whole great and involved complex of physical and human factors which make up a geographical entity or environment. If location were all, Europe is a part of Asia, Siberia a part of Europe, and northern Africa a part of Europe, except for Egypt which is a part of Asia... 'Africa begins at the Pyrenees', and conversely Europe at the Atlas. A very much stronger argument could be made for any of these statements than for the local variant.

In fact, the names of the continents are only convenient short-hand symbols, derived from the vastly different world of classical antiquity, for traditional groupings of land-masses and countries. In particular – as, to be fair, the late Mr Holt once remarked – there is no such thing as a monolithic entity 'Asia'. Few regions in similar latitudes are so dissimilar as Arabia and south-east Asia, few expressions of the human spirit more alien each to each than Islam and Hinduism, to say nothing of the more modern ideologies which dominate the greater part of the continent in the USSR and China. The only real factor of unity in Asia has been afforded historically by the European connections of the imperialist age, and contemporaneously by the new empires of ideology, capitalist or Communist, which have replaced the old territorial empires. But this is the interlocking of world power politics, not the unity of Asia.

But in truth those who speak of Australia as part of Asia tacitly omit most of that continent from the reckoning. This was sharply pointed up by the fact that when Nehru and Shastri died, Britain, America, and Russia sent to the funerals personalities of the standing of Mountbatten, Hubert Humphrey, and Kosygin; Australia sent her local High Commissioner. 'Asia' is in fact reduced to a fringe, albeit an important one, of the Asian continent, roughly those countries from Korea to Indonesia inclusive: fourteen states out of forty-five, 1,665,000 square miles out of 17,153,000, and 370 out of 1,945 million souls. The only countries of great weight in the list are Japan and Indonesia, and their position is ambivalent.

In its origins the slogan may have been useful as a reaction to a too exclusively Eurocentric view of the world, one unfitting our geographical location – this is its kernel of sense; it may have served

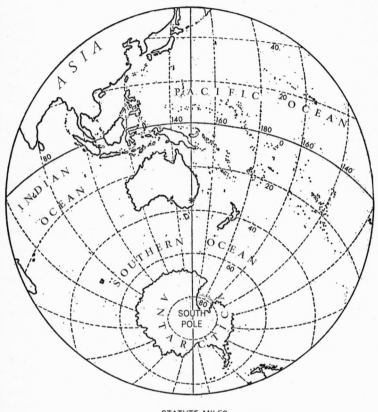

STATUTE MILES

0   1000 2000 3000 4000 5000 6000

Scale to read off distance from Canberra∗

The Hemisphere around Australia
Zenithal equidistant projection centred on Canberra

as a challenge making Australians aware of their involvement with their 'Near North', a much more meaningful phrase. It does seize on the great unresolved question which is specifically Australian, as distinct from such far more general unresolved questions as those of nuclear war and world food and population rations: the problem of living with Asia. But the proponents of 'a part of Asia' do not seem to have begun to think of what this would really mean, and the phrase has become a question-begging cliché burking real thought on this very real and vital problem. As such, it has its perils.

For one thing, there is the danger that our close relations with those marginal Asian countries which are really meant by the cliché might delude us into thinking that we are accepted as Asian, and hence lead us seriously to miscalculate our real influence: but if even the Filipinos seem often to be not quite accepted as fully Asian, what chance do we have? Will Asians, to whom cultural values are so important, respect us if we are apparently so ready to forget or deny our European heritage for a get-together slogan? Must we proclaim ourselves in advance, to parody Sukarno, as a New Submerging Force? Would we have anyone but ourselves to blame if any expansionist Asian country took, or pretended to take, the slogan seriously, and based on it an outright onslaught on 'White Australia'?

'White Australia' is indeed not what it was, and it was always to some extent a misnomer. Gradually, and more by administration than by legislation, restrictions on coloured entry are being eased. Long before recent modifications it was not impossible, though by no means easy, to secure permanent residence, and there are several thousand naturalised Australians of Asian race, apart from the pre-Federation Chinese. Tacitly or overtly, the political programmes of all parties now water down or remove the old *non possumus* attitudes to Asian immigration, and there is an increasing body of minority opinion in favour of controlled intake rather than a colour bar; it seems almost certain that sooner or later there will be some sort of quota system. Whatever the official attitudes, however, one should not over-estimate the extent of the change in popular feeling; there is still a considerable residue of prejudice, disguised perhaps in economic terms, reflected for instance in suspicion or open hostility towards the employment of skilled Japanese personnel in northern post and mining projects.

In any case, the sort of Asians that Australia needs and, in the not too distant future, might accept in more than derisory token numbers are the well-trained and the well-to-do: these are precisely those whom Asian governments think, and rightly, should be getting on with the job of development at home. Moreover, any foreseeable immigration from Asia would have no perceptible effect on Asian demographic problems. Assuming the capital and shipping could be mobilised, it is most unlikely, as we have seen p. 154), that more than a score or so millions of Asian farmers could be settled in 'empty Australia' within a couple of decades, and this is as nothing to the flow of new mouths in Asia. What is needed is not the peopling, in such terms, of tropical Australia, but a better use of its land to enhance Australia's already not inconsiderable contribution to feeding and clothing the world, together with a more sustained and expanded effort in technical aid.

Aid and trade

In the spheres of technological aid and the changing patterns of trade, the ambivalence of the Australian situation and the pragmatism of Australian attitudes are well displayed. In the initiation of the Colombo Plan and of the South Pacific Commission, which has been a useful co-ordinator of advance in the scattered islands of Oceania, Australia played a notable and imaginative part, and certainly nobody would wish to depreciate the devotion which many Australians have brought to the task of aiding underdeveloped countries, the businesslike competence of official support (especially to the admirable Colombo Plan), and the gains in human welfare which have resulted. Nevertheless, for a society which on the whole is rather given to boasting of its affluence and high technology, Australia's aid record is far from outstanding: well under 1 per cent of Gross National Product, which places her well down on the list of aid-giving nations. Even so, the official calculation includes the Commonwealth subventions to New Guinea – much of which goes to Australian salaries; and this seems a somewhat dubious calculation ethically, at least until New Guinea does attain self-government. And, most paradoxically, it would not be altogether fanciful to suggest that one of our major single items of 'aid' – although it was aid paid for on the nail – was by way of wheat shipments to mainland China.

Here indeed we are really a part of Asia, considering Asia as a trade complex. Japan now runs Britain neck and neck as a customer: she has long been an important wool buyer and in recent years has taken nearly all the Australian coal export (which amounts to nearly half Japan's imports of coking coal), and the bulk of the very rapidly increasing iron ore export will feed Japanese industries. Trade based essentially on wool and minerals is of course liable to fluctuations, but still the general trend is upwards and is likely to keep Japan a close second to Britain as a customer, if she does not take first place; and clearly a country with the varied manufacturing development and commercial adroitness of Japan will not be content indefinitely with too unfavourable terms of trade, so that the already important Japanese export to Australia (for instance, motor vehicles, electrical gear, textiles) is likely to expand and diversify. The rapid growth of trade has been accompanied by Japanese investment, especially in connection with mining development in the north, and this too is likely to expand. There is likely to be less permanence in China's role as an importer of Australian produce, since this rests on a narrow base – in effect, wheat; but the great wheat sales of the mid-'sixties made her Australia's fifth customer, and without them the major agricultural industry of Australia might well have been in a precarious position.

The United States often ranks second both as customer and supplier, and the intrusion of American development capital and know-how over a wide range of industries (including mining and pastoral development in 'empty Australia') will mean closer trade ties; indeed, these are already so complex that there are difficult questions of balance, reflected for instance in allegations that openings for wool in America have been sacrificed to secure tobacco exports, small in the general picture but electorally important to the Country Party.

In this rather fluid situation, Britain's entry into the Common Market, if and when it comes about, could be not so much a disaster as a stimulus to the diversification both of export lines and markets which Australia so badly needs. Unfortunately, apart from Japan and China, Asian markets for Australian primary products are limited, and their growth would depend on changes in food habits (for instance, a turn to wheat and meat diets) which would be rather unlikely in any case for social reasons, and most unlikely without a great rise in Asian living standards, and this itself would be largely dependent on political stability and general economic advance, both so far sadly lacking in much of south and east Asia. As for manufacture, much the same applies: as we have seen (p. 142), much of Australian secondary industry depends on licenses from international firms, and these often specifically bar exports to south-east Asia; and clearly also countries like India, Japan, China, and even Hong Kong, with vast reserves of cheap labour and/or mass markets, are in a strong competitive position.

In the circumstances it is natural, though again unfortunate, that Australian thinking should still be too often defensive. Although with the rise of mineral exports the primacy of wool is challenged, and may indeed be displaced, as an exporter Australia still relies basically on primary products, and given the environment these will probably hold a preponderant share of export values for as long as can be foreseen. But there seems to be a reluctance to accept the fact that specific priorities are not likely to remain unchanged indefinitely, and to take really active steps to diversify the export basis, particularly on the manufacturing side, let alone to contemplate phasing out marginal activities and replacing them by new ones. The desperate protection of dairy products and the relative lack of interest in oilseeds is a case in point. Perhaps the most positive reaction to the 'threat' of the Common Market has been a desire to explore the possibilities of closer trade relations with New Zealand, but this comes up against the difficulty that the two countries, as of to-day, are essentially competitive rather than complementary. Any closely integrated tariff policy, for example, would meet the opposition of the struggling established dairy industry in Australia and the struggling nascent manufacturing interests of New Zealand.

Meanwhile, it would perhaps not be too cynical to say that Australia loves America as a brother, except that it makes difficulties about taking our meat and wool; and loathes China (which it does not officially recognise) except that it makes no difficulties about taking as much wheat as we can supply. Could ambivalence and pragmatism go further?

The Chinese syndrome and the American alliance

This ambivalence affects Australia's relations not only with the unrecognised People's Republic but also with the recognised Republic of China in Taiwan. The latter has had an Embassy in Canberra continuously since the war, but there was no Australian mission opened in Taiwan until 1966, almost simultaneously with the recognition of Outer Mongolia, a move probably as unwelcome in Taipeh as in Peking. The motivation is obscure. Yet one thing is not ambivalent: there is no reasonable doubt that the overwhelming psychological factor in the Australian world outlook is fear of Communist China, though only the DLP – in marked contrast to the Country Party – is consistent enough to oppose wheat sales. There is little recognition that a powerful China would present problems whether Communist or not; again perhaps only the DLP, though its main animus is anti-Communist, has had sufficient realism to admit this; perhaps this failure is merely the pragmatism of 'sufficient unto the day is the evil thereof'. Yet the Chinese Empire and the Kuo Min Tang both laid claim to considerable areas of northern Burma, and Red China has at least formally waived these and settled the boundary, not unfavourably to Burma, by treaty, precarious as this may be. Again as regards Tibet (and at least some of the claims against India), the difference between Red and KMT China might seem to be a difference in power to act rather than in policy.

Any régime in control of a strong China would wish to extend considerable influence over the mainland states of south-east Asia, or at least to exclude over-strong influences from outside the region. It would perhaps be difficult, since the promulgation of the Monroe Doctrine, to regard such a sphere of influence as illegitimate in itself, as distinct from the means taken to exercise it. Recognition of this fact is not an argument for the admission of a Chinese right of 'suzerainty', only of the fact that any Chinese régime having the power to do so would wish to repel any other suzerainty. It is argued, with sincerity, that Chinese suzerainty is exactly what the Americans are fighting to repel; it could be argued that they might well feel impelled to do so whatever the nature of the Chinese régime, but that only the aggressive nature of Chinese Communists has enforced the taking up of arms as against diplomatic measures. In practice, however, the line between repelling someone else's suzerainty and establishing and extending one's own may be exceedingly difficult to draw and to respect. This obviously applies to both parties, and even were the Maoists far more correct in the conduct of international relations than they are, it is difficult to see south-east Asia being left in a neutralist position – immeasurably happier as that state would be for the Vietnamese North and South, and immeasurably tragic as has been the American and Australian involvement in that country.[1] This is the core of the dilemma; action and reaction are equal and opposite, and though the 'domino' theory may well have been erroneous when first enunciated, now that the stakes have been raised again and again this might be a very hazardous assumption.

Such considerations seem desirable to avoid over-simplification of the issues, but they are doubtless academic over against the facts that the formidable resurgence of Chinese power has taken a revolutionary Communist form, and that the American reaction has been one of militant containment. This reaction has appeared to offer Australia the opportunity of an insurance policy, and the opportunity has been eagerly grasped – so eagerly that she has left herself little room for manoeuvre, and hence little opportunity to exercise any influence in the alliance. Whatever the outcome of the long agony of Vietnam, whether Australia emerges in the role of client to a triumphant or a defeated intervention, in the long run this stance can hardly fail to reflect adversely on the wished-for image of 'a part of Asia', an honest broker between East and West – except, of course, in the eyes of such irretrievably committed régimes as those of Thailand and Taiwan. The position is defended on the ground that Australia must earn the gratitude of her 'great and powerful friend' the United States. Whatever one may think of more altruistic motivations, such as a determination to let the South Vietnamese choose freely their own form of government, this defence is not only plausible but sincere, and it is acceptable to the great bulk of Australian opinion. Yet one cannot but wish that there had been more finesse, more flexibility.

That such adroitness is not beyond Australian capabilities may be indicated by the remarkable success of her policy in Indonesia during the confrontation with Malaysia. She was handicapped by a bad start, in that she had appeared to resist, almost alone, and until the last feasible moment, the transfer of West Irian to Indonesia; yet she managed to back Malaysia to the extent of having support troops in Malaya itself, and even a few combat troops in the Borneo jungles, without arriving at a break even with the hyper-nationalist and/or crypto-Communist Djakarta of Sukarno and Subandrio. This seems to have been largely owing to the understanding of the Australian diplomats on the spot, and in the nature

[1] In the writer's personal view, a tragic mistake.

of things one cannot draw a recipe from it; every diplomatic situation is a special case to be decided on its own special merits. But it shows, at least, that with calm, patience, and understanding the role of honest broker can be sustained. Unfortunately a similar effort in Cambodia, where Australia has represented American interests, broke down, apparently by the collision of a somewhat stiff Australian stance with the elusive, not to say devious, policy and personality of Prince Sihanouk.

Are there any possibilities for flexibility, on the Indonesian model, in the wider Asian scene? Probably they have been lost by default. The American alliance is now the cornerstone of Australian foreign policy; nor can one see that isolation or non-alignment would have been a feasible alternative. But between a complete neutralism and an automatic total commitment there is, or rather in this specific case there probably was, some range of choice. At the very least, if Australia hoped to receive real respect or consideration – apart from Texas-style junketings – one might have thought it desirable that she should have put some price on her favours. It is now quite impracticable to attempt any sudden or dramatic disengagement; but a change of government might enable some modest potentiality for initiative to be regained: 'regained', because in an earlier phase conservative Australian governments have certainly (if usually privately) maintained significantly different views from those of the State Department.[1]

Alignments and defence

Apart from standard adherence to the United Nations Organisation and the [British] Commonwealth of Nations, the most important formal bases of Australia's foreign policy are her membership of the Australia, New Zealand and United States Treaty (ANZUS) and the South-East Asia Treaty Organisation (SEATO).

The course of the second World War in the Pacific brought home the vital interest of Australia in some form of regional defence arrangements, and ANZUS (1951) was the first step. It was made possible partly as a sort of solatium to Australia for the 'soft' peace treaty with Japan – not unnaturally, Australians were much less ready to accept Japan into the comity of nations than were the

[1] See for example Sir Alan Watt's authoritative study of *The Evolution of Australian Foreign Policy 1938–65* (Cambridge University Press, 1967), pp. 243–46.

Americans, with their eyes on Communist China and much less exposed to imminent peril in 1941–42 – and partly as a result of the Australian contribution in Korea. From an Australian point of view, the key fact about ANZUS is that, unlike SEATO, it commits the United States (or at least tends to commit her, for precise action would depend on the nature and scale of the threat) in the event of an attack not only on Australia itself but on New Guinea, and this with no limitation to Communist attack. Although the threat of an Indonesian 'liberation' intervention in New Guinea has receded since the fall of Sukarno and the disruption of the Indonesian Communist Party, there is no guarantee that it might not emerge in another form, and indeed – again from a narrowly Australian point of view – the risk of American disinterest is clearly greater were the threat non-Communist.[1]

SEATO (1954) is far more complex, indeed a strange and confusing institution. Only three Asian countries are members – Thailand, the Philippines, and Pakistan, and of these Pakistan from the first has clearly been interested in the pact merely as an insurance against India, and has not been averse to relations with Communist China which seem incompatible with the spirit of SEATO, while the Philippine Republic has at times been restive. Britain's adhesion was at first reluctant, and since the avowal of a policy of running-down commitments east of Suez its continuance seems at best luke-warm, while France has to all intents openly withdrawn.

Quite apart from these signs of stress in SEATO, there are two very marked qualifications to its working as a concert of powers designed to maintain peace and stability in the area. The United States, and only the United States, limited its adherence by an 'understanding' that it agreed to act only in the event of specifically Communist aggression.[2] And, although Article IV of the Treaty speaks of 'unanimous agreement', in 1962 a joint Thai-American declaration affirmed that American help to Thailand would not depend on prior agreement of the other parties, 'since the Treaty obligation is individual as well as collective'. Furthermore, the

[1] Paradoxically, an anti-Indonesian insurgency in West Irian, which is not inconceivable and in which Peking might well be interested, could present Australia with serious difficulties, in view of the indigenous suspicion of Indonesia rife in Australian New Guinea.

[2] Conversely, Australia opted out in advance from any involvement in an Indo-Pakistani conflict.

reference to the strengthening of 'free institutions' has little relevance to Pakistan and Thailand; all the Asian members have
expressed dissatisfaction at the extent of non-military aid provided;
and of the three 'protocol states' – non-members to whom the
protection of SEATO was offered – Laos and Cambodia have withdrawn, leaving only South Vietnam.

This is of course a very simplified picture, and doubtless the
microscopic eye of the expert may find virtues in the machinery of
consultation which SEATO provides. But the uninitiate, not privy
to its councils, must wonder what the point of it all really is. This
wonderment will not be diminished by the observation that neither
American nor Australian (nor again, more obviously, South
Korean) intervention in South Vietnam has been called for under
SEATO auspices. Perhaps the real achievement of SEATO has
been confined to stiffening Thai morale.

The material strength at Australia's disposal to meet her overseas
commitments, which are not likely to diminish but rather to expand,
has until recently been very small. Three examples, one from each of
the Services, will suffice. In 1965 the sending of one battalion to
Vietnam, in addition to the Australian component of the Commonwealth Strategic Reserve in Malaysia, meant that nearly half the
available field troops were overseas. When in February 1964 the
aircraft carrier *Melbourne* collided with and sank the destroyer
Voyager on night exercises in Jervis Bay, a few seconds sufficed to
lose one-third of the Royal Australian Navy's destroyer strength
and to put its only capital ship out of commission for months.
Finally, until F111 supersonic bombers become available from the
United States in 1969–70 – and the drawing-board history of this
aircraft does not inspire much confidence in delivery dates, still less
prices – the Royal Australian Air Force will have no effective strike
capacity, its Canberra bombers being obsolete. There has been expansion, and the regular Army is said to be at its highest peace-time
level; yet the maintenance of 8,000 troops in Vietnam imposes strain.

It reflects very ill on the conservative governments in power since
1949; it is strange that, in a political climate so threatening, a more
determined effort was not made to break away from the general
insouciance of the Australian electorate, politically unpopular as
that might have been. To some extent this has been due to a too-
sharp dichotomy between the priorities of development and defence;
even at ministerial level, it has been suggested that development

expenditure, by strengthening the productive capacity and population of the country, in effect does defence work. There is of course something in this argument, but it is no use building for a higher defence industry potential if for lack of defences the country is swamped or disrupted before it can go into production. Meanwhile, it is with an ill grace that Australia complains of the British retreat from east of Suez when Britain spends 7 per cent of Gross National Product on defence, Australia 4 or 5 per cent. Assuming that Australia does wish to maintain an attitude of independence, more is needed.

There is no need to stress the excellence of the material, both officer and other rank, available to the Australian armed forces. Its mobilisation and deployment, however, raise great difficulties in so vast a continent, which over most of its extent is very thinly peopled and very inadequately provided with an infrastructure of transport and service facilities. Apart from manpower, Australia is clearly not capable of producing all, or even a very massive proportion, of her needs in the complex hardware of modern war. Her iron and steel, ship-building, and general engineering capacity are very substantial defence assets, and such things as the French supersonic interceptor fighter, the Mirage, will be assembled, and an increasing proportion of the components made, in Australia, while some fairly sophisticated machines have been produced essentially by Australian initiative – the Jindivik pilotless target plane, the Ikara anti-submarine missile, the Milkara anti-tank weapon. Basically, however, such is the complexity and cost of modern armaments that 'Anything we make ourselves is likely to be obsolete before it is produced', while reliance on overseas supplies not only involves foreign exchange, but represents a continuing dependence on spares and replacements – which, as Israel's experience with the Mirage shows, is hardly an element of strength.[1] This inevitable reliance on overseas supplies of course adds greatly to the difficulty of a non-aligned position, though it does not make it quite impossible.

Some of the elements of a reconstruction of Australia's forces have been put in hand. There can be two views of the morality and justice of the government's selective compulsory service system, of

[1] See T. B. Millar, *Australia's Defence* (Melbourne University Press, 1965), p. 166; this is an admirably clear survey of the problem, almost the only serious discussion available to non-specialists, though other views may be found in M. Teichmann (ed.), *Aspects of Australia's Defence* (Political Science Dept., Monash University, Melbourne, 1966).

the way in which it was introduced, and its application to send conscripts to Vietnam; but at least it should supply a trained and readily-mobilised reserve for the ground forces. A prime need is a better development of military air transport, including heavy helicopters; this could be of particular importance in Australian geographical conditions. The Navy has now some American guided missile destroyers; considering the length and exposure of Australia's coasts, and her dependence on shipping lanes (particularly those across the Indian Ocean), a build-up of submarine strength, already initiated, seems essential; and the projected naval base on the west coast, probably at Cockburn Sound south of Perth, would seem to warrant a high priority, with or without British co-operation as the retreat from east of Suez comes into play. Once the Mirages and F111 bombers are operational in numbers, much improved ground facilities, especially a more highly developed radar net, will be essential.

All this would mean a much tougher effort by Australian governments and their taxpayers. But the case can be made on either view of Australia's position, committed or non-aligned. In the former view it obviously adds to Australia's value to the alliance, and is indeed essential to self-respect and outside respect. And, in the world to-day, any neutralist stance by Australia would unfortunately have to be an armed neutrality, or one of absolute pacifism; and this last is a gamble which few Australians would be prepared to take.

Nuclear clouds

Although such a build-up as T. B. Millar suggests, some items of which are mentioned above, would represent a serious effort, it would be far from a commitment to a war-oriented economy; and this relatively modest tooling-up should suffice to meet any local troubles which might arise in the Indonesian-Malaysian region. Far more serious would be Australia's position in the event of a general war; and here, of course, the imminence of effective nuclear power in Chinese hands adds a new and alarming dimension to the discussion. Doubtless when China possesses sufficient nuclear weaponry for massive assault or retaliation on the United States, Australia would strategically dwindle to a secondary target, on which there would be little or no temptation to waste bombs. Before that time, however, China might have sufficient capacity to use Australia as an object of nuclear blackmail. Alliance or no alliance, this bluffing of the 'paper tiger' would probably produce an American counter; but that is no compensation for a devastated continent. And we have already given hostages to fortune in the shape of the Woomera Rocket Range and the American radio-communications base at North-West Cape in Western Australia. Both of these are 'legitimate' targets, if any such there be.

So far, Australia seems content to rest under the American nuclear umbrella; few people have seriously proposed the institution of an independent nuclear deterrent. This would not be beyond Australia's power, though its cost would mean a very serious distortion of the country's productive capacity. On the other hand, there is naturally and rightly a very serious antipathy to any further nuclear proliferation. Should a general treaty restricting the spread of nuclear weapons become effective, with China as odd man out, this would seem to imply some responsibility on the existing nuclear powers to extend guarantees to those excluded from the club. On the other hand, the adoption of a non-aligned stance might be held to carry with it an implication that an independent deterrent would warrant consideration.

Living with Asia

All this discussion, however it may have appeared to diverge, really hinges on and comes back to Australia's position as a non-Asian nation not a part of but next to Asia. As Millar puts it,

> Australia's strategic problems, like her national interests, are shared by no other country. As large as the United States, and with a population roughly that of New York City; with vast resources awaiting only labour, capital, technology and enthusiasm; rich, satisfied, and rather lazy; still aggressively 'white' in culture and outlook although separated from Europe by Asia and from America by the Pacific, we are only slowly learning to live with Asia. . . .[1]

As we have seen, the whole question is oversimplified by the 'part of Asia' approach: a nation with so different a heritage can never be that, but it must have increasingly close links with Asia. To those whose vision of the West is its technology, its administrative competence, and its military power, the answer is easy – too easy: support 'free Asia', without too much definition of where and what

[1] *Op. cit.*, p. 42.

'free Asia' is. What is left out is too often not only 'which Asia' but 'which West': the West of efficient military imperialisms and materialist capitalisms, or the West of cultural and spiritual achievement which, despite the self-abasement of a guilt-ridden intelligentsia, need fear no comparison with 'the wisdom of the East'. The indications are that Australia has backed the first two of these concepts of the West.

Yet a nation firmly convinced of the non-material values of Western civilisation and committed not to forcing them upon Asian peoples but to sharing both these values and the fruits of material technology, might yet achieve great things as a mediator: Western by heritage, Eastern by location. This would indeed be an honourable and magnificent ambition; but it needs a long view, patience and foresight, an appreciation of intangibles in culture and politics. It does not, unfortunately, seem to fit into the Australian pragmatic tradition.

And yet, was Mr Holt perhaps right after all? Distasteful as it is, may not 'All the way with LBJ' be the only answer for a small Western nation on the edge of the Asian immensity? Is the only alternative to an unbearably perilous an precarious isolation to be servile dependence, which itself has its perils? Or can we not, by an effort of will, aspire to a position not of power, but of respected independence, respected as an honest broker, a mediator? Australia's freedom of international action must always be limited by her small population and her location; but it may not be impossible to attain some flexibility, some room to manoeuvre within those limits.

For this, Australia must come to terms with herself; must translate her myths into a rationale for action. 'Australia is a part of Asia', 'peopling the north' are dangerous myths; 'Australian involvement with Asia', 'using the north' are reasonable bases for action. They will be difficult to interpret and apply, but since no sensible interpretation or application is possible of clichés that have no meaning, the effort of translation must be made.

Epilogue

This book has sought to trace the way in which a vast and generally harsh land, inhabited firstly by wandering bands of aborigines and then by a few hundred felons and their gaolers, has developed into a nation of twelve million people, who contribute disproportionately to the feeding and clothing of the world, and not inconsiderably to its culture. The society harbours within itself many unresolved dichotomies: loyalties are difficult to pin down. Australians no longer think of Britain as 'Home', yet there persists a vague nostalgia for the British connection, though the once-dazzling images of the Crown and the British Empire and Commonwealth seem gradually fading. Again, loyalty to the continent and the culture is strong, and the States still stand for proud and individual traditions over against a less personally compelling Commonwealth of Australia. Unresolved are the extent and nature of the assimilation of both the 'New Australians' and the oldest Australians, the aborigines. There are the tensions of simple pleasures against get-with-it sophistication, of the bush virtues against the values or non-values of suburbia, of élite against mass, of a genuine snobbism against an often equally genuine egalitarianism, of the desire in the arts for a full and rich expression of the local genius against that for cosmopolitan expertise and acceptance, of a Puritan tradition in a hedonist society, of internal complacency over against international anxieties.

Often Australia gives the impression of being a tired society; there seems at times a certain sourness in the mateship and the democracy, a lack of spring and tempo in the people. Yet these same people retain their gift for energy and improvised collective action when under challenge. In the last resort the British (or other) migrant would find it easy to compile a long list of failings and frustrations and irritations; less easy to isolate the intangible charm of living in Australia and among Australians. Somehow, despite the politics and the suburbias, there is a freshness in the air; the lines of individual destiny seem less easily and less firmly chalked out than in Britain. Often one thinks of Auden's line: 'affectionate people, but crude their sense of glory'. But perhaps the very concept of glory carries with it some element of crudity; and although the building of the Australian Commonwealth has been pragmatic, disjointed and discontinuous in some fields and phases, at times even inept in detail, 'the extent of empire' which Watkin Tench foreshadowed in the miserable Sydney of 1788 has not been without 'grandeur of design'. Much was poorly done, very much remains to be done; yet one looks back at those dismal, even squalid, beginnings, one marvels at what has been done by so few people, in so vast a land, in so short a span of human history.

*   *   *

When Harold Holt, Prime Minister of Australia, stepped into the sea for a dip before lunch on 17 December 1967, never to return, this innocent action was in the event not only personally tragic but politically significant. Mr Holt, whose tenure of office, after the outstanding triumph of the November 1966 elections, had not been particularly happy, had shown signs of returning grip in the decisive reaction to the British devaluation. The speed and firmness of the decision not to devalue the Australian dollar may have owed something to the absence overseas of Mr John McEwen, the Country Party Minister for Trade; in his absence the Country Party members of Cabinet, able men but junior, were unable to take a really firm stand in defence of the threatened primary industries.

Normally – though by no means necessarily – the logical successor would have been Mr William McMahon, Commonwealth Treasurer and Deputy Leader of the Liberal Party. It is doubtful if this succession would have been very welcome in the country at large; but in any case, Mr McEwen immediately interposed a veto in the most decisive manner: neither he nor his party could serve under Mr McMahon. It had of course been common knowledge for years that Mr McEwen and Mr McMahon were rather more than just political rivals; and their approaches to economic policy diverged seriously. While Mr McEwen stood on the whole for a high protectionist policy, and had publicly expressed apprehension at the influx of American and Japanese capital especially in mining (where it might 'leave us just with big holes in the ground'), Mr McMahon was more flexible in fiscal matters and saw nothing but an unmixed blessing in continuing capital inflow. To Mr McEwen, he was under serious suspicion of being in much too close touch with personalities and groups whose thinking was anathema to the Country Party.

As Mr Holt's Deputy Prime Minister, Mr McEwen took over the substantive office pending the election of a new leader of the majority party. The coalition was of course under strain, probably greater than at any time since it came to power in 1949, but despite the much greater numerical strength of the Liberals in Parliament, there was really no practical alternative to accepting the veto on Mr McMahon. There were minor contenders, but in effect the choice lay between Mr Paul Hasluck, Minister for External Affairs, and Senator John Gorton, Minister for Education and Science. The former was much respected for his integrity and moral courage, but also regarded as somewhat doctrinaire and lacking the human touch; his relations with the Press, to which he was usually incommuncative, were bad. Senator Gorton was on the whole less well known, but was clearly a man of weight, and was elected on the second ballot.

The new Prime Minister describes himself as left of centre in the Liberal Party; he had some reputation as a Vietnam hawk, but proclaimed his unalterable opposition to bombing escalation. In domestic politics, he had given rise to some suspicion of centralising tendencies. He took over in difficult circumstances: apart from the need of walking warily on coalition matters (Mr McMahon remained as Liberal Deputy Leader), he was faced externally by the problem provided by the acceleration of the British withdrawal from east of Suez, internally by a very serious postal strike. All that can be said of his initial performance is that the congratulatory telegram from Mr Whitlam, Leader of the ALP, stated no more than the truth: 'Your colleagues have given me a formidable opponent.'

A Note on Books

The books mentioned below are a very small, and very personal, selection from the great mass of useful, and often delightful, literature readily available. Books cited in the text or footnotes are normally not included here. A & R=Angus & Robertson, Sydney; ANU=Australian National University Press, Canberra; MUP= Melbourne University Press.

For general reference, the annual *Year Book of the Commonwealth of Australia* (Government Printer, Canberra) is remarkably comprehensive and remarkably cheap; the Department of National Development, Canberra, issues an admirable *Atlas of Australian Resources*. The ten-volume *Australian Encyclopaedia* (1958) is unfortunately only available in libraries, but there is a very useful one-volume *Modern Encyclopaedia of Australia and New Zealand* (Horwitz-Grahame, Sydney, 1964). There is really no good modern general geography, other than textbooks, but Griffith Taylor's *Australia: A Study of Warm Environments and their Effect on British Settlement* (Methuen, 7th ed. 1959) though old and highly idiosyncratic is still stimulating. A very readable account of the physical aspect will be found in C. F. Laseron, *The Face of Australia* (Angus and Robertson, 1953), the basic facts in *The Australian Environment* (CSIRO, Melbourne, 3rd ed. 1960).

So far only the first two of the four volumes of Manning Clark's *A History of Australia* (MUP, 1962, 1968) have appeared; they offer a highly individual and debatable but very significant reinterpretation. More conventional in attitude, but lively in style, are Hartley Grattan's volumes on *The South-west Pacific to 1900* and *since 1900* (University of Michigan, Ann Arbor, 1963). Russell Ward's *The Australian Legend* (Oxford University Press, 1958) explores the bush mythos and the origins of 'mateship', while Geoffrey Serle, *The Golden Age* (MUP, 1963) is a vivid history of Victoria in the decade 1851–61 which saw so much and so crucial change. The life of the great graziers is vividly displayed in Mary

Durack, *Kings in Grass Castles* (Constable, 1954) and Margaret Kiddle, *Men of Yesterday* (MUP, 1961) – the latter, dealing with the Western District of Victoria, is our best regional social history so far. The selectors and their like left little written record, but Samuel Shumack's 'autobiography', *Tales and Legends of the Canberra Pioneers* (ANU, 1967), is both unique and fascinating, and the woman's side is presented in the sketches of Eve Pownall's *Mary of Maranoa* (Johnston, Sydney, 1964). On Canberra itself the standard work is H. L. White (ed.), *Canberra: A Nation's Capital* (A & R, 1954), while Lionel Wigmore's *The Long View* (Cheshire, Melbourne, 1963) is a very readable history.

S. W. Wadham, G. L. Wood, and R. K. Wilson, *Land Utilization in Australia* (MUP, 4th ed. 1964) is a standard review of the rural industries; a specialised but important book on Murray irrigation is T. Langford-Smith and J. Rutherford, *Water and Land* (ANU, 1967). The ramifications of wool growing and the wool trade are carded out in Alan Barnard (ed.), *The Simple Fleece* (MUP/ANU, 1962), and Geoffrey Blainey's *The Rush that Never Ended* (MUP, 1963) is an account of mining history both exciting and authentic.

There is no good single volume devoted to the formal history of the Commonwealth as such; Brian Fitzpatrick's *The Australian Commonwealth* (Cheshire, 1956) is lively, Leftish, scholarly, but hardly formal. Geoffrey Sawer's two volumes on *Australian Federal Politics and Law 1901–29* and *1929–49* (MUP, 1956, 1953) are much more readable than their austerely legalist approach would suggest. There are three biographies which cover much of the ground: J. A. La Nauze, *Alfred Deakin* (MUP, 1965); L. F. Fitzhardinge, *William Morris Hughes* (A & R, Vol. I 1964); L. F. Crisp, *Ben Chifley* (Longmans, n.d. [?1961]).

Books on the north and the aborigines are noted in the text; on New Guinea Gavin Souter, *The Last Unknown* (A & R, 1963) is a fascinating history, and E. K. Fisk (ed.), *New Guinea on the Threshold* (ANU, 1966), a series of authoritative essays on current problems.

Turning to the cultural side, Peter Coleman (ed.), *Australian Civilization* (Cheshire, paperback ed. 1966) brings together the views of a number of leading intellectuals. Bibliographies of the leading writers will be found in Geoffrey Dutton (ed.), *The Literature of Australia* (Penguins, 1964); Penguins also have two good anthologies,

Modern Australian Verse and *Australian Ballads*; the latter should surely be accompanied by *Songs from Queensland* and *Across the Western Plains* (both Wattle Recordings, Sydney). Dobell, Drysdale and Nolan are available in handsome volumes by Thames & Hudson, who have also J. D. Pringle's perceptive *Australian Painting Today* (1963), though his geography might be queried. Bernard Smith, *Australian Painting 1788–1960* (Oxford University Press, 1962) takes a wider range. On architecture, Morton Herman's *The Early Australian Architects* (A & R, 1954) is lavish and scholarly, but unfortunately confined to New South Wales; there is a biography of *Francis Greenway* by M. H. Ellis (A & R, 1949), but the versatile James Blackburn awaits a study. Two lively surveys of private building, Robin Boyd's *Australia's Home* (MUP, 1952) and J. M. Freeland's *The Australian Pub* (MUP, 1966) are highly recommendable not only as studies of their ostensible subjects but as social history.

For reviews of 'the state of the nation', the reader might wish to compare with this book the more iconoclastic and perhaps 'with it' surveys by Donald Horne, *The Lucky Country* (Penguins, 1965), and Craig McGregor, *Profile of Australia* (Hodder & Stoughton, 1966). Not entirely a curiosity is Geoffrey Dutton (ed.), *Australia and the Monarchy* (Sun Books, Sydney, 1966), the first avowedly Republican manifesto, perhaps not the last.

Finally, apart from Trollope, Froude, and the Webbs, who all left some record of their travels, the only English writer of high standing to write specifically on Australia is D. H. Lawrence. *Kangaroo* (1923) is indisputably a remarkably perceptive novel, with a fine sense of environment, magnificent pictures of landscape, and an astonishing anticipation of the New Guard movement (cf. p. 85 above). But it is curiously ambivalent: much of the book is avowedly observation of the curious *mores* of the natives, but Lawrence, being Lawrence, can never quite detach himself and simply observe. One has at times an uneasy feeling that Somers, who is the 'observer' standing for Lawrence himself, actually exemplifies some of those traits that he disliked and distrusted in Australians; though he certainly penetrates into the depths, or the emptiness, underlying 'mateship'. To be read, surely; but perhaps with caution, and certainly *not* as a first introduction to Australia.

Index

Printed in Great Britain by
Western Printing Services Limited
Bristol